America Is Not Post-Racial

America Is Not Post-Racial

Xenophobia, Islamophobia, Racism, and the 44th President

Algernon Austin

 PRAEGER™

An Imprint of ABC-CLIO, LLC

Santa Barbara, California • Denver, Colorado

Library of Congress Cataloging-in-Publication Data
Austin, Algernon.
    America is not post-racial : xenophobia, islamophobia, racism, and the 44th president / Algernon Austin.
        pages cm
    Includes bibliographical references and index.
    ISBN 978-1-4408-4125-5 (alk. paper) — ISBN 978-1-4408-4126-2
(EISBN)   1. Obama, Barack—Adversaries.   2. Right-wing extremists—United
States.   3. United States—Politics and government—2009–   4. Racism—United
States.   I. Title.
    E908.A89 2015
    305.800973—dc23   2015016083

ISBN: 978-1-4408-4125-5
EISBN: 978-1-4408-4126-2

19   18   17   16   15   1   2   3   4   5

This book is also available on the World Wide Web as an eBook.
Visit www.abc-clio.com for details.

Praeger
An Imprint of ABC-CLIO, LLC

ABC-CLIO, LLC
130 Cremona Drive, P.O. Box 1911
Santa Barbara, California 93116-1911

This book is printed on acid-free paper ∞

Manufactured in the United States of America

Contents

Preface

This is the only book to identify and analyze the 25 million Americans who are the most angry and afraid of Barack Obama as president. These Obama Haters are so extreme in their political views that they make average Tea Party supporters look like moderates. Obama Haters are more likely than other Americans to vote in a presidential primary or caucus, to contact their U.S. representative or senator, and to donate to a political campaign. This high level of political participation gives them political power greater than their numbers. Even after Obama's presidency, they—and their xenophobia, Islamophobia, and racism—will likely continue to shape American politics.

This study emerged out of my confusion over Obama-hatred. To me President Obama does not seem like the radical his opponents paint him to be. For example, the Republican Party is apparently incensed over Obamacare, yet Obamacare looks an awful lot like an expansion of "Romneycare," the health insurance reform put in place by the former Republican presidential candidate Mitt Romney when he was governor of Massachusetts. Why is Obama attacked by Republicans for advancing a Republican idea? To unpack where conservatism ends and where irrational hatred begins, I closely examine the views of Obama Haters and compare them with conservatives who are not angry and afraid at the thought of Obama. I find that Obama Haters are motivated by much more than simply conservatism.

There are essentially three different analyses occurring in these pages. The first is a detailed quantitative and qualitative analysis of the Obama Haters. I move the discussion of Obama-hatred beyond suspicion and speculation and provide solid evidence about who the Obama Haters are and what motivates them.

At another level, this book is a type of case study of America's response to a nearly perfect black male. Obama is, in the words of Vice President Joe Biden,[1] "articulate and bright and clean and a nice-looking guy." If America is post-racial, Obama's race should not matter in America's response to him. For many Americans, it does not. But for more of us than we have been willing to admit, it does. We think that people who voted for Obama are free of antiblack prejudice, but I show that this is not the case.

Finally, I am also using the Obama Haters to highlight issues that may be useful to engage to reduce racial hatred. Beyond the Obama Haters, many more moderate Americans are anxious about the idea of a more racially and ethnically diverse America. As the proportion of people of color in the U.S. population increases, a body of social science research predicts that there will be more racial animosity. We must take action to see that America's increasing diversity does not lead to increased racial and ethnic conflict.

I received support and encouragement from many people in many different ways while writing this book. I'll highlight only a few for special recognition. I thank the five D.C. policy wonks I interviewed for their time and insight. I really appreciated learning their views on the Obama administration. Thanks to Janelle Wong, Zoe Sullivan, James Mwombela, Enid Logan, Roberta Gold, and Roger Clay for their useful feedback on drafts of the proposal and manuscript. Thanks to Brian Smedley for hosting a discussion of my research.

Obama-phobia in America

All American presidents are subject to outrageous attacks. As one presidential historian has noted:

> Harry Truman was condemned for being soft on communism and thereby risking the deliverance of America to Russia. Franklin Roosevelt was called a socialist. Thomas Jefferson was called the anti-Christ. Andrew Jackson was called a Caesar. Over-the-top criticism of presidents has a long history.[1]

But there still appears to be a difference in the anti-Obama attacks. President Obama has been called all of the above—and much more. He has been called a "communist" *and* a "socialist" *and* "the anti-Christ" *and* a "dictator" as well as an "illegal immigrant" *and* a "Muslim" *and* a "nigger." In terms of the variety of over-the-top criticism of presidents, Obama can't be beat. "The most sustained attacks on a president's legitimacy have been directed at Barack Obama," argues the political scientist, Gary C. Jacobson.[2] The political writer Paul Waldman agrees: "It's safe to say that no president in modern times has had his legitimacy questioned by the opposition party as much as Barack Obama."[3] It is doubtful that any other president has had to deal with such widely believed misinformation about his place of birth and his religion.

Obama has faced a strong and unified opposition. Republicans disapprove of Barack Obama more than any other Democratic president on record. It may be expected that the popular presidents Kennedy, Johnson, and Clinton would have higher Gallup-poll approval ratings by Republicans than President Obama. But Obama is also rated lower than the relatively unpopular presidents Truman and Carter.[4]

This dislike of Obama by Republicans should be surprising because, argu-ably, Obama has been the most Republican-friendly of recent Democratic presidents. President George W. Bush's tax cuts were going to expire, but President Obama saved them for 99 percent of taxpayers and made them permanent.[5] On national security policies, Bush's former director of the Cen-tral Intelligence Agency sees a "powerful continuity between . . . George W. Bush and Barack Obama."[6] Obamacare was developed from a conservative proposal, and a version of it was first implemented by Obama's 2012 Repub-lican opponent for the presidency, Mitt Romney.[7] Barack Obama was called the "deportation president" by the head of the nation's largest Latino advo-cacy organization[8] because he has put more agents on the border[9] and has removed more unauthorized immigrants than any other president.[10] Obama has repeatedly argued the conservative viewpoint that many African Amer-icans "are trapped [in poverty] by their own self-destructive behaviors."[11] He even signaled that he was willing to consider cuts to Social Security,[12] one of the most sacred New Deal programs.[13] Much to the annoyance of many on the left, Barack Obama has worked very hard to appease those on the right. He has been hated by many conservatives in spite of his efforts.

Obama has been hated for reasons that cannot be explained by his pol-icies; he's a centrist politician.[14] The strongest evidence that it is not sim-ply his policies that are behind Obama-hatred is the fact that some people change their policy positions after becoming aware that Obama agrees with them. A 2015 survey found that 76 percent of Americans support Obama's 2014 executive action deferring the deportation of unauthorized immigrants. However, when survey respondents were informed that the policy is Pres-ident Obama's, support for it drops 11 percentage points to 65 percent.[15] Other researchers have found that as Obama became more associated with health insurance reform, more people became opposed to reform.[16] Hatred of Obama caused some people to change their policy positions from agreeing with Obama to opposing him.

Part of Obama-hatred is due to the increasing partisanship and vitriol in American political life.[17] But part of it is also about race. And ethnicity. And religion.

Others have examined the attacks on Obama by media personalities and partisan politicians, but these analyses leave some of the most important questions unanswered. It is not surprising that professional anti-Democrats like Rush Limbaugh, Sarah Palin, Glenn Beck, and Michele Bachmann would attack a Democratic president. Essentially, doing so is their job.

An analysis of the professional anti-Democrats cannot tell us what pro-portion of the American public hates Obama and why. Or whether Obama is hated more than one would expect or less. Or whether he is hated for rational reasons or irrational ones. Analyzing individuals like Rush Limbaugh and

Sarah Palin does not give us a sense of the size nor solid evidence about the motivations of the Obama-hating public. This book does.

My analysis reveals that there are 25 million Obama Haters in America, more than 90 percent of whom identify as Republican or as Republican-leaning. Obama Haters are people who do not merely disapprove of the job President Obama is doing; they are angry and afraid at the thought of him. They are convinced that he aims to destroy America.

Obama differs from other presidents, of course, not just in the quantity and quality of over-the-top attacks that he has received. He differs because of his race. My analysis shows that race is a motivating factor for the Obama Haters. Haters exhibit a high level of hostility toward African Americans. In addition to this hatred of blacks, many Haters see whites as an oppressed minority group in the United States. Many of them believe that whites face more discrimination than that faced by blacks and that whites are a politically weak group confronting a country with politically powerful blacks. Their hatred of Obama therefore is just a specific example of their hatred and paranoia about black people.

While antiblack racism is a powerful factor behind being an Obama Hater, Haters are also motivated by anti-immigrant and anti-Muslim sentiments. Nearly two-thirds of Obama Haters believe the false "Birther" idea that Obama was born in another country. They are almost unanimous in their support of the police stopping and checking the legal status of individuals suspected of being unauthorized immigrants. A third of Obama Haters simply want to arrest and deport all unauthorized immigrants. The Haters are not too fond of immigrants, and, in their minds, Obama is an immigrant.

Three-fifths of Haters also believe incorrectly that Obama is Muslim. They argue, for example, "He's a Muslim, and the proof is all over the place, but people refuse to see it. . . . If he has to choose between Americans and Muslims, he will side with his Muslim brethren."[18] For many of the Haters, one cannot be American *and* Muslim since they see Muslims as anti-American. One can only be American *or* Muslim, and they have decided that Obama is Muslim.

Obama Haters are among the most antiblack, anti-immigrant, and anti-Muslim Americans. They believe Obama to be foreign-born and Muslim, and thus, they hate Obama because he is black, "an immigrant," and "Muslim." While race is crucial to Obama-phobia, it is also about xenophobia and Islamophobia.

Many people took the 2008 election of Barack Obama as president of the United States as evidence that the country is now post-racial. But a careful examination of the evidence would have revealed that antiblack attitudes and antiblack discrimination were (and are) still common in American society. The fact that a black man raised by a white mother and white grandparents, with two degrees from Ivy League universities, and who is "articulate and bright and clean and a nice-looking guy"[19] can still be subject to virulent racial hatred should make us definitively reject claims of post-racialism. If Obama, nearly the perfect black man in many respects, can be the target of racial hatred, all blacks can be affected. And it is for this reason, ultimately, that Obama-phobia is important. Obama-phobia serves as an important illustration of the obstacles that even the best-educated blacks can face at this time in American history.

Obama Haters are more politically engaged than the rest of the general public. They are more likely to vote in a presidential primary or caucus, to contact their elected representatives, and to contribute to political campaigns. For this reason, they have a greater political influence than their numbers. Obama Haters will likely play an obstructionist role to progressive change in American politics beyond the Obama administration. Because they are anti-immigrant and anti-Muslim, they can be expected to continue to be agitated as the country becomes more racially and ethnically diverse. As the nation becomes more nonwhite, they can be expected to hate more.

While the Obama Haters stand out for their mixture of intense hatreds, it would be a mistake to assume that they are the only Americans with antiblack, anti-immigrant, and anti-Muslim attitudes. Sadly, as the nation becomes more nonwhite, more Americans may come to resemble the Obama Haters. Currently, nearly a third of whites express anxiety about the idea of whites not being the numerical majority.[20] Sociological theory and research suggests that as a racial minority group grows in size relative to the majority group, there is more racial competition and conflict.[21] Unless we intervene positively, there may be many more haters in America's future. One way we can begin to address this problem is to use the Obama Haters to help craft an anti-prejudice agenda.

CHAPTER OVERVIEW

Chapter 1, "Why Obama Haters Should Love Obama," presents the case for why conservatives should be "Obama lovers." Given that conservatives had to have a Democratic president, since the Republican candidate lost the 2008 and 2012 elections, a Republican-friendly Democrat like Obama is ideal for them. I interview five liberal Washington, D.C., policy wonks who highlight different reasons why the left has been disappointed in Obama and why the right should be happy to have him. I present the case that on tax policy, national security, border security, and several other issues—including health insurance reform—Obama has been quite friendly to conservative ideas.

Chapter 2, "The Not-Post-Racial Election," discusses the many flaws in the thinking that led to the claim that the 2008 election of Obama made the country post-racial. I present evidence that individuals with strong antiblack prejudice voted for Obama and that on the most important measure of racial liberalism—support for addressing institutional discrimination—there is no evidence that Americans today are any more racially-liberal than they were 20 years ago.

Chapter 3, "Angry, Afraid, and Cold: Defining the Obama Haters," explains the criteria by which one is classified as an Obama Hater and presents a profile of the Obama-hating public based on data from the 2012 American National Election Study (ANES). Based on the qualitative data, a major reason why Obama Haters hate Obama is that they think that he is not American and wants to destroy America.

Chapter 4, "Obama Haters' Racial Attitudes," reviews the qualitative and quantitative ANES data for evidence of antiblack bias among Obama Haters. Obama Haters have a strong dislike of African Americans. Many of them also see whites as victims of powerful blacks and Latinos. I conclude that their hatred of Obama is just a specific example of their general fear and hatred of black people.

Chapter 5, "Othering Obama, Part I: Xenophobia among Obama Haters," discusses the Othering of Barack Obama as an immigrant. It reviews the qualitative and quantitative ANES data and finds a high level of xenophobia among Obama Haters. Nearly two-thirds of Obama Haters believe incorrectly that Obama was not born in the United States. Xenophobia is a factor in their hatred of Obama.

Chapter 6, "Othering Obama, Part II: Islamophobia among Obama Haters," presents the role of Islamophobia in Obama hatred. Obama Haters have very negative views of Muslims. I conclude that Haters believe that Obama is unpatriotic and working to destroy America because they believe he is Muslim.

Chapter 7, "Hot Tea: Obama Haters and the Tea Partiers," compares Obama Haters to supporters of the Tea Party. These groups overlap, but most Tea Party supporters are not Obama Haters. While Tea Party supporters exhibit a fairly high level of xenophobia, Islamophobia, and antiblack racism, they seem moderate in comparison to Obama Haters.

Chapter 8, "Thinking Like a Hater," compares Obama Haters' responses to conspiracy theories about the George W. Bush administration versus the Obama administration, and it examines their public policy priorities. Obama Haters reject conspiracy theories that reflect negatively on the Bush administration, but they accept conspiracy theories that are connected to the Obama administration. Because of their hatred of Obama, any negative stories about him are seductive and believable to them. Haters want to reduce government spending on welfare and to increase government spending on national defense.

Chapter 9, "The Future of Hate," addresses what can be done to improve the fate of black people and other people of color not named Barack Obama. While the concentration of negative racial and ethnic attitudes is stronger among the Obama Haters than among the Non-Haters, no hateful attitude is unique to the Haters. Further, there is reason to believe that as the country becomes more nonwhite, racial fears and hatreds will increase. Only a long-term project of sustained racial-justice organizing and anti-stereotyping communication can lower fears and anxieties.

"Afterword: Obama Unleashed in the Second Term?" discusses some of the more prominent executive actions President Obama took in 2014. Obama's executive actions were the administration's attempt to address long-standing problems and campaign promises under the constraint of the two most recalcitrant Congresses on record in U.S. history. Obama's actions were in line with public opinion and generally in line with mainstream policy thinking. None of his actions challenge the idea that he is a centrist politician.

A NOTE ON QUOTES AND TABLES

There are numerous quotations in this book taken from survey responses and from the comments sections on websites. Individuals entering comments on a survey or website generally do not have built-in access to a spell-check or other resources to improve the readability and clarity of their writing. There are a number of quotations with numerous spelling and grammatical errors, and with missing punctuation. Rather than litter these quotes with "[sic]," I have lightly edited these comments so that readers can focus on the ideas and not on the errors. When changes are made, the verbatim text can be found in the notes.

Individuals interested in data can find tables by chapter in the appendix. This will allow those interested to explore some of the quantitative findings in a bit more detail. Unless otherwise specified, the data is from the 2012 ANES.

CHAPTER 1

Why Obama Haters Should Love Obama

Listening to the professional anti-Democrats (i.e., people like Rush Limbaugh, Sarah Palin, Glenn Beck, partisan Republican politicians, and Fox News personalities) one gets the impression that Barack Obama is a far-left-leaning president with a radical leftist agenda. It can be difficult for individuals to develop a good perspective on Obama because most popular media tend to feature centrist and right-wing voices. As the ombudsman for NPR stated, on NPR, "The voice that's being left out is the left voice, not the right voice." The voice "to the left of President Obama and to the left of Bill Clinton" is the voice that is rarely heard.[1] For people who lack a good sense of the left, Obama might seem to be taking left-wing positions because the professionals in what one author calls "the Obama hate machine"[2] have been so effective in getting their hate messages out. But if one has a good sense of what the left position on issues is, Obama does not appear to be pursuing a far-left agenda.

In fact, from a position on the left, one could argue that Obama should be loved by conservatives because much of his agenda supports the traditional Republican conservative agenda. To be clear, Obama is a Democrat, not a Republican. But he is a centrist Democrat, and he has been eager to work with Republicans. Republican leaders have either been too busy hating him to notice this fact, or, more likely, they decided that it was more to their political advantage to hate Obama than to work with him.

The Republican nominee for president lost the 2008 and 2012 elections. Given that Republicans had to have a Democratic president, what type of Democrat would be best for them? One argument is that a Democrat who would seriously listen to Republican ideas, and who might even share some of them, would be best for the Republican Party and American conservatism. Barack Obama has been this type of Democrat.

In a sense, this view was first put forth by conservative students at Harvard Law School. Barack Obama became the first African American president of the *Harvard Law Review* because the conservative editors "felt he would give us a fair shake," said a former *Harvard Law Review* editor and a former member of the George W. Bush administration.[3] This view is also supported by the African American Harvard Law School professor Charles Ogletree. Ogletree recalls,

> When I first encountered Barack Obama, I thought he was a Republican. That Obama, a man even then deeply committed to progressive values, could be mistaken for a conservative was, I think, an early indication of his exceptional personal thoughtfulness and inclusiveness as a leader.[4]

The journalist Ezra Klein dubbed Obama a "moderate Republican" after pointing out that several of Obama's major policy positions, including the design of his health insurance reform, are positions that Republicans advocated for in the 1990s.[5] Bruce Bartlett, a former policy analyst for President Ronald Reagan, also pointing to Obama's major policies, argues that Obama is a "moderately conservative" politician.[6] Obama sees some validity in this characterization. He has said, "The truth of the matter is that my policies are so mainstream that . . . back in the 1980s, I would be considered a moderate Republican."[7]

To show that President Obama's agenda is not a far-left agenda and that it has had elements that have been traditionally appealing to conservatives, in the middle of 2014, I asked five left-leaning Washington, D.C., policy wonks to give their assessment of the president. The names of the wonks have been changed to maintain their confidentiality. Confidentiality allowed them to speak freely. These are individuals who have for years worked in liberal think tanks, progressive advocacy organizations, and Democratic Party politics.

The wonks gave Obama a letter grade and discussed what they see as Obama's successes and failures from their left-leaning perspective. Averaging all of their grades, Obama receives a C+ grade, with individual grades ranging from a low of a D+ to a high of B-. Obama has been far from their dream president. These policy wonks also identify areas where they feel Obama has been too conservative. It is in these areas that conservatives should be happy that they have had a centrist president and not a leftist one. The paraphrased and condensed interviews are provided here. These summaries do not cover all of the points discussed. It is important to remember that these interviews were conducted before Obama's executive actions after the 2014 midterm election. I discuss these executive actions of President Obama in the afterword.

LIBERAL POLICY WONKS GRADE THE PRESIDENT

Curtis Thompson: Obama Disempowered His Base and Made Them Passive, B–

I expected President Barack Obama to keep his campaign promise to conduct the health insurance reform in the open. But instead he held negotiations behind closed doors just as the Bill Clinton administration did. There were too many former Clinton administration staff, and they were very worried about not making the same mistakes that Clinton did in his attempt at health insurance reform. The Obama administration spent a lot of energy gaining the support of the Senate Democrats and various special interests to prevent the effort from failing. They were willing to make any deal to get the legislation to pass. This process led to cynicism among the public, and to many of the things that ended up embarrassing Obama about the reform.

Obama also made the mistake of not empowering his base around health insurance reform. He told his base to "go away, sit down. I'm going to get you health care. Trust me." This disempowered his base and made them passive. His approach to gay civil rights, on the other hand, has empowered the movement. He has empowered the LGBT community by having the president, the attorney general, and the federal government stand with the movement against states trying to deny gay civil rights. This has strengthened the gay civil rights movement.

The administration tries too hard to be bipartisan. Obama should have seized the bully pulpit to lay out a broad vision that would change the national conversation. Instead of Obama using his advantage to put his opponents on the defensive, he quickly allowed himself be put on the defensive.

For example, on health care, Obama has not changed the president Ronald Reagan conversation. He played into the Reagan conversation in the way in which he fixed health care. To change the conversation, Obama should have said something like, "government's responsibility is the health of the people." This could have been argued based on the statement in the Declaration of Independence that Americans have the right to "life, liberty, and the pursuit of happiness." Good health is an essential ingredient to these rights. Instead Obama has put forward the uninspiring technocratic message that it is government's responsibility to make sure that you buy health insurance.

Overall, Obama didn't respond to the enormity of the task facing the country during the Great Recession. He acted as if he was the president for the second Clinton administration, rather than the president of a country in a tremendous crisis. The Great Recession was essentially the same as the Great Depression. The only difference was that we had in place the safety net that we developed out of what we learned from the Great Depression. It was mainly these protective measures that prevented the economic situation from being much worse.

While the Great Depression gave us a new and stronger foundation in terms of economic policy, Obama has not built a new and stronger economic foundation from the Great Recession. The Great Depression gave us the minimum wage, but the Great Recession has not even led to an increase in the minimum wage. Obama will likely be the only president other than Ronald Reagan not to have increased the minimum wage.

Obama deserves credit for rescuing the financial system, achieving health insurance reform, and ending the wars in Iraq and Afghanistan. Obama has shown us that there was something really incompetent about the George W. Bush administration when it came to responding to terrorism. Obama has been able to get many specific terrorists that Bush could not. He got bin Laden.

Katrina Nivens: It Is Not Even Clear That Obama's Judicial Appointments Should Be Called Democrats, C+

I have been disappointed with President Barack Obama's appointments. This is a lost opportunity to create a progressive federal government and to build a broader progressive movement. I expected that, in 2009, Barack Obama would make numerous appointments of people with a strong commitment to social justice to his administration. Only in the case of the Supreme Court can I say that the Obama administration has done well. The appointment of Justice Sonia Sotomayor is probably the best thing that Obama has done as president.

The political right always looks for extreme and committed conservatives for its judicial appointments. Obama's judicial appointments, aside from the Supreme Court, are so ideologically lukewarm that it is not even clear that they should be called Democrats.

Obama has done poorly with his political appointments also. And, in too many cases, he has left important positions vacant. It is ridiculous that the administration left the Department of Labor's Wage and Hour position open when it is such an important position to deal with the effects of the Great Recession.

Obama did not use his appointments tactically to build a progressive movement. Conservatives cycle individuals through political appointee positions, and then once individuals have served in the administration, they gain legitimacy that can be used to advance conservative causes in roles outside of government. Obama has not adopted this conservative tactic.

Obama did not truly support the few progressive political appointments that he did make. The administration muzzled progressive appointees like the former secretary of labor Hilda Solis, and it did not let them engage in progressive activity. The forced resignation of Van Jones from his position as green jobs advisor is an example of the Obama administration failing to support people who had been strong Obama supporters.

Obama's governing style has also been too conservative. In general, he has not made his base happy because he compromises on progressive goals before engaging with Republicans. This pre-negotiation-compromise tactic has failed to win over any Republicans. It has been a lose–lose approach to governing.

After Obama's reelection, I hoped that Obama would let loose since he did not have to worry about being elected again. I hoped that he would make bold progressive moves, but I haven't seen this happening. I have been greatly disappointed in Obama's second term.

One positive thing the Obama administration did is the Deferred Action for Childhood Arrivals. But I'm upset that he continues to remove unauthorized immigrants at a rate higher than the George W. Bush administration. It is clear now that the high level of deportation will not win over any Republicans and cause them to support comprehensive immigration reform. So why continue to do it? The continued high deportation rate has been a slap in the face to progressives. Once again we have been duped.

There are a few other areas where the Obama administration has done well. On some of the LGBT issues, he has done better than I expected. We have so many more openly LGBT people in powerful positions in the government. Obama's ending of the military's "don't ask, don't tell" policy for gays and lesbians is a key advance.

Colin Davies: Worse Than the George W. Bush Administration, D+

The Obama administration has not done many good things. I am only able to identify a couple of positives. The administration has evolved in a positive direction on gay and lesbian issues with its support of marriage equality. But this evolution was because of pressure gays and lesbians have put on the administration. Also, Obama's support for immigration reform is a positive. Obama will sign any immigration reform bill that comes to him. Obama deserves credit for protecting the DREAMers from deportation. These positives for immigrants, however, are balanced with the negative of the high level of deportations of unauthorized immigrants during Obama's tenure.

I think that the high level of deportations of unauthorized immigrants under the Obama administration was a political move done to coax conservative leaders to support immigration reform. If this is the case, it has been a win for conservative hardliners on unauthorized immigration. We have had increased boarder enforcement, increased deportations, but no path to legalization or citizenship for the unauthorized.

I am particularly upset with the violation of civil liberties under the Obama administration. The Obama administration has been worse than the George W. Bush administration in this area. I agree with the ACLU's assessment that the Obama administration has failed to eliminate some of the worst policies put in place by President Bush such as military commissions and indefinite detention, the use of drones for assassinations, and the surveillance by the National Security Administration. I am angry that the administration encourages secrecy and has waged a war on whistleblowers instead of being a transparent administration as Obama promised.

I am bothered by many other things the administration has failed to do. I wished that Obama had pushed for a single-payer universal health insurance system. I would have accepted something less than this type of system, but only if the something less was the result of hard-fought negotiations. The Affordable Care Act is based on a conservative plan developed by a conservative think tank. Obamacare is an ultra-capitalist reform. The administration botched potentially effective climate-change policy negotiations led by Senators John Kerry, Lindsey Graham, and Joseph Lieberman. I feel that the administration did not push hard enough to close the Guantanamo prison, and to achieve comprehensive immigration reform. Obama's "Beer Summit" was a huge embarrassment. Obama was completely spineless in his response to the controversy.

Barack Obama in 2008 struck me as a moderate liberal. I hoped that there was a secret lefty Obama that would emerge, but I have yet to see this person. Obama has only turned out to be more moderate than I thought he would be. Obama is definitely not a socialist as can be seen by the great performance of the stock market under the Obama administration. Capital, as measured by the stock market, is doing very well, but the wages of average workers are stagnating. The administration has been very lenient on Wall Street given the role of Wall Street in the financial crisis that caused the Great Recession. This is because Obama has needed money from Wall Street and the "one percent" to get elected.

Sarah Hughes: Obama Caters More to Republicans Than to Democrats, B–/C+

I worked on Barack Obama's first presidential campaign, and I had high expectations for him. I thought that because Obama came from a community-organizing background, he would be very sensitive to the needs of average Americans, and that he would work to build thoughtful, systemic, progressive change. Instead, I think that Obama has been too close to business elites, and that much of what he has done has been small Band-Aid-type policies. Today, I see Obama as just a typical, very pragmatic, middle-of-the-road politician.

I hoped that as the first African American president, Barack Obama would change the landscape of American politics. I thought that he would achieve comprehensive immigration reform, focus intensely on job creation, insure that people of color had power and influence in the government, run an open and transparent government, and shift priorities so that policies benefited poor people and people of color. I have been very disappointed.

Immigration reform has not been achieved, and its prospects are dim. I think that the administration did not fight hard enough on this issue. I am happy, though, about the Deferred Action for Childhood Arrivals policy.

In terms of race, I feel that the administration has gone out of its way to avoid the issue. Obama has even slighted the minority caucuses in Congress. Too few people of color have been appointed to the administration. Obama has not done enough to address the needs of people of color who were disproportionately hurt during the Great Recession. I am annoyed by the conservative personal-responsibility themes in his speeches toward African Americans.

I am also disturbed by the emphasis on the military in the Obama administration. It seems like Obama is trying to prove to white America that he is indeed American, and to prove that he is patriotic. It is unfortunate that Michelle Obama has been forced to work so much on the issue of military families and has had to repeatedly pose for military photo-ops. Michelle Obama's full potential has not been used by the administration.

The administration has made many mistakes in its education policies. It has supported charter schools, but these schools have often excluded limited-English-proficient students and students with disabilities. The administration's Race to the Top program has exacerbated inequalities, because it is the most advantaged school systems that are most likely to win the competition. This competition leaves poor and rural school systems behind. The White House's My Brother's Keeper initiative on boys and young men of color is heavily focused on education, but it is too little and too late. There is nothing new and innovative in its recommendations. If the issue was more important to the administration they could have done something larger, with a bigger impact, earlier on in Obama's tenure. The administration does get credit though for trying to increase access to high-quality early childhood education, and for making investments in Pell grants and in minority-serving colleges and universities. It is also positive that the administration is attempting to reform for-profit colleges.

As someone involved in the Obama campaign, I saw the large numbers of people that he engaged. I saw that he had a strong progressive following. Progressives were campaigning for him all over the country. It is a shame that this people power was not used by the administration. In my eyes, Obama caters more to Republicans than to Democrats. He has appointed too many Republicans to positions. Some people feel that he doesn't have any loyalty to his party.

Erik Naylor: Hillary Clinton Might Have Been Better for Black Progress Than Obama, C+

Obama is a fairly mainstream liberal, but the Great Recession forced Obama to enact more left-leaning, progressive policies to save the economy than he would have otherwise. While Obama has been forced to be progressive, Obama has squandered opportunities to establish a more long-standing progressive era. Many of what I would call the positives of the Obama administration are tainted by the missed opportunities to do much more in terms of progressive politics.

From the start, Obama made substantial mistakes. Obama thought that he could bring the country together. He believed it; I didn't. This led Obama to immediately shutting down an important source of power. He created a movement around himself to get elected, and then he demobilized it in favor of a political strategy of compromise with the right. Obama should have used the movement to push forward a people's agenda. Obama has not been power strong in his approach to politics.

On the other hand, I did not expect the ferocious intensity of the opposition to Obama. Even moderate, centrist policies put forth by Obama have been opposed.

Obama did well by enacting the American Recovery and Reinvestment Act (ARRA), which is an important progressive legislation. ARRA is the largest investment in decades for job creation for middle-class and working-class people and for poverty reduction. However, ARRA is also Obama's greatest missed opportunity. The economic stimulus needed to be bigger. If Obama was not so determined to reason and compromise with the right, he could have fought for and won a larger stimulus. Obama also did not put in ARRA targeted help for communities of color. ARRA could have been used to make true advances to reduce racial inequality, but the vision needed to do this was never there in the administration.

I never thought that Barack Obama would be very progressive, and Obama has lived down to my expectations. The only area where my expectations were not realized was in the area of foreign policy. Obama has been more conservative, and therefore worse than I thought he would be, in this area. Obama's foreign policy looks a lot like President George W. Bush's foreign policy. Obama is conducting a 2.0-version of the Bush foreign policy but with drones where Bush had boots on the ground. Conservatives should be happy generally with Obama, and they should also be happy about how many members of Al-Qaeda have been killed under the Obama administration.

I have been irked by Obama's racial politics. It drove me crazy the way he did and didn't deal with the issue of race. I couldn't stand his major address on race. The Philadelphia speech on race was so self-serving. My critique of that speech is that his major address on race happened only because he was in trouble. It wasn't coming out of a spirit of dealing with the racial divide. It was about saving his political career. And it was crafted to get past the issue so that he could deal with other things. That's not helpful for dealing with racial inequality.

I think that there may have been more racial progress and more progress in terms of progressive politics generally if Hillary Clinton had been elected. This is not because Clinton is more progressive than Obama, but because people on the left would have been more willing to criticize her for not doing more. Black and white liberal activists have been reluctant to criticize Barack Obama for being too conservative because he is the first black president.

On race, however, Obama faces heightened scrutiny. If Obama enacted legislation with the purpose of helping African Americans, he would run the risk of being seen as racially biased in favor of blacks and not as simply trying to address the legitimate needs of a segment of the American population. For this reason also, I wonder if Hillary Clinton might have been better for black progress than Obama. It's clear to me that Hillary would have had more space to deal directly with race particularly as it relates to African Americans.

Conclusion

Barack Obama has been a disappointment to many on the political left. He has taken a centrist path and has missed great opportunities to advance progressive causes. For those on the left, he has done some good things, but mainly because outside forces forced him to be more progressive than he probably desired to be. The C+ grade of these policy wonks is in line with an assessment of Obama's first term by progressives. *Grading the 44th President: A Report Card on Barack Obama's First Term as a Progressive Leader* gives Obama a C- grade.[8] In the following discussion I use the insights of the wonks to examine more carefully why conservatives might not love Obama and why they should love Obama.

WHY CONSERVATIVES MIGHT NOT LOVE OBAMA

It is to be expected that Republicans would find things that they do not like in a Democratic administration. This is the reason why they identify as Republican. Many conservative Democrats may also disagree with some mainstream Democratic ideas. In this section, I am focusing not on Obama's support for long-standing Democratic policies but on policies where he moved the Democratic Party significantly forward on an issue or championed a new issue. It is in these areas, where, I would say, it is most legitimate for Republicans or conservatives to be upset with the administration.

The policy wonks do identify areas where Obama has made advances that conservatives might not like. If one is opposed to gay and lesbian civil rights, then one could legitimately dislike Obama. Obama signed legislation expanding hate-crimes law to include sexual orientation and legislation permitting gays and lesbians to serve openly in the military.[9] He expanded the Family Leave Act to include same-sex couples,[10] issued an executive order preventing federal contractors from discriminating against employees based on sexual identity or gender orientation,[11] and supported the Supreme Court's striking down of the Defense of Marriage Act.[12] The end of the Defense of Marriage Act means that married same-sex couples can now obtain federal benefits.[13] For individuals opposed to gay and lesbian civil rights, these are all moves in the wrong direction.

Individuals who want the administration to take the hardest line on unauthorized immigrants may be upset that the administration has begun Deferred Action for Childhood Arrivals. This action enables individuals who were brought to the United States without authorization when they were under 16 years old the possibility of avoiding deportation for two years.[14] While an anti-unauthorized-immigrant person might not like this administrative action, it is a very modest program. In the following section I discuss why an anti-unauthorized-immigrant person might feel positive about the administration. (I discuss the 2014 Deferred Action for Parental Accountability in the afterword.)

Individuals favoring limited government involvement in the economy— even in times of extreme economic crisis—would likely be upset by the American Recovery and Reinvestment Act (ARRA or the Obama economic stimulus), and the Patient Protection and Affordable Care Act (ACA or Obamacare). ARRA was based on the principles of Keynesian economics, which was developed from the analysis of the Great Depression. It is not a far-left economic theory but a long-standing part of mainstream economics.[15] Obamacare was based on a conservative health insurance reform proposal, and it works by requiring those who can afford it to purchase *private* health insurance.[16] A version of Obamacare was implemented at the state level by the former Republican governor Mitt Romney.[17] Because ARRA and Obamacare are mainstream and conservative policies, respectively, they should not automatically offend average conservatives. Only extreme conservatives or conservatives who were misinformed about the policies should be opposed to these policies.

A recurring theme of this book is that there has been tremendous misinformation hounding Obama at every step. Although the economic stimulus was attacked by conservative anti-Democrats as a "trillion-dollar socialist experiment"[18] among other things, for serious macroeconomists, there is consensus that ARRA was effective in halting the decline in the U.S. economy.

The economic analysts at Goldman Sachs, Macroeconomic Advisors, Global Insight, and JPMorgan all see ARRA as adding strength to the American economy.[19] A survey of a geographically and politically diverse group of 44 of the nation's leading academic economists found that 36 thought that the Obama economic stimulus reduced unemployment, 1 disagreed, and the remaining 7 did not respond. When asked if they think that the benefits of the stimulus exceeded the costs, 25 economists agreed, 2 disagreed, and 10 were uncertain.[20] The nonpartisan Congressional Budget Office also finds that the stimulus worked.[21] Below the national level, the stimulus found some support among Republican governors, mayors, and county executives.[22] Obama's economic stimulus was based on mainstream economic theory, and it was widely seen as effective by experts. It is really only the most ideologically extreme of conservatives who should oppose ARRA.

Of the items here that could upset a Republican or a conservative, the major issue is for antigay-rights conservatives. The Obama administration has hurt their cause, but it seems likely that there would have been similar changes with any Democratic administration. Some progressive critics argue that the Obama administration has been following public opinion on this issue, not leading it.[23] With regard to unauthorized immigrants, what the administration did up until 2014 was quite modest. As the wonks and others argue, the administration could have done much more. On the Recovery Act, given the choice between the stimulus and another Great Depression, the rational choice is the stimulus. Republicans in the Senate were also able to change ARRA so that it was more in line with their conservative ideals.[24] It is also worth noting that there have been several cases of lawmakers who voted against the Recovery Act but then sought to bring more of its benefits to their districts.[25] The Obama administration has not pushed an extreme left-wing agenda that could account for the extreme level of hatred directed at it.

WHY CONSERVATIVES SHOULD LOVE OBAMA

Conservatives should love Obama because he has achieved conservative goals, supported conservative policies, endorsed conservative beliefs, failed to build a stronger progressive movement, and has been willing to compromise with conservatives on just about anything. It is hard to think of a Democratic president who has, in a sense, loved conservative ideas more.

In terms of domestic policy, there probably isn't a goal more important to Republican leaders than cutting taxes. For this reason, Republicans should be swooning over President Barack Obama. In his first two years as president, Obama cut taxes more than President George W. Bush did in his first *four* years.[26] There has been little attention paid to the fact that about a third

(36 percent) of the Recovery Act was tax cuts. Of the $816.3 billion of the stimulus, $290.7 billion were in the form of tax benefits.[27] In 2010, Obama approved a tax cut package worth $801 billion.[28] In 2013, Obama did what President Bush could not: he made the Bush tax cuts permanent for 99 percent of American taxpayers. All of the Bush tax cuts were scheduled to expire, but Obama allowed them to expire only for the richest 1 percent. Over 10 years, this revised continuation of the Bush-Obama tax cuts is valued at $4.6 trillion.[29] As a result of Bush and Obama tax cutting, middle-income families are paying a lower rate for federal taxes than they have in several decades.[30] Many conservatives love tax cuts; therefore, they should love Obama.

As the wonks mentioned, the Obama administration has run a relatively strong national-security state. The Obama administration has killed a large number of individuals presumed or known to be major terrorist leaders against the United States, including Osama bin Laden, the mastermind behind the September 11, 2001, attacks.[31] Obama has been eager to remove the United States from George W. Bush's wars in Iraq and Afghanistan, but, in terms of the rest of the American "war on terror," Obama has continued Bush's policies. The blogger Kevin Gosztola reports on a speech where Michael Hayden, Bush's former director of the Central Intelligence Agency and the National Security Agency, outlines the continuities between Bush's and Obama's national-security policies:

> The former CIA director highlighted Obama's failure to close Guantanamo, the administration's invoking of the state secrets privilege in "war on terror" cases and supporting the continued legalization of the Bush administration's warrantless wiretapping program through the reauthorization of the FISA Amendments Act.[32]

Hayden stated that there is a "powerful continuity between two vastly different presidents, George W. Bush and Barack Obama . . . when it comes to this conflict."[33] Conservatives who support Bush's "war-on-terror" tactics should support Obama.

President Obama has also continued and expanded George W. Bush's policies with regard to the U.S. border and unauthorized immigration. There are more border security agents now than at any other time in U.S. history. Along the Southwest border, specifically, the number of agents increased from about 9,000 in 2001 to about 19,000 in 2013.[34] An immigration expert, Douglas Massey, states, "We know from various surveys that the cost of hiring a smuggler to get into the U.S. has increased significantly as enforcement has been ramped up. We also know that Mexicans have been pushed into more remote areas to try to cross where it is physically more difficult and dangerous."[35] The increased patrols of the Southwest border has led to some reduction in the number of immigrants entering the United States illegally.[36]

The Obama administration has removed about two million unauthorized immigrants. These are more removals than in any other administration.[37] It has also adopted a "near zero-tolerance" policy at the border. In 2013, nearly two-thirds of the deportations by Immigration and Customs Enforcement were of immigrants caught as they were trying to enter the country illegally. The administration also has a policy of "fast-track" deportations in which immigrants receive no screening by immigration officers or hearings by judges to challenge their deportation.[38] Conservatives who want strong border security and who want unauthorized immigrants deported should love the Obama administration since it has a strong record in this area.

More often than not, President Obama's approach to African Americans has been in accord with the dominant conservative thinking on race. Conservatives tend to argue for a color-blind or post-racial perspective. They see racial prejudice and discrimination as largely things of the past and as not important to contemporary life. Consequently, there is no need to have policies to address antiblack prejudice and discrimination since it is claimed that these things do not exist today. Conservatives see the lower standing of blacks on various socioeconomic measures, not as evidence of racial discrimination but as evidence that blacks are being held back by their bad cultural values and behaviors.

Barack Obama agrees that bad cultural values and behaviors hold blacks back. In his 2006 book, *The Audacity of Hope*, he states, "We know that many in the inner city are trapped by their own self-destructive behaviors" and that "perhaps the single biggest thing we could do to reduce [inner city] poverty is encourage teenage girls to finish high school and avoid having children out of wedlock."[39] In 2008, Senator Obama lectured a black congregation,

> If we are honest with ourselves, we'll admit that what too many [African American] fathers also are is missing—missing from too many lives and too many homes. They have abandoned their responsibilities, acting like boys instead of men. And the foundations of our families are weaker because of it.[40]

In 2013, at the graduation ceremony of the historically black and male Morehouse College, Obama stated, "We know that too many young men in our community continue to make bad choices."[41] Conservatives who believe that blacks are to blame for their low socioeconomic standing should be happy to have Obama as president.

President Obama's signature legislation, the ACA (Obamacare), should also be loved by conservatives. It is true that the ACA serves the liberal ideal of providing health insurance coverage to more Americans, but it is done within a conservative framework. Rising government health care costs in Medicare, Medicaid, and the Veteran's Administration are "the single largest cause of the federal government's long-term budget problems."[42] All rich countries do a better job than the United States at providing health insurance to *all of their citizens at a lower per capita cost.*[43] Health insurance reform is absolutely necessary to begin reducing U.S. deficits and the debt, which are very important goals for fiscal conservatives.

The simplest reform and the one favored by many on the left was to expand Medicare to cover all Americans. This single-payer option would have low costs, but it would have eliminated the private insurance industry.[44] Antigovernment conservatives would object to a universal government-provided health insurance system. President Obama, however, did not push for the left-leaning Medicare-for-all option. Instead, the ACA is based on a reform plan from the conservative think tank, the Heritage Foundation.[45] The ACA is, in a sense, a compromise between the fiscally conservative ideal of lowering government health care costs and the antigovernment conservative ideal of maintaining lots of private companies in health insurance. If one is conservative and has to have health insurance reform, one would prefer a reform designed by a conservative think tank than a liberal one. Obamacare is that health insurance reform and the reason that conservatives should love Obamacare.

The wonks generally agree that Obama has squandered opportunities to build and strengthen the progressive movement. They argue that he did not use the many people mobilized by his campaign to advance a progressive agenda and that he did use his power to make judicial and political appointments to build a progressive movement. According to Thompson, Obama told his base to "go away [and] sit down." Thompson argues that this governing style disempowered his base and made them passive. Nivens believes that Obama's judicial and political appointments have been ideologically lukewarm. Hughes feels Obama has failed to utilize his strong progressive following after his first campaign. Naylor argues that Obama created a movement around himself to get elected, and then he demobilized it in favor of a political strategy of compromise with the right. In this instance, Obama did not do something to further the conservative agenda, but he failed to seize opportunities to advance a progressive agenda. This is another reason that conservatives can be happy to have Obama as president.

Perhaps the most appealing Obama quality for conservatives is the fact that Obama has been eager to compromise with conservatives. Robert H. Mnookin of the Harvard Negotiation Research Project states, "President Obama's natural inclination, in my view, is to really try very hard to understand the other side's perspective, try to reach common ground."[46] The journalist Michael Grunwald states, "Obama was by nature a conciliator, even when his enemies were vowing to kick the hell out of him."[47] Grunwald reports about the negotiations for the Recovery Act:

> [Republicans] demanded tax cuts; [Obama] gave them tax cuts. They complained about sod on the Mall, condoms, herpes prevention, and "smoking cessation"; he killed all those Democratic cats and dogs. Obama showed unprecedented deference by visiting the Republicans on their turf in his first week; they signaled he was wasting his time before he even got into his motorcade.[48]

This inclination to constantly try to appease Republicans even when it is clear that they have no interest in compromise has irritated liberals as can be seen in the interviews with the wonks earlier.

Paul Krugman stated that Obama has a "deeply self-destructive tendency to echo his opponents' arguments."[49] But there is reason to believe that Obama sometimes repeats conservative arguments because, as a centrist Democrat, he finds many of those arguments appealing. Grunwald writes:

> [Obama is] more comfortable in the role of dad taking away the credit card than teenager binging at the mall. He seemed defensive about the stimulus, often noting that he never planned to start his presidency with a spending spree, complaining it reinforced the Republican narrative that he was a typical liberal Democrat. Deficit reduction better suited his self-image as a centrist, a maker of hard choices, a cleaner of Bush-era messes; he joked about his "inner Blue Dog."[50]

One White House economist told Grunwald, "In his heart, I think the president was a deficit hawk,"[51] a person who supports the conservative position on federal spending.

President Obama has disappointed those on the left, including everyone I interviewed, repeatedly, because he is a centrist Democrat. Obama proved his commitment to being open to conservative ideas even if it meant angering his liberal base by offering to cut Social Security benefits with the "chained Consumer Price Index."[52] Cutting Social Security benefits has been a big, long-standing goal of conservative deficit hawks.[53] Liberals see Social Security as one of their major policy successes because it has been very effective at reducing poverty.[54] Left-leaning liberals argue for increasing Social Security benefits, not decreasing them.[55]

Barack Obama has repeatedly, massively cut taxes. He did what Bush could not do: he made nearly all of the Bush tax cuts permanent. He has continued and expanded Bush's war-on-terror policies and, as Thompson argues, has probably been more effective in executing those policies than Bush. Osama bin Laden, for example, was caught under the Obama administration, not Bush's. He has secured the border more and has removed more immigrants than any other president in history. He believes the conservative idea that blacks' self-destructive behaviors play a major role in their low socioeconomic status. He has thrown cold water on the progressive movement. He has based his health insurance reform on ideas from a leading conservative think tank. He has shown that he is willing to negotiate with conservatives on anything. Despite being, perhaps, the most Republican-friendly of all Democratic presidents, Obama is the most disliked president among Republicans on record.[56]

Obama's example teaches us that our current political system and media can be quite good at spreading and maintaining lies. A centrist Democrat who endorses conservative ideas can be painted as a socialist at war with conservatism. Despite doing many things that should lead him to be loved by conservatives, Obama is hated.

CHAPTER 2

The Not-Post-Racial Election

The 2008 election of Barack Obama as president was a high point for the belief in the idea of a post-racial America. From as early as the 1960s, some scholars have downplayed, if not completely dismissed, racial prejudice and discrimination as important factors in racial inequality.[1] By the 2000s, liberal (or formerly liberal) black public intellectuals like Bill Cosby, Juan Williams, and Orlando Patterson loudly proclaimed that it was the bad behavior spawned from a culture of poverty that held blacks back.[2] Barack Obama, the senator, joined this chorus when he argued in *The Audacity of Hope*, "We know that many in the inner city are trapped by their own self-destructive behaviors" and that "perhaps the single biggest thing we could do to reduce [inner city] poverty is encourage teenage girls to finish high school and avoid having children out of wedlock."[3] For many, the successful election of Barack Obama—the nation's first black president—was the final proof that it is not race but bad values that hold blacks back. Obama's 2008 election seemed like the triumph of the argument that America had moved beyond a place where nonwhite race limited opportunities.

NPR news analyst Daniel Schorr argued that Obama's campaign successes signaled the emergence of a "post-racial era . . . where civil rights veterans of the past century are consigned to history and Americans begin to make race-free judgments on who should lead them."[4] The African American Harvard University professor Henry Louis Gates, Jr., declared that the election was "the symbolic culmination of the black freedom struggle, the grand achievement of a great collective dream."[5] The African American journalist Jonetta Rose Barras claimed that "with Barack Obama's ascension to the highest office in the United States, most African Americans feel that we have arrived as fully equal citizens."[6] One young Californian woman argued,

"At this point, the whole race thing is over . . . it doesn't matter anymore. We've transcended it. Now we have a black president, so clearly we are not racist."[7] The success of Obama led many to believe that antiblack racial bias and discrimination had ended.[8]

Today, after the arrest of Professor Gates, after the killing of Trayvon Martin, after the hostility toward unauthorized immigrants from Mexico and Central America, after the events in Ferguson, Missouri, after the attacks on black voting rights, after the protests in Baltimore over the death of Freddie Gray, we hear far fewer assertions that America is beyond race. In fact, in December 2014, Americans rated racism one of the most important problems facing the country.[9]

The fact that the erroneous claim of post-racialism was made by so many reveals that there are many things we do not understand about racial prejudice and discrimination. A reexamination of the election and the post-racial argument can help to correct the flaws in our thinking. As the nation becomes more racially and ethnically diverse, increasingly there will be similar situations of people of color being selected for positions of power that tempt us to assume more racial progress than may actually exist. By understanding our errors in 2008, we will be better able to distinguish true racial progress from superficial racial progress.

WHAT DID VOTING FOR OBAMA MEAN FOR ANTIBLACK RACIAL PREJUDICE AND DISCRIMINATION

The argument about the arrival of a post-racial America rested on false assumptions about what the election of a black man as president of the United States signified. Obama's victory was historic, but, as I will show later, in itself, it revealed almost nothing about racial attitudes in America and even less about racial discrimination in America.

Although we often think that elections provide unambiguous answers about what the public wants, the fact of the matter is that the typical American election cannot be used as an indicator of majority public opinion. One problem with American elections is the low participation rate. In 2008, only 57 percent of the voting-age[10] population actually voted.[11] Obama received slightly more than half of these votes. He was supported by 29 percent of the voting-age population—nowhere near a majority of the American people.[12] Even if we were to accept the assumption that people voting for Obama are post-racial, the overwhelming majority of American adults did *not* vote for Obama. We cannot conclude that non-Obama voters are post-racial.

The same error in thinking about elections was present in the response to the 2014 election of Mia Love as the first black Utahan woman in Congress.[13] The turnout rate for that election was about 25 percent.[14] Love received half of the vote[15] giving her support from about 13 percent of voting-age Utahans in Congressional District 4. Again, this is nowhere near a majority, and these results cannot be used to declare the District 4 Utahans colorblind as Love has suggested.[16]

In fact, there is reason to wonder if race hurt Love significantly in the election. Love is a Mormon Republican in a very Mormon and very Republican state, yet she received only 50 percent of the vote. The *Cook Political Report* declared Mia Love the "top Republican underachiever for only barely winning in a strongly Republican area."[17] Rather than celebrate that 13 percent of District 4 Utahans voted for a black woman, we should be asking why so many of them did not.

It is also incorrect to assume that voting for a black candidate means that one is post-racial. For decades, sociologists have been aware that individuals can feel different degrees of comfort in different situations with racial groups.[18] Someone may be fine with working with a person of a different race but may still not want a person of that race to be his or her neighbor or a member of his or her family.[19] What does voting for a black person for president mean? While the presidency is a very important position and the president represents the country in a variety of ways, for most voters the president is not someone that they interact with every day. He doesn't live in their neighborhood. His kids do not attend school with their kids. Being president does not make him part of their family. We don't know what voting for a black man for president means in terms of one's comfort in interacting with blacks more generally. This is a second reason why we cannot use an election of a racial minority candidate as a broad measure of racial attitudes.

There is evidence that there was a "racists-for-Obama" vote. In American politics, it is not uncommon for voters to choose the candidate who they feel is the lesser of two evils. A vote for a candidate is often much less than an enthusiastic endorsement of that candidate. There were a number of political, economic, and strategic factors that drove voters to support Obama and that could have caused some voters to put aside their dislike of blacks temporarily. For the voter who told a canvasser, "Ma'am, we're voting for the n***er," it probably wasn't post-racialism that motivated him.[20] Another said, "I've got to vote for him," but he also reluctantly admitted, "I'm not crazy about him . . . I don't know, maybe 'cause he's black."[21] Union organizers in Pennsylvania were able to convince a number of voters who did not want to vote for a black man to forget Obama's race for a moment and just vote according to their policy positions.[22]

It was possible to vote for Obama and still not like black people very much. In 2008, the political scientist Charles Franklin found that more than a fifth of Americans with negative attitudes toward blacks supported Obama.[23] My analysis, using a different dataset and a different measure of racial prejudice, finds that of the people who voted in 2008, 3 in 10 individuals who express a high level of antiblack racial resentment voted for Obama. (In 2012, a quarter of them planned on voting for Obama).[24] Voting for a black politician does not mean that an individual is free of racial prejudice.

One way that people who dislike black people could vote for Obama is by seeing him as not black. The Obama campaign, in a variety of ways, high-lighted that Obama was raised by a white mother and white grandparents,[25] leading many to think of him as biracial. On the other hand, Obama personally identifies as black.[26] In the United States, the dominant historical pattern has been for individuals with a black and a white parent to identify as black.[27] It is only since the emergence of the biracial or multiracial movement in the 1990s that this pattern has been strongly contested nationally.[28] Most African Americans have white ancestry.[29] Many individuals with a similar skin color to Obama identify as black and are assumed to be black by strangers on the street. Thus, it is possible for individuals to see Obama as black *or* as black–white biracial.

For some people, they could vote for Obama when they thought of him as biracial but not when they thought of him as black. One woman, a lifelong Democrat, struggled with the idea of voting for a black man for president. Finally, her sister convinced her: "My sister said, 'You don't understand—he is white, too. He has a white mom and white grandparents.' That had a lot to do with [me voting for Obama]."[30] At least some Obama campaign volunteers used this strategy to move people to support Obama. A volunteer reported:

> If this issue [Obama's race] comes up, even if obliquely, I emphasize that Obama is from a multiracial background and that his father was an African intellectual, not an American from the inner city. I explain that Obama has never aligned himself solely with African-American interests—not on any issue—but rather has always sought to find a middle ground.[31]

Another volunteer reports telling an admittedly prejudiced voter: "One thing you have to remember is that Obama, he's half white and he was raised by his white mother. So his views are more white than black really."[32]

There is reason to believe Obama's biracial background played a role in his winning the election. A slight majority of Americans (52 percent) see Obama as biracial. Only 27 percent categorize him as black. The remainder see him as either both, neither, or they don't know how to categorize him. Whites and Latinos are more likely than blacks to categorize Obama as mixed-race.[33] Further, individuals who see Obama as having different values and interests from blacks are more likely to perceive him as being mixed-race.[34] Given these facts, it is possible that a majority of people voting for Obama did not see themselves as voting for a black man.

Obama probably also benefited from his biracial background in a more subtle way because it conferred onto him a relatively light complexion for a man who identifies as black. The political psychologist Drew Western argues, "Barack Obama had light-colored skin, and that made a big difference." Western feels that had he a dark complexion, "it is not at all clear to me that he could have made it."[35] Other researchers have found that darker skin leads to worse social and economic outcomes for blacks.[36]

Another way that someone could vote for Obama and separate him from blackness is to see him as exceptional. One white woman stated,

> [Obama's] "black characteristics" (if you will) are not there. The way that African Americans speak, the way that they behave—a lot of things about him radiate "white" not "black." And maybe that's why I don't even think about his race.[37]

When someone views a black person as "not really black," this way of thinking allows the person to remain uncritical about his or her antiblack biases and stereotypes while reacting positively to a particular black person.

A person's attitude toward a particular individual of a racial or ethnic minority group cannot be assumed to be his or her attitude toward the group generally. Even individuals who voted for Obama and who hold him in positive regard cannot be automatically assumed to be free of prejudice against black people generally. Some Obama supporters did not see themselves as voting for a black man because they see him as biracial or because they perceive him as being not really black. For these individuals, supporting Obama and having antiblack attitudes would not be inconsistent, because Obama is not black in their mind.

A more significant error in the thinking that the election of Barack Obama means that the country is post-racial is the way it fundamentally avoids the issue of institutional racial discrimination. Racial discrimination is more than simply interpersonal interactions. The day before Obama's election America's schools were still—more than a half century after the *Brown* decision—racially segregated and unequal. The inferior schools that black children attend place them at a disadvantage relative to white students.[38] White youth who use and sell illicit drugs are much less likely to be incarcerated than black youth who do the same.[39] These and other societal inequities are the result of institutional practices, not simply interpersonal animus. Obama's election did not make these and other forms of institutional discrimination go away.[40]

Institutional discrimination can be best addressed when there is strong public support to address these types of problems. The political scientist Vincent L. Hutchings examined whether whites in the Obama era showed signs of being more willing to support policies to address institutional discrimination than whites did two decades ago. He first examined whether whites thought that the government should ensure that blacks do not face discrimination in the labor market or whether they thought it was not the government's business. In 1988, 48 percent of whites felt that the government should ensure that blacks received fair treatment. In 2008, basically the same share of whites (44 percent) agreed. Hutchings also examined whether whites supported the idea that the government should try to improve the social and economic position of blacks. In 1988, 40 percent of whites did. In 2008, again, basically the same share (37 percent) agreed. Hutchings's final item for examination was support for affirmative action. In both 1988 and 2008, 11 percent of whites expressed support for affirmative action.[41] Based on Hutchings's findings, there is no evidence that whites in the Obama era are any more racially progressive than in the past. The biggest obstacle to black equal opportunity is still institutional discrimination, and the American public is still largely opposed to addressing it.

THE MOST RACIALIZED RECENT ELECTION

For those who bothered to look for it, there was evidence that the 2008 election of Barack Obama as president was not a sign of a post-racial America. Of course, many people would not come out and say that they opposed Obama because of his race. But as the Arkansan journalist Suzi Parker stated,

> In 2008, white people I have known my entire life confessed to me that they would not vote for Obama because of his race. They won't go on record. They will say otherwise in public. But in a comfortable environment over iced tea when they forget I'm a reporter, they will say this.[42]

She added:

> They will crack racist jokes. They will insist Obama is a Muslim, a socialist and a Nazi. These are not Republicans necessarily. In fact, many of these people have voted Democratic their entire lives.[43]

While many people with these views might be reluctant to share them, it was not impossible to find some who would.

In addition to the "racists-for-Obama" voters, there were "racists-against-Obama" voters. In some pockets of the country, the Obama campaign field-workers encountered a level of antiblack animosity that shocked them.[44] When Danielle Ross was campaigning for Obama in Indiana, she recalled that the first person she encountered said bluntly, "I'll never vote for a black person." This response set the tone for a horrible day for Ross that was filled with people expressing antiblack sentiments. Some Obama field-workers and phone-bank volunteers had to deal with being called racially derogatory names and with hearing hateful rants and ugly racial stereotypes. One phone-bank volunteer was told that someone should "hang that darky from a tree!"[45]

In Texas too, a man blurted out, "String him from a tree!" recalls Nadia Y. Kim, another Obama campaign volunteer. A white woman told Kim, "Not only will I not vote for him, but I wouldn't help him if he was dying at my feet!" In Las Vegas, a campaign worker recalls being told essentially, "I'm not going to vote for [Obama] because he's black," from three different people.[46] An Obama volunteer reports that in Virginia, "volunteers were distressed when respondents dismissed Obama as a worthless 'nigger' before hanging up the phone or slamming the door."[47] In Pennsylvania, a campaign worker reported that his jaw dropped when someone forcefully said, "I ain't voting for no 'f-ing n-word.'"[48] Another Pennsylvania Obama volunteer said that 1 in 10 people he spoke to said they would not vote for Obama because of his race.[49] In North Carolina a woman told an Obama volunteer, "I'd never vote for a [racial slur]."[50]

Beyond these reports, the evidence from a statistical analysis of survey data reveals that not only did race play a role in the 2008 presidential campaign and election, but 2008 was the most racially polarized election in recent history. The political scientists Michael Tesler and David O. Sears determined that an individual's level of antiblack racial resentment was a powerful predictor of support for Obama versus Hillary Clinton and versus John McCain. Individuals low in resentment toward blacks were more likely to favor Obama versus his opponents even after taking into account other factors that predict vote choice. Individuals with high levels of antiblack racial resentment were more likely to favor Obama's opponents all else equal.[51]

Tesler and Sears conclude:

> We can say with a great deal of confidence that the election of our first black president was not a post-racial moment. Rather, racial attitudes were heavily implicated in every aspect of Barack Obama's quest for the White House. From Americans' earliest evaluations of Candidate Obama to their primary voting to their general election vote choice, Obama was heavily judged in terms of his racial background. Racial attitudes were strongly associated with both support for and opposition to Obama throughout the election year. With these positive and negative effects largely canceling themselves out in Obama's aggregate vote tallies, many mistakenly took his victory as a sign that race no longer mattered in American politics. Behind such success in the primaries and general election, however, lay perhaps the most racialized presidential voting patterns in American history.[52]

Obama's 2008 victory was therefore precisely the opposite of a post-racial moment.

After the election, individuals who disliked blacks were, if anything, feeling more hateful than before. The Southern Poverty Law Center, which tracks hate crimes, found that there was an increase in these incidents after the election,[53] including on several college campuses.[54] For example, on the campus of North Carolina State University, students spray-painted, "Let's shoot that Nigger in the head" and "Hang Obama by a noose."[55]

The scholar Mark Orbe documented the experiences of black students at two historically black colleges in Alabama. The students had to limit or stifle their celebrations of Obama's victory because of the anger in the broader community about the election. After one of the schools received a bomb threat, the administrators told the students not to wear Obama t-shirts. In addition, someone drove through one of the campuses with a Confederate flag on the back of a truck.[56] One young woman described her experience off-campus the day after the election:

> My boyfriend and I were out at the store after the election—the day after the election. And we just got stared down. And I'm used to getting stared at down here, but it was like . . . I mean with hatred. I mean conversations would cease when we walked by. We were like, "Holy crap! We have to get back to campus!" . . . [We heard] stories about people being shouted at as they walked to their cars. Stuff being thrown at people's cars as they drove by. So, we decided to spend the day on campus.[57]

It is clearly wrong to declare an election the beginning of post-racial era when in Alabama and elsewhere blacks, fearing racial violence, are too afraid to celebrate the results of the election.

WHY AMERICANS HAVE DIFFICULTY SEEING RACIAL PREJUDICE AND DISCRIMINATION

> *I didn't think it was so prevalent, but boy, the [racist] billboard signs and these [racist] laminated pages—it shows that in the rural community I live in, there is a race problem. . . . I knew there was prejudice but didn't think it was to that extent.*[58]
>   —a white canvasser for the 2008 Obama campaign

One reason so many pundits could declare the election of Barack Obama as a post-racial moment is that the Obama campaign and news organizations chose to make the racial animosity directed toward him during the 2008 campaign largely a nonstory.[59] The campaign strategists were aware of the negative role that race could play for Obama in the election. They needed to do everything possible to prevent people from thinking of Obama as a black candidate as opposed to a candidate who just happens to have African ancestry. Gwen Ifill reported that Cornell Belcher, the Obama campaign's top pollster, told her after the election, "The thing is, a *black man* can't be president of America, given the racial aversion and history that's still out there . . . However, an extraordinary, gifted, and talented young man who happens to be black can be president."[60] Talking about the fairly common occurrence of antiblack racial slurs directed at campaign workers would make more voters think about blackness and Obama together. Although Obama campaign workers could report receiving racist comments with some regularity, these experiences rarely made news. Pundits could easily miss them.

They could also easily miss these sentiments because we are an increasingly ideologically polarized nation.[61] People low in racial prejudice tend to hang out with other people with similar beliefs. These individuals are then susceptible to thinking that all of America is racially liberal. So, racially liberal pundits with their racially liberal friends did not see any news reports about racist attitudes directed at Obama, and they then declared that the election of Barack Obama proves that the country is post-racial.

But the deeper question is, why, given our knowledge of America's racial history, didn't news editors and pundits *seek out* stories about the racist attitudes directed at Obama campaign workers? The campaign workers were ready to tell their stories but few reporters asked for them.[62]

There are several answers. One reason, to paraphrase the former Attorney General Eric Holder, why we are cowards about discussing racial prejudice and discrimination is that prejudice and discrimination runs so strongly against our ideas of America and of individualism in American culture. We tell ourselves that America is the greatest country on earth because we love freedom and because anyone who works hard can succeed in America through his or her own efforts. If we acknowledge the long, deep, and persistent reality of American racial subjugation, we have to fundamentally revise the story we tell ourselves about America. We may have to change the way we feel about our American identity. We want America to be the America of our ideals, and this desire makes it hard for us to engage with the ways America has not achieved those ideals. One way we can try to resolve this American dilemma is to deny, avoid, and repress the evidence of racial prejudice and discrimination.[63] The story of a post-racial America makes us feel better as Americans than a story of America still struggling to achieve full racial equal opportunity.

TRANSFORMING AMERICAN REALITIES INTO AMERICAN IDEALS

We need to see American ideals as ideals that we work toward. The only way the country will get closer to its ideals of equal opportunity for all is by first facing the ways in which we fail to meet these ideals. The racial-justice activist Jay Smooth gives advice on how to talk about interpersonal racism which can be applied to how to begin to think about America and racism more broadly. He argues that "we need to move away from the premise that being a good person is a fixed, immutable characteristic, and shift toward seeing being good as a practice. It is a practice that we carry out by engaging with our imperfections."[64] America becomes a more perfect union when we work to overcome racial prejudice and discrimination, not when we pretend that it does not exist. In fact, America becomes a less perfect union with every denial and whitewashing of the continued existence of racial prejudice and discrimination.

America has had roughly 200 years of racial slavery[65] followed by 100 years of Jim Crow. We should not assume that antiblackness is a trivial and passing phenomenon in American culture. The only way we will end antiblack bias and discrimination in American society is by seeking it out and shining a light on it.

To assess if we have made progress in achieving racial equality, we need to go beyond assessing America by particular successful minority individuals. As America becomes more racially and ethnically diverse there will be more minority superstars, but the light of a few hundred or even a few thousand superstars should not blind us to the millions who suffer from disadvantage.

We cannot assume that because we haven't personally heard about anti-black racial prejudice and discrimination that it is not occurring. In the following chapters, I use some of the more appropriate sample-survey data to measure prejudice and discrimination. While liberals today may acknowledge that we are not post-racial, many conservatives still insist that we are. In Chapter 4, I engage this conservative viewpoint more directly.

Although America has a ways to go before providing full equal opportunity for all regardless of race, it is important to acknowledge that we have made considerable progress over our history. This progress is not trivial. It is much better to be black today than a century ago. But a careful examination of the history of America's movements for racial progress shows that we have always achieved much less than we initially assumed. This too was the case with the election of Barack Obama.

CHAPTER 3

Angry, Afraid, and Cold: Defining the Obama Haters

> **Obama Hater 220:** He is a Socialist/Communist. He is not a loyal American and does not love this country.
>
> **Obama Hater 306:** He's a Muslim radical set to destroy the country, replace the Constitution with Sharia law, and become a dictator. He is an illegal sitting as president, and he should be on trial for treason with the senile Democratic leadership.[1]

Every president is hated by somebody. Typically the president will be blamed if the economy is bad.[2] The people who hate the president may think that the president is a liar. If it is the president's second term, the "haters" will see the president as having done a bad job in his first term. These are typical attacks, and President Barack Obama is the recipient of them. But Obama is also the recipient of some more unusual attacks.

Obama Haters 220 and **306** quoted earlier express some of the more atypical reasons why some Americans are "angry, afraid, and cold" toward Barack Obama. Many Obama Haters see him as a socialist, a Muslim, a radical, an "illegal," or a dictator bent on destroying America. In this chapter we will explore who are the Obama Haters and why they say they hate Obama.

DEFINING OBAMA HATERS: ANGRY, AFRAID, AND COLD TOWARD OBAMA

While some authors have looked at the people who can be called the professional anti-Democrats—people who make money or secure political positions by saying outrageous things about Democrats—I have chosen to examine average Americans who hate President Obama. The professional anti-Democrats like Rush Limbaugh will attack any Democratic president. Essentially doing so is their job. Therefore, there are limits on what we can learn about American society by knowing that professional anti-Democrats are criticizing a Democratic president. A key question is to what extent their attacks are believed and supported by the American public. This book provides information on this issue. Because I begin with the American public and focus on the attitudes driving the hatred of President Obama, I can also capture motivations and ideas that may have not been primed by the Republican attack corps. And I include individuals who are not right wing but who may nonetheless hate Obama.

An "Obama Hater" can be defined in a number of ways. I use data from the 2012 American National Election Study (ANES).[3] The ANES is a sample survey of the voting-eligible population—U.S. citizens who are 18 years of age and older. The ANES is designed to allow one to use the data to obtain information that is representative of the entire voting-eligible population. I define *Obama Haters* as individuals who are (1) angry, (2) afraid, and (3) cold toward President Obama.[4] The ANES asked respondents to indicate whether President Obama has, "because of the kind of person he is or because of something he has done, ever made you feel: angry" and whether he has ever made the respondent "afraid." Individuals who indicate that President Obama makes them feel angry "always" or "most of the time" fulfill my first requirement. Those who also say that President Obama makes them feel afraid "always" or "most of the time" fulfill my second requirement.

The "cold" assessment is a bit more complicated. The ANES allowed respondents to provide a "feeling thermometer" rating of President Obama. Individuals were able to rate Obama from 0 to 100 "degrees." The higher the rating above 50, the more favorable or warmer one feels about the president. The lower the rating below 50, the less favorable or colder one feels about the president. Individuals were also able to rate the Republican presidential candidate Mitt Romney on a feeling thermometer.

I decided to create a measure that would allow me to assess individuals' feeling thermometer ratings of Obama relative to their ratings of Romney. This relative scale allows me to better capture individuals who are emotionally cold toward Obama. For example, an individual who rates Obama 0 and Romney 100 sees Obama as a worse choice than an individual who rates Obama 0 and Romney, also, 0. The latter individual is likely cold to all mainstream politicians, while the former individual is cold specifically toward Obama. The latter individual likely sees the election of Obama as more of the same for the country, while the former likely sees Obama's election as a very bad turn for the country.

This adjusted feeling thermometer ranges from 0 to 100, but 50 means that an individual rated Obama and Romney equally. A rating above 50 means that the individual is warmer or feels more favorable toward Obama than to Romney. A rating below 50 means that the individual is colder or feels less favorable toward Obama than to Romney. "Cold"—the third criterion of being an Obama Hater—is defined as an individual rating Obama less than or equal to 32 "degrees"—"freezing"—on this relative feeling thermometer.

I occasionally compare Obama Haters to Romney Haters. Romney Haters are defined in the same fashion—(1) angry, (2) afraid, and (3) cold—but with the focus on feelings toward Romney. In the ANES, 11.2 percent of respondents are Obama Haters and 10.2 percent are Romney Haters. Because of the margin of error, these percentages are statistically equivalent. It is important to note that Haters are individuals who express *extreme* dislike for the presidential candidates. It does not include those with merely moderate dislikes. It is not comparable to a simple disapproval or un-favorability rating.

Obama does not appear to be subjected to more hate than one would expect for a recent president. The share of the population that hates him according to my definition is basically the same as the share that hates Romney. Because of a difference in one of the relevant survey questions from the 2004 ANES to the 2012 ANES, it is not possible to perfectly compare George W. Bush Haters to Obama Haters. But the available data suggests comparable shares of hatred for both presidents.[5] While Obama is *disapproved of* more than any Democratic president since Truman,[6] he is not more *hated* than recent presidents and presidential candidates. Hate requires more interest in politics and more anger than simple disapproval.

The question now is whether he is hated for reasons that seem legitimate or illegitimate.

WHO ARE THE OBAMA HATERS?

The average Obama Hater, or simply Hater, is in his or her mid-50s, is non-Hispanic white, has some higher education, and is doing a bit better than average economically. Haters are split evenly between men and women. Nearly three-tenths (29.3 percent) of Haters are over 64 years old, making them older on average than the voting-eligible population as a whole. Nearly nine-tenths of (88.7 percent) Haters are non-Hispanic white. This rate makes them significantly whiter than the voting-eligible population. Educationally, Haters look like the population overall.[7] In terms of income, Haters are a little better off than the population overall. A little more than half of Haters (51.8 percent) have a family income of $55,000 or above. They are also wealthier than average. Nearly 9 out of every 10 (86.5 percent) Haters own their own home, and more than half (55.9 percent) of them have investments in the stock market. (See Appendix, Table 3.2, for additional details on these findings.)

Politically, Obama Haters tend to be conservatives, and they lean toward the extreme end of the political spectrum. More than four-fifths (82.3 percent) of Haters identify their political ideology as conservative, with 16.5 percent saying that they are extremely conservative. For the voting-eligible population overall, only about two-fifths (39.6 percent) identify as conservative and only 4.7 percent identify as extremely conservative. More than 9 in 10 (92.7 percent) Haters identify as Republican or Republican-leaning, and more than half (56.5 percent) identify as strong Republicans. For the population overall, 4 in 10 (41 percent) identify as Republican or Republican-leaning and less than a fifth (15.8 percent) as strong Republicans. Seven in ten (70.3 percent) Haters support or lean toward supporting the Tea Party compared to about 3 in 10 (26.9 percent) for the population overall.[8]

Obama Haters indicate that they are more politically engaged than the public generally. Nearly three-quarters (71.5 percent) of Haters reported that they pay attention to politics always or most of the time compared to only half (49.9 percent) of the population overall. About half (53.2 percent) of Haters voted in a presidential primary or caucus compared to about a third (35.6 percent) for the population overall. Nearly a third (31.1 percent) have contacted their U.S. representative or senator in the prior four years while the rate was a fifth (20.9 percent) for the population overall. About a sixth (17.1 percent) of Haters have contributed to a specific candidate's campaign, while about a ninth (11.8 percent) of the general public have done the same. About half of Haters (51.3 percent) were contacted by a political party in 2012 compared to about two-fifths (43.9 percent) for the voting-eligible population overall.[9]

WHY DO OBAMA HATERS HATE OBAMA?

In this section, I will discuss my analysis of short open-ended responses by the Obama Haters to the question "Is there anything in particular about Barack Obama that might make you want to vote against him?" A total of 95 percent of the Haters—554 individuals in the sample—provided valid responses ranging from one word to a paragraph. One benefit of open-ended responses is that it allows the respondent to express what is most salient in his or her mind rather than being forced to choose among items determined by the designer of the survey. We get to see what is most important to the respondent at the moment the survey is completed.

Because respondents are creating their own responses, these data cannot be treated as typical poll data. For example, *if asked* about the American Recovery and Reinvestment Act (ARRA) or "the stimulus," a large percentage of Obama Haters would probably say that this was one of the reasons that they disliked Obama. In 2012, however, ARRA was no longer a major news story, and it was mentioned only by one Hater.[10] Thus, we have only the most prominent thoughts in the respondents' minds, not a comprehensive accounting of all of their dislikes.

There are a few points one should keep in mind as one reviews the analysis of these responses. The respondents controlled the length of the responses. They were as brief as they wanted to be, and many chose to be brief. They were not asked to clarify or elaborate on their responses, just to list as many dislikes as they could think of. The categories in the analysis are not mutually exclusive. Many individuals are counted in more than one category. It is important to remember that these are the opinions of people expressing the most intense dislike for President Barack Obama. Their remarks are not nice. We cannot assume that they are accurate. In fact, in many cases, they are not.

Obama Is Seen as Being Not American and Out to Destroy America

A quarter of Obama Haters would not vote for Barack Obama because they see him as not American or as antagonistic to the American people and to American values. They say:

Hater 118: . . . [he] tramples on our Constitution, illegally bypasses Congress, and seems to want to bring down our country so that it is not the greatest country in the world anymore. He is not a proud American; he is a Globalist. The horrible economy in the United States can be directly laid at his and his appointees' feet.[11]

Hater 210: He is a Muslim, socialist and wasn't born in this country. He is a liar and is taking this country down. He is a TERRIBLE president!

Hater 301: He's a communist dictator wannabe who has no respect for God, our history, our Constitution, our freedoms, our culture, our borders, our military, our tax money, Israel or the truth. Also, he's a pro-terrorist, Muslim anti-colonialist with an animus toward Whites in general and American Whites in particular. He has no love for this country or its people. He's . . . a man to be feared not respected.[12]

Hater 424: I think he HATES this country. Everything has gone the wrong way ever since he became president. I do not like the way he is always apologizing for our country. He is very bad for our country, and it seems he is doing everything he can to ruin our country.[13]

Obama is seen as consciously working against the Constitution and the well-being of Americans. Probably no other president has been seen as actively trying to harm the country by so many.

Obama Is Blamed for Bad Economic Conditions

Presidents are typically assessed, rightly or wrongly, on the state of the economy.[14] This is also the case for the Haters and President Obama. The Haters see his administration as having "out-of-control spending" and as failing to fix the bad economy. Twenty-five percent of Haters refer to bad economic conditions for why they dislike the president.

Many Haters are upset specifically about the level of spending, the national debt or the national deficit under the Obama administration.

> **Hater 30:** Obama's bad mishandling of finances has resulted in astronomical budget deficits and a continuing weak economy. He also seems to be totally ideological, and has not adjusted his policies despite past clear-cut failures.[15]
>
> **Hater 86:** He's dug the country deeper and deeper into debt, and takes no responsibility for it. He has weakened our country, and continues to downsize our military forces.
>
> **Hater 88:** He's taken us into bankruptcy, our whole country. He's raised our debt, and we have almost no chance of getting out of it. He has made us a laughing stock. He's made us a weak country. He has disgraced our military. He took away our space program. I mean there's no good thing that he's done.[16]
>
> **Hater 497:** (1) He rules by executive order rather than by legislation. (2) Out-of-control spending. (3) Excessive regulations by the EPA and other agencies.[17]

In addition to the major theme of federal spending, minor themes concern Obama as a poor commander in chief of the military, Obama as a dictator ruling by executive order, and the Obama administration stifling business with excessive regulation. So, we see that typical Republican or conservative critiques of Democrats are part of the reason for disliking Obama.

Other Obama Haters, instead of simply being focused on federal spending, address the economy more broadly or focus on jobs.

> **Hater 145:** He has been ineffective as a president. Our family is still struggling with a weak economy he seems unable to address. . . .
>
> **Hater 519:** The economy has been the worst ever. I have been unemployed for over 2 years. I have been applying for jobs at still no avail. Mr. Obama needs to get out of office for the sake of our country.

But, for many, the problem was not that Obama failed to fix the bad economy but that Obama's policies had either created the bad economy or made it worse.

> **Hater 123:** He did not improve the economy; he made it worse.[18]
>
> **Hater 396:** I do not trust him, and he has made a lot of really bad changes that are hurting our economy.[19]
>
> **Hater 431:** I think the economy has fallen apart since he took office.

Again, this line of criticism is typical for presidents even if the Great Recession was not a typical recession.

Obama Is Seen as a Liar

A fifth of the Haters view Barack Obama as a liar or untrustworthy. Obama's supposed lying is associated with or related to many different issues as exemplified by the following response:

> **Hater 522:** He hasn't done anything in the past four years. He lies about the unemployment rate. He lies about the money he has spent. He lies that he is a Christian.[20]

One minor theme among the Haters' responses is the idea that Obama did not keep his promises.

> **Hater 450:** Liar, liar pants on fire. He kept no promises, and is hurting the economy and tax payers. If you are on the dole, he is your guy. He is a Marxist. He embarrasses our country by being weak and apologizing for the USA's prosperity. He is too weak on crime. His cabinet is full of corrupt politicians. Eric Holder is a liar.[21]
>
> **Hater 281:** He said he would be transparent—he lied. He said things would get better for America—he lied. We are not in a better place. He has spent money we do not have. He has given money to people without a payback plan. He, I feel, is destroying the America I grew up knowing and believing in.[22]

Not only is Obama seen as untrustworthy; another minor theme is that his advisors and appointees, like Attorney General Eric Holder, are also untrustworthy, corrupt, or inept.

> **Hater 270:** He lies. He abuses the Constitution. He doesn't do his job, and he had led this country down a path that is hell. He is more interested in schmoozing with movie stars than in attending necessary briefings. He surrounds himself with Chicago Mafia—and look what has happened to some of them. They don't tell the truth either.[23]
>
> **Hater 14:** He acts like a used-car salesman. He doesn't produce what he says. He has lied to the American people. There is something fishy about his birth certificate. I don't think he is an American citizen. He is more for himself than for the American people. He takes money from Medicare to support Obamacare. It is not that he is black [that I want to vote against him]. He is even worse than President Jimmy Carter.[24]

Two other minor themes in the responses are that Obama is more interested in spending time with celebrities than in doing the work of the presidency and that he cares only about himself and does not care about the American people.

Obama Is Seen as Having Done a Bad Job

A fifth of Haters felt that Obama had already done a bad job as president and, therefore, he should not be reelected. They argued:

> **Hater 9:** Four years of nothing but debt and Obamacare. The man has done nothing but travel and play. I don't think he really knows what's going on.[25]
>
> **Hater 238:** He is leading this country into financial disaster. I would vote for anyone that is qualified before voting for our current president.[26]
>
> **Hater 432:** I work very hard for my income, 60 to 70 hours a week. I currently make less than half of what I made four years ago before he was elected; plus, all my expenses went up. He is an amateur and has no idea what he is doing. Everything he has tried has failed, the companies he has backed etc., and yet he still wants to take what I have and give it to people that don't want to work at all.[27]

A minor theme in the responses was the questioning of Obama's ability to competently execute his duties as president. A number of respondents saw him as unqualified and as an amateur.

Obama Is Seen as Being a "Socialist"

About a fifth of Obama Haters consider Obama to be a socialist, a Marxist, a proponent of class warfare, antibusiness, or some similar thing. For anyone who examines the Obama administration, this claim is hard to understand. Yet it is one of the main charges made against Obama by Haters. The question then is, what do Haters mean when they say that Obama is "socialist" or something similar?

The "socialist" charge is to varying degrees an epithet. Individuals want a socially legitimate way to express their hatred of Obama. It is also a new way to say liberal. To the extent that capitalism is seen as integral to the American way of life and what has made America great, the "socialist" charge is another way for Haters to express their view that Obama is anti-American and harmful to America. We can see "communist" and "socialist" being used simply as words of hatred by **Hater 44**. The all-capitals are in the original text.

> **Hater 44:** COMMUNIST. SOCIALIST. ATHEIST. DISCIPLE OF SAUL ALINSKY.[28]

The following responses reveal the association of "socialist" with the stereotypical ideas about and terms for liberalism.

> **Hater 32:** Barack Obama has followed the tenets of a European socialist. He seems to see the government as a solution to our problems. More people have become dependent on the government under this administration than any other, save possibly FDR.

Hater 36: Big government, socialist, large deficits, out of control spending and regulation, not focused on the economy, not focused on jobs, will sacrifice the common good of people just to stay elected.[29]

Hater 153: He is a socialist liberal that only does [things] to suit himself and not the American people.[30]

Hater 347: His love of huge government, communism, and his undying support of the Muslim faith. So, pretty much everything he is for.[31]

Hater 451: He is a Marxist anti-colonialist. He is destroying the country with the other progressives.[32]

What these Haters mean by "socialist" and other similar terms is essentially "evil liberal." In their view, Franklin Delano Roosevelt (FDR), progressives, and anyone who thinks that government can solve problems are "socialists."

They Hate the Affordable Care Act

The Affordable Care Act or Obamacare is perhaps President Obama's signature legislation. Therefore, it is not surprising that it would be a major theme in Haters' dislike of Obama. But it is less prominent than one might expect. Only about a sixth of Haters express dislike for Obama because of his health care policies. The five themes discussed earlier seem to be more important in the Haters dislike of Obama (see Table A).

Also, surprisingly Obamacare, although seen as "socialized medicine" by some, does not appear to be linked to the perception of Obama as a socialist. Only 16 percent of those who dislike Obama for Obamacare also mention being against him for his "socialism." Perhaps these two issues were linked at one point, but they are no longer. This finding also supports the idea that "socialist" is merely a new term on the right for "liberal" and nothing else.

Table A Haters' Top Reasons for Voting against Obama and Romney

	Obama Haters' Top Reasons for Voting against Obama		Romney Haters' Top Reasons for Voting against Romney
25%	He is not American and wants to destroy America	41%	He only cares about the rich
25%	Bad economic conditions	20%	He is a liar and can't be trusted
21%	He is a liar and can't be trusted	19%	He is sexist/against women's rights
20%	He's done a bad job so far	14%	He is a flip flopper
19%	He's a "socialist"	14%	I don't like or don't agree with him
16%	Obamacare	14%	He will destroy the safety net and Obamacare

Comparing Obama Haters to Romney Haters

To better assess the reasons the Obama Haters give for disliking Obama, it is useful to compare them to Romney Haters as done in Table A.[33] As mentioned earlier, the shares of Obama Haters and Romney Haters in the voting-eligible population are comparable. Obama Haters are as likely to call Obama a liar as are Romney Haters to call Romney a liar. As also mentioned earlier, it is not surprising that Obama is blamed for the bad economy. It is not possible to evaluate highly subjective statements that people feel that Obama has done a bad job or that they do not like Romney.

The Obama Haters' view that Obama is not American and anti-American, however, is startling because it is not remotely connected to any reality. Obama could not be elected president if he were not American. He has even released his birth certificate—something no other American president has been forced to do. He has not been "palling around with terrorists."[34] In fact, Osama bin Laden was killed during his administration. The view that he is not American and anti-American is pure fabrication. Although this idea is completely false, it is a major reason why Haters hate Obama. This is reason for Obama hatred that lacks legitimacy.

All of the Romney Haters' views, excluding the "liar" and "don't like" ideas, are at least connected to some reality. The view that Romney cares only about the rich comes from various controversial statements that he made during his campaign. His "47 percent" comment, which disparaged the poorest half of the American population based on misinformation,[35] and his suggestion that everyone has parents who can lend their children tens of thousands of dollars,[36] among other things, gave many people the impression that he really did not know and could not empathize with the experiences of middle- and low-income Americans. Romney took a very hard line against abortion during the campaign,[37] and this explains the view that he is against women's rights. Even Republican Party activists seem to consider Romney a flip-flopper.[38] Attempts to reduce safety-net spending has been a long-standing Republican goal. The U.S. House of Representatives has voted more than 50 times to repeal Obamacare.[39] Romney shares these goals.[40]

Romney hatred is grounded in reality and real, if subjective, feelings. A major component of Obama hatred, however, is based on a fictional claim that Obama is not American and desires to destroy America. Romney is hated for who he is; Obama is hated, in part, based on prejudicial fantasies.

Summary

The Obama Haters dislike Obama for typical and atypical reasons. It appears that people who hate a president (or a presidential candidate) tend to think he is a liar and cannot be trusted. A fifth of Obama Haters and a fifth of

Romney Haters see the respective candidate as a liar who cannot be trusted. Given that presidents are evaluated based on economic conditions, it is not surprising that Obama is blamed for the condition of the economy. Obama is also disliked for supposedly not doing a good job as president.

Aside from these more generic dislikes, Haters also dislike Obama for things more specific to the Obama administration. The Affordable Care Act or Obamacare draws ire, but it is not the most prominent issue. Obama is called a "socialist" but since he has not nationalized any companies or industries, this label cannot be taken literally. (A major component of the Affordable Care Act is requiring those who can afford it to buy *private* health insurance.) Given that the Haters see Franklin Delano Roosevelt and progressives as "socialists," the term seems to be a new way of referring to liberals.

One of the most prominent themes in Haters' dislike of Obama is the view that Obama is not American and that he wants to destroy America. About two-thirds (65.1 percent) of Haters believe that Obama was "probably" or "definitely born in another country" compared to about a quarter (24.8 percent) of the voting-eligible population in general.[41] Since Obama was born in the United States, and is not trying to destroy America, this is quite shocking. This reason for hating Obama is linked to the xenophobia, Islamophobia, and racism of the Obama Haters, which will be examined and discussed more in the following chapters.

CHAPTER 4

Obama Haters' Racial Attitudes

How dare you state that Republicans are criticizing Barack Obama because he is black? What evidence do you have of that? We judge him by the content of his character, not the color of his skin. We criticize him because his ignorance, incompetence, and arrogance are destroying this country, the greatest one on earth.[1]

—hate mail from a Tea Party supporter to Tea Party researchers

There are still conservatives who deny that racial antipathy has had any role in the criticism of President Barack Obama. When Democratic senator Mary Landrieu stated "The South has not always been the friendliest place for African-Americans" and that "It's been a difficult time for the president to present himself in a very positive light as a leader," Republican leaders called on her to apologize.[2] It is wrong to say that race has been the only reason for opposition to Obama, and, it is also true that blacks have found many unfriendly places outside of the South. But Senator Landrieu is correct in implying that race has played a role in opposition to Obama.

In the following discussion I analyze the views of Obama Haters to find out whether they hate Obama because he is African American or because of his policies. To answer this question, I will first turn to some of the qualitative American National Election Study (ANES) data. Then I will examine the quantitative ANES data and compare the racial attitudes of Obama Haters, politically Conservative Non-Haters, and Moderate and Liberal Non-Haters. For brevity, I will often refer to these groups as Haters, Conservatives, and Moderates-Liberals, respectively.

As we review the data on racial attitudes, it is important to consider that most Americans do not wish to be seen as being racially prejudiced or racist.

Thus, even when people truly believe negative ideas about racial minority groups, they tend to be reluctant to share them with strangers. As a result, it is very difficult for surveys to capture people's true feelings on these issues. It is generally understood that direct survey questions significantly underestimate the extent of negative racial attitudes toward groups. With this limitation in mind, it is still useful to see how Haters, Conservatives, and Moderates-Liberals compare on these questions about their racial attitudes toward blacks and other groups.

THE QUALITATIVE DATA

There is no unambiguous evidence of antiblack attitudes in the qualitative data. But there are hints that at least some Haters may see Barack Obama and his family through racial stereotypes. The idea that Barack Obama—a man with a law degree from Harvard University, a former lecturer in Constitutional law at the University of Chicago, a former Illinois state senator, and a former U.S. senator—is unqualified to be president may rest on racial prejudice and not on an assessment of his qualifications. For example, **Hater 25** argues that Obama is "inept and over his head." **Hater 370** states, "He was and still is unqualified for the office of President of the United States."[3] **Hater 355** claims, "He is the least qualified president we have had." **Hater 432** states, "He is an amateur and has no idea what he is doing." **Hater 546** argues that Obama is "totally unequipped to be the president of the USA." Criticisms of presidents' experience and abilities are typical, but this criticism seems to echo an antiblack stereotype.

It appears that some Haters are also challenging the work ethic and ability for self-control of Obama and his family. The ideas that blacks are lazy and that blacks lack self-control are common negative stereotypes. The Haters say:

> **Hater 9:** . . . The man has done nothing but travel and play. I don't think he really knows what's going on.[4]
> **Hater 277:** He prefers to play golf, go on talk shows, and play basketball with friends than take care of business. He prefers to spend his time with movie stars and not pay attention to world affairs. His wife and he are on vacation all the time.[5]
> **Hater 296:** . . . [Obama has a] lack of appreciation for hard work.
> **Hater 479:** . . . He has cost more than any president in history to keep in the White House; his personal spending is out of control.

While these views may be motivated by racial stereotypes, one cannot be certain. They are not clear enough to be definitively categorized as motivated by racial bias.

It is possible that some Haters see Obama through antiblack stereotypes. They see him as unqualified, lazy, and lacking in self-control. It is possible for someone to think these things about a president, however, without racial stereotypes. Because these ideas were not explicitly linked to blackness, we cannot be certain about whether there is a racial motivation behind them.

THE QUANTITATIVE DATA

If Obama Haters are motivated by political issues and not race, they should appear to be very similar to Conservatives on racial attitudes toward African Americans. Obama Haters span the political spectrum from liberal to conservative, but they are far more likely to be conservative than anything else. More than four-fifths of Haters (82.3 percent) identify as politically conservative.

If the United States is post-racial, then no group should exhibit antiblack racial attitudes, and all three groups—Haters, Conservatives, and Moderates-Liberals—should be very similar on all of the survey questions examined here. If, on the other hand, Obama Haters are racially motivated and hate Obama, in part, for his blackness, they would have more negative views of blacks than Conservatives. The designers of the ANES appear to provide a simple way of answering the question of race and the dislike of Obama: they asked survey respondents: "What about Obama's race? Did this tend to make you prefer or vote for Obama or Romney or did it make no difference?" For the voting-eligible population as a whole, 7.9 percent indicated that Obama's race made them prefer him, and 5.5 percent indicated that it made them prefer Romney.[6] When one considers the margin of error, these percentages are basically the same.

Haters, however, indicated that Obama's race pushed them to support Romney at greater rates than for the comparison groups. A total of 14.9 percent of Haters said that Obama's race caused them to support Romney; 6.8 percent of Conservatives and 3.1 percent of Moderates-Liberals said the same.[7] Thus, Haters were twice as likely as Conservatives and nearly five times as likely as Moderates-Liberals to favor Romney because of his race. This is the first sign that race plays a role in the hatred of Obama.

Some may argue that, of course, there are a few bad apples among Haters, but that for all of the other Haters race is not a factor behind their attitudes toward Obama. To address this argument, *I will remove everyone who indicated that Obama's race influenced their preference for or against Obama in the remaining analyses in this section.*

While the question about Obama's race may appear to answer the question about the role of race in attitudes toward Obama, social scientists know that people are not always completely honest in their responses to sensitive topics. There may be some people for whom Obama's race did matter to them in their preference for the 2012 election, but they did not say so. At a deeper level, some people may have been affected by Obama's race, but they may have difficultly admitting it at a conscious level even to themselves. We can use other questions in the 2012 ANES to probe at individuals' racial attitudes to see if they harbor negative views of blacks, but, as discussed earlier, this approach will likely deliver an underestimate of the significance of blackness to respondents.

A Dislike of Blacks and Latinos

Haters have the strongest dislike of and the lowest regard for African Americans among the three groups. In addition, they have the highest level of hostility toward blacks as measured by the antiblack racial resentment index.

Of all the measures to gauge antiblack sentiment, the racial resentment index is probably the best. Haters registered the strongest racial resentment of the three groups. The racial resentment index ranges from 0.0 to 1.0, with 1.0 being the highest level of resentment. Haters have an average score of 0.81, Conservatives 0.70, and Moderates-Liberals 0.57. More than a quarter (26.2 percent) of Haters have a score of 1.0—the most antiblack score possible. This rate of maximum antiblackness is more than twice that of Conservatives (11.4 percent) and nearly four times that of Moderates-Liberals (7.0 percent).[8]

Other measures of feelings toward blacks, Latinos, and Asians, while probably less sensitive at gauging attitudes, are nonetheless useful for gaining some insight into the Obama Haters. Haters express the most dislike of blacks and Latinos of the three groups, rating them the coldest on a feeling thermometer. Haters are colder toward Asians than Moderates-Liberals, but not Conservatives. Haters and Conservatives are also more likely than Moderates-Liberals to view blacks as lazy. All three groups see Hispanics as just as hardworking as whites and Asians as more hardworking than whites. Haters have negative views toward Hispanics, but these views appear to be somewhat less intense than for blacks. (See Appendix, Tables 4.3 and 4.4, for additional details on these findings.)

A White-Victimhood Mentality

A lot of white people honestly think they have been significantly deprived of various things because of minorities. And it's hard to overstate how deeply these feelings run. It's not so much animosity toward people who are different—it's the animosity of the aggrieved. They feel like they are victims.[9]
                                                            —an online comment to a *New York Times* article

Many Haters perceive the United States to be a country in which whites are an oppressed minority. For many of them, whites face a great deal of discrimination, as much or more than that faced by African Americans and Hispanics. They believe that whites are a politically disenfranchised group confronting a country with politically powerful blacks and Latinos. They also believe that the Obama administration favors blacks over whites. These views are startling since there is no evidence to support them.

Haters are the most likely to say that there is "a great deal" or "a lot" of discrimination against whites in the United States, and they are the least likely to say the same about blacks and Hispanics.[10] Two-thirds (66.4 percent) of Haters perceive whites as facing equal or greater levels of discrimination than blacks. This rate is higher than that for Conservatives (52.2 percent) and Moderates-Liberals (30.7 percent). The picture is very similar when discrimination against whites is compared to discrimination against Hispanics. Nearly two-thirds (64.3 percent) of Haters perceive whites as facing equal or greater levels of discrimination than Hispanics. Again, this rate is higher than that for Conservatives (46.7 percent) and for Moderates-Liberals (29.9 percent).[11]

For social scientists who have studied the research and who have looked at the data, these views are astounding. There is no question that African Americans and Latinos face levels of racial discrimination far greater than that faced by whites. For example, the nation's schools are still largely segregated and majority black and Hispanic schools are still inferior in quality to majority white schools.[12] Employers will respond more favorably to a résumé with the name Emily than to *the same résumé* with a name more commonly found among African Americans like Lakisha.[13] This fact no doubt plays a role, in the black unemployment rate being, decade after decade, about twice the white unemployment rate.[14] Blacks who use marijuana are more than three times as likely to be arrested as whites who use marijuana.[15] This fact and other criminal justice policies contribute to the strong overrepresentation of blacks in America's prisons.[16] In 2012, blacks were 14 times as likely to be victims of hate crimes as whites. Hispanics were twice as likely as whites.[17] But this estimate for Hispanics is likely an underestimate because hate crimes against unauthorized Hispanic immigrants are likely to be underreported and therefore undercounted in official statistics.[18] These are just a sample of the findings that make it clear that the degree of discrimination faced by blacks and Latinos greatly exceeds that faced by whites.

Haters also are the most likely to perceive whites as having too little influence in American politics. A fifth (19.9 percent) of Haters believe this compared with about a tenth (11 percent) of Conservatives and a twentieth (5 percent) of Moderates-Liberals.[19] Haters are the most likely to perceive blacks and Latinos as having too much influence in American politics.

A third of Haters (33.7 percent) say that blacks have too much influence, and nearly 3 in 10 (29.2 percent) say that Latinos have too much influence.[20]

In 2012, when the ANES data was collected, Hispanics made up 17 percent of the U.S. population and non-Hispanic blacks made up 12 percent.[21] At that time, the United States had had one nonwhite president—Barack Obama—out of 44 representing 2 percent of the total. There were zero U.S. senators who were African American and two who were Hispanic, making the Senate 2 percent Hispanic. In the U.S. House of Representatives, there were 41 African American voting members making up about 9 percent of the body. For Hispanics in the House of Representatives, the number was 29, making up about 7 percent of the body.[22] There was one African American and one Latina on the Supreme Court. This left the court about 80 percent non-Hispanic white. In terms of the highest officials at the federal level, there is no evidence of blacks or Latinos possessing too much influence in American politics. Both groups are *underrepresented* in the nation's most powerful political positions.

A more recent and more comprehensive examination of all federal, state, and county elected officials from the spring of 2014 found that 90 percent of these elected officials were white.[23] Non-Hispanic whites only made up 62 percent of the population.[24] Thus, whites are significantly *overrepresented* in positions of political power.

Another way of looking at influence is in terms of voting power and economic power. Elected officials need votes and money to win office. Individuals or groups can have influence over elected officials if they have votes or money. Here again whites have a considerable advantage. They are the majority group making up 71 percent of the voting-eligible population in 2012. Blacks and Hispanics combined made up only 23 percent of the voting-eligible population.[25] Hispanic voting-power is significantly lower than their population share because significant numbers of Hispanics are foreign-born. Many blacks are ineligible to vote because they are ex-offenders.[26] Further whites' voting power is amplified by the fact that they typically have a higher voter-turnout rate than blacks and Hispanics.[27]

Whites also have significantly greater amounts of disposable income and wealth to spend on political campaigns. In 2013, the white (non-Hispanic) median household income was $58,000, while the Hispanic median income was $41,000 and the black median income was $35,000.[28] In 2013, at the median, blacks had only 8 percent of the wealth whites had. Hispanics had 10 percent.[29]

It is not possible to make a fact-based argument that blacks and Latinos have too much influence in American politics or that whites have too little. It seems that at least some of Haters' beliefs about people of color are not based on reality.

We can see a white-victimhood mentality among Haters again in their strong belief that the Obama administration favors blacks over whites. Three-fifths (61.6 percent) of Haters believe this compared to a third (33.0 percent) of Conservatives and about a tenth (11.4 percent) of Moderates-Liberals.[30]

And again, there is no evidence of this being the case. President Obama has explicitly stated, "I'm not the president of black America. I'm the president of the United States of America."[31] In his first two years in office, Obama mentioned race fewer times than any Democratic president since 1961, according to research by the political scientist Daniel Gillon.[32] There have been no major government policies targeted specifically to help blacks in the Obama administration although there have been policies targeting business owners,[33] immigrants, gays and lesbians, veterans, and other constituencies. (See the afterword for a discussion of why the My Brother's Keeper initiative does not change this conclusion.)

Obama Haters Are Racially Motivated

Individuals who have the most intense dislike for the nation's first black president also have the most intense negative feelings toward black people generally among the three groups compared. Although more than 80 percent of Haters are conservatives, their attitudes toward blacks are more negative than those of the Conservative Non-Hater group. Haters dislike blacks more, and they are more likely to perceive whites to be victims of powerful blacks and Latinos than Conservatives. And it is important to remember that (1) these analyses were done excluding the 14.9 percent of Haters who admitted racial bias by saying that they voted for Romney because of Obama's race and (2) survey questions of the type analyzed here tend to underestimate the degree of antiblack sentiment. Given Haters' feelings and attitudes toward blacks generally, it is not surprising that they would hate the nation's first black president, Barack Obama.

WHY ARE OBAMA HATERS SO ANTIBLACK?

Are Obama Haters so antiblack because they are older than the other groups and grew up in a time when antiblack attitudes were more common and more accepted? Is it because many of them are not simply conservative but extremely conservative? Is it because they are above average in economic status and feel hostility to lower-income groups? I explored these questions by conducting a multivariate statistical analysis. The analysis allowed me to parse out the influence of several factors that might lead to antiblack attitudes simultaneously.

I used the black–white relative feeling thermometer and then the anti-black racial resentment index to capture antiblack sentiments. The analysis controlled for, or took into account, a variety of demographic factors and individuals' political orientation.[34] The analysis also included individuals who said they favored Romney because of Obama's race.

After taking all of these factors into account, negative black attitudes were still a significant factor in predicting whether one would be an Obama Hater.[35] It is not simply age, political views, or economic circumstances that lead one to hate Obama. The hatred of Obama is related to deep-seated racial attitudes. I conducted the same analysis to see if racial attitudes played a role in being a Romney Hater. In the case of Romney, the racial-attitudes measures did not predict that one would be a Romney Hater.

People who feel hostility toward blacks are more likely to hate Obama, but people who feel sympathy for blacks are not more likely to hate Romney. As the analysis in Chapter 3 suggests, Romney-hatred appears to be driven mainly by things that he actually said and did, not by wild fictions about who he is. Obama-hatred—at least a component of it—is driven by racial prejudice. This suggests that a president or a politician or some other public figure may be hated by a segment of the American public for being black, but he or she won't be hated for being white.

CONCLUSION

It turns out that there is a lot of evidence that many people are criticizing Obama because of his race. Of course, not all Obama criticism is racially motivated, but it is clear that a significant portion is. Many individuals have plainly stated that they do not like Obama because of his race. Sometimes they have said this using a racial epithet or an offensive racial stereotype (see Chapter 2 for examples). My research shows that the most anti-Obama segment of the American population is also a strongly antiblack segment of the American population. Their hatred of Obama is just a specific example of their general fear and hatred of black people.

CHAPTER 5

Othering Obama, Part I:
Xenophobia among Obama Haters

"F*ck Obongo from the Ocongo," wrote one Obama hater on a conservative, pro-gun website. Another declared, "Obongo for president = a big win for Osama." This website experienced a spike in negative nicknames for Barack Obama after he won the presidential election in 2008. The two most popular names were "Obongo" and "The Kenyan."[1] "Obongo" is a disparaging linking of Obama to Africa, Obama's supposed continent of birth. "The Kenyan" also fits within the "Birther" narrative that Obama is foreign-born. The comment connecting Obama to Osama bin Laden, the most hated anti-American Muslim terrorist, suggests that Obama is sympathetic to bin Laden's cause. Another statement on the website asserted that Obama's full name is "curious obongo The Kenyan pigmonkey," merging to the "classic" racist monkey association for blacks with the Birther idea.[2] These comments reveal the mix of xenophobia, Islamophobia, and racism swirling around in the "haters'" minds.

Barack Obama has often been portrayed as "a foreign, dangerous, alien other" by his opponents. This portrayal, as the sociologist Enid Logan observes, is different from associating him with antiblack stereotypes. In this case, rather than "being seen as a lesser member of the nation"—as is common in racist representations of African Americans—Obama is being presented as "inherently foreign to the nation"—as an alien other.[3]

The sociologist Nadia Y. Kim concurs with Logan that Obama has been subject to two different types of racialization. Kim sees Obama as also being subject to "foreigner racialization." She argues that this "racialization of Obama hinged on a combination of subordinating Muslims as perpetual racial foreigners and fearing the 'browning of America' brought on by immigration, especially from the global South."[4]

This foreigner racialization of Obama came from a multitude of sources. Mark Penn, a campaign strategist for Hillary Clinton in 2007, stated that Obama's multicultural background

> exposes a very strong weakness for him—his roots to basic American values and culture are at best limited. I cannot imagine America electing a president during a time of war who is not at his center fundamentally American in his thinking and in his values.[5]

During the 2008 presidential campaign, Sarah Palin accused Obama of being

> someone who sees America, it seems, as being so imperfect, imperfect enough, that he's palling around with terrorists who would target their own country. This is not a man who sees America as you see America and as I see America.[6]

For Palin and many other critics, Obama does not simply have values that are different from the mainstream of America, Obama's values are antithetical to American values.

Logan argues,

> For some, it must have seemed that their worst nightmare was coming to life. Obama's ascendance was the culmination of the immigrant take-over, the beginning of a new era of white racial oppression, the end of the real America.[7]

Given the strong negative views of immigrants and of Muslims by some in the United States, Barack Obama's opponents could find it politically beneficial to convince the public that he is Muslim and foreign-born.

BARACK OBAMA AS RACIAL OTHER

President Obama was born in the United States and is Christian, yet he and his supporters have been forced to refute false claims that he is foreign-born and that he is Muslim over and over again. The challenges to Obama's religion and place of birth are quite bizarre. These are not issues on which individuals are typically challenged. If a person says that he is Christian and born in Hawaii, a controversy does not usually follow.

One has to wonder about the role of race in serving as the kindling for these attacks. Barack Obama's Republican opponents for the presidency was John McCain in 2008 and Mitt Romney in 2012. John McCain, like Barack Obama, was not born in any of the 48 contiguous states of the mainland United States.[8] Mitt Romney's father, like Barack Obama's father, was not born in the United States.[9] Yet neither McCain nor Romney has been subject to a social movement questioning and challenging their citizenship and American-ness as Obama has.[10] There is reason to suspect that a white president, born in Hawaii, named Barry O'Hara would never have had such a controversy over his birth certificate.

Asians who were born and raised in the United States frequently report not being seen as real Americans. After telling questioners that they are from the United States, they often get the response, "No, where are you really from?"[11] The retired American figure skater, Michelle Kwan, who was born in California and who won several medals for the United States, has had the dishonor of being presented as not American in the U.S. media twice. In the 1998 Olympic Games, Tara Lipinski, a white American won the gold medal in figure skating. Kwan won the silver. MSNBC's headline stated, "American Beats Kwan."[12] In the 2002 Olympic Games, the white American Sarah Hughes won the gold, the Russian, Irina Slutskaya, won the silver, and Kwan won the bronze. The *Seattle Times*'s headline stated, "American Outshines Kwan, Slutskaya in Skating Surprise."[13] Once again, an Asian *American* was treated as a "perpetual foreigner."

The thinking that led to Michelle Kwan being presented as not American is, of course, not limited to journalists. The association of Asian Americans with foreign-ness is common in American culture. Social psychologists have found that at the subconscious level, Americans are more likely to associate whites than Asian Americans with American-ness.[14]

The problem of being seen subconsciously as foreign is not limited to Asian Americans. Social psychologists have found the same dynamic with African Americans relative to whites. Americans more easily associate whites than blacks with American-ness. In fact, in an experiment, respondents associated the former prime minister of the United Kingdom, Tony Blair, with symbols of America more readily than they did Barack Obama. At the subconscious level, Americans could more easily see a white Englishman as American than a black American.[15]

The social psychologist Mahzarin R. Banaji concludes, "[This research] shows our minds will not just distort our preferences but distort facts. African Americans in their [own] minds are fully American, but not in the minds of whites."[16] For these reasons, one suspects that a white version of Barack Obama would have been less likely to be challenged on his American-ness. If that alternate Obama were challenged, one suspects that the idea of him being not American would have been less successful.

The data from the 2012 American National Election Study supports the idea that Obama's blackness is implicated in the challenge to his American-ness and Christian-ness. Individuals scoring highest on the racial resentment index, a measure of feelings of hostility toward blacks, are the most likely to believe that Obama was not born in the United States and that he is Muslim. Individuals scoring high in racial resentment are 11 times as likely as individuals low in racial resentment (43.6 percent vs. 4.0 percent) to think that Obama is "probably" or "definitely born in another country."[17] The finding is similar for the issue of Obama's religion. Individuals scoring high in racial resentment are 17 times as likely as individuals low in racial resentment (46.7 percent vs. 2.7 percent) to think that Obama is Muslim.[18] Even after controlling for demographic and political identity characteristics, and anti-immigrant and anti-Muslim sentiments, high racial resentment remains a powerful predictor of whether one believes Obama to be foreign-born and to be Muslim.[19] If Obama were white, and therefore not a victim of antiblack racial resentment, it is likely that there would be no challenge to his citizenship and religious faith.

XENOPHOBIA IN AMERICAN CULTURE

There is a long history of ambivalence toward immigrants in the United States. Americans have often viewed immigrants as a valuable source of labor for economic development, and Americans have often viewed immigrants as a force that would produce cultural and economic decline. The *New York Times* columnist, Anand Giridharadas, captures this conflicted thinking well.

> We want them to work harder than us, to inject new energy into the republic, but not to take our jobs. We want them to melt their culture into our proverbial pot, but not to change who we are. We want them to help sustain America's self-image as a nation that takes the world's tired, huddled masses, but we don't want their tired, huddled selves going on welfare and deepening our debt. We want them to prove to us and the world that anyone with pluck can rise here from lowly origins, but we'd prefer it if they were already engineers with a job when they arrived.[20]

Many of the negative feelings about immigration, however, have been shaped by animosity toward particular racial and ethnic groups and not simply to the idea of immigration.[21]

Immigration to the United States was largely unregulated prior to the nineteenth century and citizenship was easily obtained. The nineteenth century saw the rise of strong anti-Irish, anti-Catholic, and anti-Chinese sentiments. The anti-Irish and anti-Catholic sentiments were comingled since the Irish immigrants were Catholics. The native Protestants viewed Catholics as plotting to subject the country to the rule of the pope. While there was violence and discrimination directed at the Irish, the first non-diseased and noncriminal group to be banned from the United States was the Chinese.

After being used to build the Central Pacific railroad in the 1860s, Chinese immigrants found growing forces arrayed against them. In 1882, Congress enacted the Chinese Exclusion Act. This act and its extensions outlawed Chinese immigration, denied citizenship to Chinese residents, and made possible the deportation of Chinese immigrants without certificates of residence. The first "illegal" immigrants in America were Chinese. Prior to the Chinese Exclusion Act, this status did not exist.[22]

Ideas of race in nineteenth- and early-twentieth-century America were somewhat different than today's. While the anti-Asian sentiments by whites may make sense within our contemporary understanding of racism, the opposition to immigration by the Irish, European Jews, and Southern and Eastern Europeans may be surprising. Race is fundamentally the product of cultural ideas and social practices. Because of this fact, race changes with time and place. In nineteenth- and early-twentieth-century America, notions of whiteness were narrower and more restrictive than they are today. The Irish, European Jews, and Southern and Eastern Europeans were seen as racially inferior to Christian whites of English and Northern European descent.[23] In the 1920s, quotas were set in place to severely restrict the immigration of Southern and Eastern Europeans. While Southern and Eastern European immigration was severely restricted, new early-twentieth-century laws prevented all Asians, not just the Chinese, from entering the United States.[24]

Today, the ambivalence about immigrants remains. While a majority of Americans view immigrants as strengthening American society, a sizable minority feel that immigrants threaten traditional American customs and values. Americans feel similarly about the economic impact of immigrants. A majority say that "immigrants strengthen our country because of their hard work and talents," while a sizable minority believe "immigrants today are a burden on our country because they take jobs, housing and health care." On unauthorized immigration, about half of Americans think that illegal immigration helps the economy by providing low-cost labor, and about half think that it hurts the economy by driving down wages.[25] On the important questions about immigration, significant numbers of Americans can be found on opposing sides. Given that there remains a reservoir of ill-feeling toward immigrants, falsely portraying President Obama as foreign-born does not simply make him seem to be an illegitimate holder of the office, for some, it also serves as a reason to believe that he is a treat to traditional American customs and values.

XENOPHOBIA AMONG THE OBAMA HATERS

Nearly two-thirds (65.1 percent) of Obama Haters believe incorrectly that Obama was "probably" or "definitely born in another country." This rate is more than twice that of Conservative Non-Haters (30.9 percent) and nearly five times that of Moderate-Liberal Non-Haters (14.0 percent).[26] To what extent are the Haters' hatred of Obama colored by negative attitudes toward the foreign-born? In this section, we will explore whether there is a correlation between anti-immigrant attitudes and being an Obama Hater using qualitative and quantitative data from the 2012 American National Election Study.

The Qualitative Data

The overwhelming majority of people who immigrate to the United States do so because of positive things that they see in the United States. They wish to be part of America, not destroy it. When an immigrant wishes to serve in a position of elected office in the United States, the assumption usually is that the individual has the same desire to serve as a natural-born citizen. Although Senator Ted Cruz was born in Canada, he is not viewed as an enemy of the state. Cruz has aspirations to be president, but so far, at least, there does not appear to be a xenophobic backlash.[27] Arnold Schwarzenegger, the former governor of California, was born in Austria, but his critics did not view him as having had a secret agenda to destroy California. Schwarzenegger has said that he would like to be president of the United States,[28] and there is no uproar that he wishes to harm the country. Even if one incorrectly believes that Barack Obama is foreign-born, this belief alone does not automatically lead one to think that he has a nefarious agenda.

The foreigner racialization of Obama has been done in a way to elicit the fears and hatreds of those prone to xenophobia. We can see this in the qualitative data from the Obama Haters below. Being foreign is assumed to be anti-American, when, in fact, most immigrants are pro-American.

> **Hater 34:** . . . I don't believe he is an American. I think he is a terrorist sympathizer. . . . He is selling us out. We are going to have a revolution in this country. Right now there are veterans, and we have all fought for our flag. We took an oath to protect our country against a[ll enemies, foreign and domestic].[29]
>
> **Hater 245:** He is not from the United States of America, and not for the people of this country.[30]
>
> **Hater 246:** He is not from the United States. He has lied for years about a false birth certificate, and he is running our country into the ground.[31]
>
> **Hater 310:** He's not an American. He lies. He disrespects America and Americans.[32]
>
> **Hater 414:** I don't trust him, and I don't think he has our best interest for the United States. I don't think he was born in the states.[33]

For many Obama Haters, Obama is not seen as an immigrant politician like Ted Cruz or Arnold Schwarzenegger but as someone who is a danger to America.

We can see some anti-immigrant attitudes among the Obama Haters in their response to the question of what they think is the most important problem facing the country. One Hater (**Hater Most Important Problem, 1st mention [MIP1] 521**) used a slur for Mexican immigrants in defining the number one problem as "Wetbacks. People from other countries that slipped into the United States."[34] **Hater MIP1 294** was less crude but still offensive when defining one of the most important problems as "the Mexicans in the United States."[35] With others one can sense the negative emotion:

> **Hater MIP1 127:** Illegal aliens are the cause of our health care crisis. With our open borders, we are also permitting terrorists to enter freely.
>
> **Hater MIP1 406:** Illegal immigrants that waste our money and time.
>
> **Hater MIP1 410:** Immigration. Get them out.[36]
>
> **Hater MIP2 144:** Immigration. Just say no!

Other Haters seem to see unauthorized immigrants through stereotypes about the "undeserving poor." One Hater sees unauthorized immigrants as having an easy life where they "get everything given to them."[37] Another claims that "illegal immigrants are getting financial aid from the government!!!!!!!!!!"[38] Another states that "too many illegals are in our country for a free ride."[39] And another says that we are "just giving out more [welfare] and to people who aren't even citizens, who are not paying into the system."[40]

The claim that unauthorized immigrants are here for a "free ride" could not be further from the facts. A major reason immigrants—authorized and unauthorized—come to the United States is for employment opportunities. Thus, there was a significant decline in the unauthorized population with the decline of employment opportunities caused by the Great Recession.[41]

One way to assess whether unauthorized immigrants are working or not is to look at the percentage of them who are employed. Unfortunately, labor force statistics are not available by immigration status, so it is necessary to examine the entire foreign-born population. Most of the unauthorized immigrant population in the United States is from Mexico. Central Americans also make up a significant share.[42] Since a relatively large share of immigrants from Mexico and Central America are unauthorized, the unauthorized should have a noticeable impact on the statistics for those groups as a whole. The data shows that immigrants from Mexico and from Central America each have a higher rate of employment than the total U.S.-born population. Mexican and Central American immigrants also have a higher rate of employment than immigrants from Germany, China, and Canada.[43] This high rate of employment would not be possible if it were the case that unauthorized Mexican and Central American immigrants were in the United States not working and living off of "financial aid" and "welfare."

Not all of the Haters concerned with immigration expressed hostility toward immigrants. Some appear to be simply seriously interested in immigration reform. The quantitative data will allow us to determine the prevalence of anti-immigrant attitudes among Obama Haters.

The Quantitative Data

In this section I compare Obama Haters to Conservative Non-Haters and Moderate and Liberal Non-Haters on xenophobia as measured by their attitudes toward immigrants. More than four-fifths of Haters (82.3 percent) identify as politically conservative.[44] Obama Haters, therefore, should appear to be quite similar to Conservatives. If, however, xenophobia is an important factor in the hatred of Obama, then Haters should have stronger anti-immigrant attitudes than Conservatives.

Obama Haters are significantly more anti-immigrant than Conservatives and Moderates-Liberals on all measures. A majority (58.4 percent) of them believe that immigrants take away jobs from people already in the United States, and they (61.5 percent) want the level of immigration reduced. They support the harshest treatment of undocumented immigrants of the three groups. They are almost unanimous (88.2 percent) in their support of state and local police stopping and checking the legal status of individuals the police suspect of being undocumented. Only a third of Obama Haters support the DREAM Act, which allows children brought to the United States illegally to obtain permanent residency, while half of Conservatives support the DREAM Act. A third of Obama Haters simply want to arrest and deport all undocumented immigrants. These negative attitudes of Obama Haters toward the undocumented are captured in their relative feeling thermometer rating of "illegal immigrants" that is well below "freezing." (See Appendix, Tables 5.5 to 5.10, for details.)

Nearly two-thirds of Obama Haters believe incorrectly that Obama was not born in the United States. Their anti-immigrant feelings are not at the same level of Conservative Non-Haters; they are more opposed to immigrants than the conservative comparison group. Obama Haters show the strongest anti-immigrant attitudes of the three groups compared.

Obama Haters' attitudes toward immigrants are not merely a function of age or their conservative politics. Anti-immigrant and anti-undocumented-immigrant attitudes remain strongly correlated with being an Obama Hater even after taking into account these and other factors in a multivariate analysis.[45] Given Haters' strong anti-immigrant attitudes, there is good reason to believe that the Haters' hatred of Obama is influenced by their anti-immigrant, xenophobic feelings.

CHAPTER 6

Othering Obama, Part II: Islamophobia among Obama Haters

Obama "just doesn't seem like he's from America," said Beth Bailey, 25. Ben Bailey, 32, noted that Obama's middle name is Hussein, "and we know what that means."[1]

—two white Democrats, 2008

Among Islamophobes, Muslims are often seen as foreign, dangerous, alien Others. Spreading the false idea that Obama is Muslim would instigate their hatred of Obama. In January 2007, the conservative magazine *Insight* published an article claiming that Obama was educated in a radical Muslim school when he lived in Indonesia as a child. The story was then repeated by a number of news organizations. A later CNN investigation, however, found that the school was a secular public school with students from a variety of religious backgrounds.[2] In January 2008, the leaders of nine Jewish organizations condemned anonymous e-mails targeting Jews claiming that Obama is Muslim.[3] In the summer of 2008, Fox News fed the false association of Barack Obama with anti-American terrorism by repeatedly "mistakenly" referring to Osama bin Laden as "Obama" bin Laden.[4] Despite being debunked, the allegations and the insinuations that Obama is Muslim have continued.

ISLAMOPHOBIA AND OBAMA

The top campaign story of the 2008 presidential season was the controversy around statements made by Barack Obama's former pastor, the Reverend Jeremiah A. Wright.[5] Obama's critics suggested that if Obama spent two decades[6] listening to supposedly radical and hate-filled sermons from Wright, then Obama must be similarly radical and hate-filled.[7] Obama was able to reassure the country that he is moderate, centrist, and conciliatory with his speech, "A More Perfect Union." As soon as the controversy about Obama's long-standing presence in Rev. Wright's church had died down, the idea that Obama was secretly a Muslim began to take off.[8]

Although Obama has declared that he is Christian,[9] has prominent Christian advisors,[10] and was embroiled in a major controversy about his membership in a Christian church, a segment of the public continues to believe that he is Muslim. In fact, according to surveys from the Pew Research Center, this segment grew from 12 percent of the public in 2008 to 17 percent in 2012, driven primarily by the views of conservative Republicans.[11] Some surveys suggest that an even larger share of the public believes that Obama is Muslim.

In the 2012 American National Election Study (ANES), 26.6 percent of the voting-eligible population state that Obama is Muslim. The ANES differs from the Pew surveys in a number of respects, but one important way is that the Pew surveys allowed respondents to say that they "don't know" Obama's religion. Nearly a third (31 percent) of Pew respondents choose that option. The ANES forces respondents to pick a religion selection. The high proportion of respondents saying that Obama is Muslin in the ANES suggests that a significant share of Americans uncertain about Obama's religion think that he might be Muslim.

The ANES and Pew surveys are very similar in the share of the population believing Obama to be Christian however. In the ANES, 51 percent of the voting-eligible population believes Obama to be Christian. In the 2012 Pew survey, 49 percent of the general public sees Obama as Christian. These estimates are equivalent when one considers the margin of error.

While 76.3 percent of ANES respondents know that Mitt Romney is Mormon, only 51.0 percent know that Obama is Christian. Obama suffers from a significant disadvantage in that fewer people have an accurate knowledge of his religion,[12] and large share of the public associates him with a negatively stigmatized religion in American culture—Islam.

ISLAMOPHOBIA IN AMERICAN CULTURE

"I'm going to throw a bomb in your f**king school."[13] This was one of the hateful messages delivered by an anonymous caller to the Islamic School of San Diego on May 18, 2013. In addition to hate speech, Muslims, and people who are incorrectly perceived to be Muslims, have also been subject to a variety of other hate crimes including murder. The head coverings many Muslim women wear have been particularly irritating to Islamophobes. In California, in 2013, two Muslim girls were attacked by a white woman who pulled the headscarf off of one of the girls and attempted to pull the headscarf off of the other girl while screaming, "I do not approve of this; this is America!"[14]

Muslim children in America's schools have been subject to rude and offensive comments such as being called a "terrorist" or being laughed at because of their religion.[15]

There is a long history of anti-Islamic sentiment in the United States. These sentiments are likely amplified by the conflicts that the United States has had with predominantly Muslim countries, the awareness of terrorist acts committed by Muslims against Americans and Israelis, and the little knowledge that most Americans have of Islam.[16] The terrorist attacks of September 11, 2001, led to a wave of anti-Islamic sentiment in the United States.[17] Given these facts, painting Obama falsely as Muslim could be harmful to him politically.

There have been divergent trends for Republicans and Democrats on attitudes toward Muslims. Republicans have been increasingly more likely than Democrats to view Islam as a violent religion. In 2004, about 55 percent of Republicans felt that Islam encouraged violence. By 2013, the share of Republicans with this viewpoint had increased to 62 percent. In 2004, about 43 percent of Democrats felt that Islam encouraged violence. By 2013, the number had declined to 29 percent.[18]

About half of Americans feel that Islam is incompatible with American values and about half of Americans disagree. Here again, there is a partisan divide. A majority of Republicans believe that Islam is at odds with American values, while a majority of Democrats disagree. Republicans are also twice as likely as Democrats to believe that American Muslims want to establish Sharia law in the United States.[19]

In response to the question "Do you think it is justifiable for law enforcement to use profiling toward Arab Americans or American Muslims?" again there was a partisan divide. A majority of Republicans say that the profiling Arab Americans and American Muslims is justifiable while a majority of Democrats disagree.[20]

ISLAMOPHOBIA AMONG THE OBAMA HATERS

The Qualitative Data

When asked to list any reasons why they would not vote for Barack Obama, 10 percent of the Obama Haters state that they dislike Obama because they believe he is Muslim or not Christian. For many of these respondents, to be Muslim is to be not American and anti-American. For example, **Hater 558** said:

> He's a Muslim, and the proof is all over the place, but people refuse to see it. . . . If he has to choose between Americans and Muslims, he will side

with his Muslim brethren. . . . He has apologized and kowtowed to every nation in the world that we should be watching like a hawk.[21]

Hater 37 declares, "He is a Muslim. He has no flags anywhere around him."[22] **Hater 50** dislikes Obama for his supposedly "un-American values, Islam values."[23] For **Hater 142**, Obama "has an unhealthy attitude toward Islam and its relationship to our democratic society."[24] **Hater 243** believes that Obama "is probably a Muslim, and he does not have American values or Christian values."[25] According to **Hater 306**, Barack Obama is "a Muslim radical set to destroy the country, replace the Constitution with Sharia law, and become dictator."[26] **Hater 449** states, "He likes Muslims more than he likes us."[27] For these Haters, being Muslim and being a patriotic American is an impossibility.

Some Haters are aware that Obama has been a member of a Christian church, but they believe that he is insincere in his professed Christianity. When asked what Obama's religion is, their responses are "Protestant with Muslim beliefs"; "[he] pretends to be Protestant while having Muslim sympathies and atheistic policies";[28] and "he is whatever the person he is talking to wants him to be." About a fifth (19.2 percent) of Haters say that Obama is not religious. Some of the responses of these Haters to the question of Obama's religion are "[a]theistic with Muslim leanings," "[c]hameleon, anti-religion," and "whatever gets him votes."

The Quantitative Data

Again I will compare Obama Haters to Conservative Non-Haters and Moderate and Liberal Non-Haters on attitudes toward Muslims. If Islamophobia is an important factor in the hatred of Obama, then Haters should have stronger anti-Muslim attitudes than Conservatives, although four-fifths of Haters are conservative.

While straightforward questions about minority groups tend to produce large underestimates of the degree of antipathy toward these groups, this problem is significantly reduced with Muslims. Americans seem fairly comfortable expressing negative attitudes about Muslims to interviewers.[29]

One way for Islamophobia to be a factor in the hatred of Obama is if a significant share of Haters believe that he is Muslim.[30] Three-fifths (62.4 percent) of Haters believe incorrectly that Obama is Muslim compared to a third (31.6 percent) of Conservatives and a sixth (16.4 percent) of Moderates-Liberals.[31] Since a majority of Haters incorrectly believe that Obama is Muslim, their attitudes about Muslims can affect their feelings about Obama.

One measure of an individual's positive or negative disposition toward groups is his or her feeling thermometer ratings. Respondents to the ANES were asked to give a thermometer rating of Muslims from 0 to 100, with the higher the number indicating warmer, more positive feelings about the group. In this analysis, the thermometer ratings have been modified so that they are relative to the rating that the individual gave Christians. A rating of 50 means that the individual gave Muslims and Christians the same rating. The lower the value below 50, the colder or more negatively the individual feels about Muslims relative to Christians. The higher the rating above 50, the more the individual has warm or positive feelings toward Muslims relative to Christians.

All three groups are cold toward Muslims, but Haters are "freezing cold." Moderates-Liberals rate Muslims an average of 41 "degrees." Conservatives rate them 32 "degrees," and Haters rate them 23 "degrees." Although Conservatives are colder toward Muslims than Moderates-Liberals, Haters are even colder than Conservatives.[32]

It is useful to compare the feeling thermometer responses to Muslims with the responses to Mormons. About half of Americans do not see Mormons as Christians.[33] The Mormon feeling thermometer has also been constructed relative to the rating individuals gave the category "Christian." On this measure Haters do not stand out. Haters rate Mormons 39 "degrees." Conservatives rate them 39 "degrees," and Moderates-Liberals rate them 40 "degrees." Haters are not statistically different from Conservatives or Moderates-Liberals in their rating of Mormons.[34] Haters are cool toward Mormons, but just as cool as the other groups. In contrast, Haters are "freezing cold" toward Muslims and significantly colder than the other groups.

Respondents to the ANES were asked how well the words "patriotic" and "violent" described most Muslims. A majority (56.7 percent) of Haters feel that "patriotic" is "not at all" descriptive of Muslims. Only about a third of Conservatives (38.3 percent) and Moderates-Liberals (32.8 percent) feel the same.[35]

In response to the question of how well the word "violent" describes most Muslims, two-thirds of Haters (67.4 percent) feel that it describes Muslims moderately to extremely well compared to about half (47.4 percent) of Conservatives and a little more than a third (39.1 percent) of Moderates-Liberals. A fifth (20.4 percent) of Haters feel that "violent" describes most Muslims extremely well, while less than a tenth (7.0 percent) of Conservatives and (7.2 percent) of Moderates-Liberals feel the same.[36]

The quantitative evidence also points to Islamophobia as a factor in the hatred of Obama. Obama is Christian, but three-fifths (62.4 percent) of Haters believe that he is Muslim. Haters feel extremely cold toward Muslims. They see them as unpatriotic and violent. Even after taking into account demographic and political identity characteristics in a multivariate analysis, anti-Muslim feelings remain correlated with being an Obama Hater.[37]

The anti-Muslim feelings of Haters are not merely an artifact of their age or extreme conservatism. Given these facts, it is likely that many Haters believe that Obama is unpatriotic and working to destroy America because they believe he is Muslim.

CONCLUSION

Ethnocentrism—the psychological predisposition to divide the world into "us" versus "them"—played a bigger role in the 2008 election than in prior recent elections. The political scientists Cindy D. Kam and Donald R. Kinder find that this ethnocentrism was not simply motivated by antiblack racial attitudes; there were also anti-Muslim attitudes.[38] My analysis suggests that both anti-Muslim and anti-immigrant attitudes played a role in motivating the Obama-Hating public.

My analysis also concurs with the findings of the political scientists Christopher S. Parker and Matt A. Barreto in their study of the Tea Party. A majority of Obama Haters support the Tea Party, so one would expect similar findings. Parker and Barreto conclude that the Tea Party's opposition to President Obama is not merely driven by conservatism:

> It does, in fact, seem that there is something unique about Obama, something that transcends politics, ideology, or race. . . . Obama represents a threat to the American way of life that Tea Party sympathizers have come to know and cherish.[39]

My analysis suggests that Obama is perceived as a threat to the American way of life, in part, because he is perceived as foreign-born and Muslim.

Race, however, also appears to play a role in the perception of Obama as foreign-born and Muslim. Were he white, it is doubtful that his identities as American and as Christian would have been challenged. Even if they were, it is doubtful that the claims that he is foreign-born and Muslim would have amounted to much. The hatred of Obama goes beyond his race, but it appears to be enabled by his race.

A majority of Obama Haters believe Obama to be foreign-born and Muslim. Obama Haters are also more xenophobic and Islamophobic than other conservatives. They perceive immigrants as harmful to the country, and they perceive Muslims as violent and unpatriotic. Given these facts, it is not surprising that they believe that Obama is out to destroy America.

CHAPTER 7

Hot Tea: Obama Haters and the Tea Partiers

The Tea Party has been an important political movement strongly opposed to the Obama administration. One Tea Party leader defines the goal of the movement simply as to "resist the president."[1] This chapter examines the relationship between Tea Party supporters[2] and Obama Haters. This issue is complicated by the fact that the groups overlap asymmetrically. Tea Party supporters make up a group that is more than twice the size of Obama Haters. There are 58 million Tea Party supporters and 25 million Obama Haters.[3] About 70 percent of Tea Party supporters are *not* Obama Haters. On the other hand, 70 percent of Obama Haters *are* Tea Party supporters. Most Tea Party supporters are *not* Obama Haters, but most Obama Haters *are* Tea Party supporters. While the groups overlap, they are different.

The Tea Party movement has been animated by a deep distrust and dislike of Barack Obama.[4] Tea Party officials argue that they are simply motivated by a love of the country, the Constitution, and conservative and libertarian values.[5] Analysts, however, regularly report evidence of racism among Tea Party activists. It is clear that most of the Tea Party criticism and activism against Barack Obama has not been overtly about race, but antiblack attitudes have been something that has repeatedly popped out of the Tea Party "closet." The political journalist Will Bunch argues that "the thing providing the movement with so much of its fuel is anxiety about race."[6] Other journalists have also concluded that racial hatred is a motivating factor behind the Tea Party movement.[7]

A number of social scientists have largely agreed with this conclusion. In their examination of the Tea Party, the political scientists Theda Skocpol and Vanessa Williamson found that "racially laden group stereotypes certainly did float in and out of interviews."[8] Skocpol and Williamson state:

A Virginia Tea Partier told us that a "plantation mentality" was keeping "some people" on welfare. These kinds of racially insensitive comments made in person were only a very faint echo of the racial slurs that appear rarely but persistently at Tea Party rallies across the country, including in signs with racial epithets and signs equating the presidency of Barack Obama to "white slavery." A sense of "us versus them" along racial and ethnic fault lines clearly marks the worldview of many people active in the Tea Party.[9]

Skocpol and Williamson note that there is also evidence of Tea Party activists who are willing to look beyond race.[10]

The political scientists Christopher S. Parker and Matt A. Barreto conducted a quantitative examination of the Tea Party. They found that individuals with higher levels of antiblack racial resentment were more likely to support the Tea Party. They also found that Tea Party supporters, although supposedly against "big government," were fairly supportive of "big government" when it came to racially profiling racial and ethnic minorities.[11] Skocpol and Williamson expand on this finding. They argue that Tea Party activists like the government when it works for them and people they care about, but they are antigovernment when the government works for the needy and for things like the education of racial and ethnic minority children.[12]

Tea Party supporters also exhibit a high level of xenophobia. While a minority of Americans see immigrants as threatening traditional American customs and values, a majority of Tea Party supporters do.[13] A majority of Tea Party supporters also say that immigrants are "a burden on our country because they take jobs, housing and health care."[14] Democracy Corps, a liberal political research organization, reports, "The Republicans, led by the Tea Party, are about as hostile to 'undocumented' immigrants in the U.S. as they are to Obamacare."[15]

Skocpol and Williamson also found Tea Partiers intensely intolerant of Muslims.[16] They report, "We never got the sense, however, that any or our Tea Party informants actually knew any Muslim-Americans personally or even foreign Muslim visitors of whom they disapproved."[17] Survey data supports this perception of strong Tea Party Islamophobia. A 2011 survey found Republicans to be more Islamophobic than Democrats, and Tea Party supporters a bit more Islamophobic than Republicans. Tea Party supporters had the most unfavorable view of Muslims. They were the most likely to think that American Muslims want to establish Sharia law in the United States. And they were the most uncomfortable with a mosque being built near their home.[18]

These findings about Tea Party supporters remind one of Obama Haters with regard to their antiblack, anti-immigrant, and anti-Muslim attitudes. The following analyses first compare Tea Party supporters with conservatives who are not Tea Party supporters to determine whether the Tea Partiers in the American National Election Study (ANES) appear as extreme as in other studies. In the ANES also, Tea Partiers register as more antiblack, anti-immigrant, and anti-Muslim than the average conservative who is not a Tea Party supporter.

The second analysis compares two segments of the Tea Party: those who are Obama Haters and those who are not. Tea-Party Obama Haters are more hateful than other Tea Party supporters. The hateful extremism of the Tea Party overall is increased as a result of the Obama Haters within the Tea Party.

The third analysis compares two types of Obama Haters: those who are Tea Party supporters and those who are not. The Non-Tea-Party Obama Haters are less politically conservative, but they are still hateful toward Obama, immigrants, and Muslims.

TEA PARTIERS VERSUS CONSERVATIVES

In the ANES, Tea Party supporters register as strongly antiblack, xenophobic, and Islamophobic. On all of the race measures examined, they express more negative attitudes toward blacks than conservatives who are not Tea Party supporters.[19] (See Appendix, Tables 7.1 to 7.3, for details.) On two of the three measures examined concerning attitudes toward immigrants and immigration, Tea Party supporters are more anti-immigrant than conservatives. (See Appendix, Tables 7.4 to 7.6, for details.) On two of the three measures of attitudes toward Muslims, Tea Party supporters are more Islamophobic than conservatives who are not supporters of the Tea Party. (See Appendix, Tables 7.7 to 7.9, for details.) In general, Tea Partiers are a pretty hateful group. But we will see that the Tea Partiers who are also Obama Haters are even more hateful than the average Tea Partier.

HOT TEA: TEA-PARTY OBAMA HATERS

Tea-Party Obama Haters are more antiblack, more burdened by false ideas of white victimization, more xenophobic, and more Islamophobic than other Tea Party supporters. Without these members, the Tea Party would be significantly less extreme.

Political Ideology, Identification, and Participation

Obama Haters who are also Tea Party supporters are the more conservative segment of the already very conservative Tea Party. More than 90 percent of them are conservative compared to about 70 percent of Tea Party supporters who are not also Obama Haters.[20] Nearly all (96.2 percent) Tea-Party Obama Haters are Republican or lean Republican compared to about three-quarters (75.4 percent) of Tea-Party supporters who are not Obama Haters. Six in ten Tea-Party Obama Haters report that they are not simply Republican but strong Republicans. The rate for Tea-Party Non-Haters is less than half that amount (28.0 percent).[21] We see additional evidence of the conservativism of the Tea-Party Obama Haters in their policy preference regarding the poor. More than half of them (55.2 percent) want the federal government to reduce spending on the poor. Only a third (34.3 percent) of other Tea Partiers feel the same.[22]

Tea-Party Obama Haters probably have disproportionate influence on the Tea Party because they are more politically engaged than other Tea Partiers. Tea-Party Obama Haters are more likely to vote in a presidential primary or caucus than other Tea Party members. They are also more likely to contact their U.S. representative or senator, and they are more likely to contribute to a campaign. (See Appendix, Table 7.12, for details.)

Antiblack Attitudes and a White-Victimhood Mentality

Tea-Party Obama Haters are also more antiblack than other Tea Partiers. They exhibit a higher level of hostility toward blacks. A third (33.5 percent) of them obtain the highest score on the antiblack racial resentment measure compared to about a seventh (13.8 percent) of other Tea Partiers. All Tea Partiers, those who are Obama Haters and those who are not, have a high rate of support for the white-victimhood mentality. A majority of all Tea Partiers believe that whites experience as much or more discrimination than blacks and Hispanics. Perhaps not surprisingly, Obama Haters who are members of the Tea Party are more likely than other Tea Partiers to feel that Obama favors blacks over whites, but both groups score rather high on this measure. (See Appendix, Tables 7.13 to 7.15, for details.)

Anti-immigrant Attitudes

Tea-Party Obama Haters are more xenophobic than other Tea Party supporters. On all of the measures examined Tea-Party Obama Haters are significantly more anti-immigrant. About 6 in 10 (59.1 percent) Tea-Party Obama Haters want to see the level of immigration into the United States decreased compared with about half (48.9 percent) of other Tea Partiers.[23] Nearly 4 in 10 (39.2 percent) Tea-Party Obama Haters want to deport all illegal immigrants. About 2 in 10 (22.2 percent) of the other Tea Partiers feel the same.[24] Tea-Party Obama Haters are colder than other Tea Partiers in their feeling-thermometer rating of illegal immigrants.[25]

Anti-Muslim Attitudes

Tea-Party Obama Haters are more Islamophobic than other Tea Party supporters. They are colder toward Muslims than other Tea Partiers.[26] A solid majority of Tea-Party Obama Haters (70.9 percent) view Muslims as violent compared to half (50.7 percent) of Tea-Party Non-Haters.[27] Six in ten (60.7 percent) Tea-Party Obama Haters view Muslims as "not at all" patriotic. Only about 4 in 10 (37.5 percent) of other Tea Partiers feel the same.[28]

Conclusion

A significant portion of the extremism of the Tea Party comes from its Obama-Hater segment. On a number of measures, Tea-Party Obama Haters are much more hateful than other Tea Party supporters. Tea-Party Obama Haters are about one and a half times as likely as other Tea Partiers to believe that Obama favors blacks over whites and to say that Muslims are violent and not at all patriotic. They are nearly twice as likely as other Tea Partiers to want to deport all unauthorized immigrants.

These findings provide some perspective on just how extreme are the attitudes of the average Obama Hater: They make the average Tea Partier look moderate. The Tea Party could possibly gain some more legitimacy and support from moderates and liberals if it purged itself of its more hateful members. On the other hand, the more hateful members appear to be the more politically active members. Without the Obama Haters, there would likely be less activism in the Tea Party.

LESS CONSERVATIVE, BUT STILL A HATER: THE NON-TEA-PARTY OBAMA HATERS

Obama Haters who are also members of the Tea Party are very conservative, very politically active, and intensely antiblack, anti-immigrant, and anti-Muslim. The Obama Haters who are not supporters of the Tea Party, while less conservative and less politically active, are nonetheless pretty hateful, particularly regarding immigrants and Muslims.

Nine-tenths (91.8 percent) of Tea-Party Obama Haters are conservative compared to six-tenths (58.9 percent) of Non-Tea-Party Obama Haters.[29] Also, on the question of whether federal spending on the poor should be decreased, more than half (55.2 percent) of the Tea-Party Haters agree while only about a third (31.2 percent) of the other Haters feel the same.[30]

Tea-Party Obama Haters are, again, more likely to vote in a presidential primary or caucus than other Haters. They are also more likely to contact their U.S. representative or senator, and they are more likely to contribute to a campaign. (See Appendix, Table 7.12, for details.)

Although Non-Tea-Party Obama Haters are less conservative and less politically active than Tea-Party Obama Haters, they are still Obama Haters. Non-Tea-Party Obama Haters are just as likely as Tea-Party Obama Haters to see Obama as favoring blacks over whites, to think that Obama is foreign-born, and to think that Obama is a Muslim. (See Appendix, Tables 7.15, 7.16, and 7.20, for details.) However, Non-Tea-Party Obama Haters may be a little less antiblack than Tea-Party Obama Haters. While a third (33.5 percent) of Tea-Party Haters obtain the highest antiblack racial resentment score, only a fifth (19.5 percent) of the Non-Tea-Party Haters achieve the same result.[31] Non-Tea-Party Haters also appear to suffer from a slightly lower rate of the white-victimhood mentality.[32]

On all of the immigration measures examined, Tea-Party Haters and Non-Tea-Party Haters have equivalent scores. Non-Tea-Party Haters are slightly warmer toward Muslims than Tea-Party Haters, but they may be similar on the view of Muslims as violent and unpatriotic. (See Appendix, Tables 7.17 to 7.19 and 7.21 to 7.23, for details.) These analyses of stereotypes of Muslims, however, may suffer from small sample sizes.[33]

While it is correct that extreme racial and ethnic hatred tends to be found among the more extreme conservatives, the Non-Tea-Party Obama Haters show that it can be present among those who are somewhat less conservative too. Chapter 9 delves into this issue more deeply by examining xenophobia, Islamophobia, and racism beyond the Obama Haters.

DISTINGUISHING OBAMA HATERS FROM TEA PARTIERS

These findings reveal the validity of distinguishing Obama Haters from Tea Partiers. While Tea Partiers are more extreme than other conservatives, the typical Obama Hater is more extreme than the typical Tea Partier. Tea Partiers are anti-Obama, but they are not anti-Obama to the intensity of Obama Haters. For example, two-fifths (42.3 percent) of Tea Partiers who are not also Obama Haters think that Obama favors blacks over whites, but more than three-fifths (65.4 percent) of Obama Haters think that this is true.[34] Tea Partiers are xenophobic, Islamophobic, and racist, but Obama Haters are more so. Obama Haters are significantly more likely than Tea Partiers to believe that Muslims are violent and not at all patriotic, and they are more likely to want to deport all unauthorized immigrants. A significant portion of the hatefulness found in studies of the Tea Party appears to come from the Obama Haters within the Tea Party. There is also reason to believe that a substantial amount of Tea Party activism is driven by the Obama-Hater element within the Tea Party.

CHAPTER 8

Thinking Like a Hater

When asked the religion of the Republican presidential candidate, Mitt Romney, 90.2 percent of Obama Haters answered correctly. Overall, 76.3 percent of the voting-eligible population gave the correct answer. When asked the religion of the Democratic presidential candidate, Barack Obama, only 13.6 percent of Obama Haters answered correctly. Overall, 51.0 percent of the population answered correctly.[1] The Obama Haters' accuracy rate for Romney's religion is impressive. It is much better than average. Their error rate for Obama's religion is astounding. It is much, much worse than average.

How could Obama Haters be more knowledgeable than average about Romney and, at the same time, be so much less knowledgeable than average about Obama? Was their high rate of accuracy about Romney a fluke or are they truly knowledgeable about American political affairs? Do they have an affinity for unconventional or conspiratorial theories that leads them to be susceptible to false ideas about Obama's religion? Or, will they simply believe anything negative about Obama because they hate him?

In the following discussion, I explore these questions. Beyond the anti-black racism, xenophobia, and Islamophobia, what other factors shape how Obama Haters think, and what are their policy priorities? I explore these issues here comparing Haters to Conservatives, and Moderates-Liberals.

IGNORANCE, PARANOIA, OR HATRED?

Liberals in favor of the Affordable Care Act (ACA or Obamacare) have often made fun of the ACA opponents who state that they want "government hands off my Medicare."[2] Since Medicare is a government program, this demand is nonsensical.

Obama Haters, however, know that Medicare is a program of the federal government. Well, nearly 9 in 10 (88.4 percent) of them do. This rate is more than the share for Conservatives (81.9 percent) and Moderates-Liberals (79.3 percent).[3] In fact, generally, on basic political knowledge questions, Haters are more likely to know the correct answer than Conservatives or Moderates-Liberals.

Out of nine political knowledge questions in the 2012 American National Election Study (ANES), a greater share of Haters answered correctly than either Conservatives or Moderates-Liberals on seven of them.[4] On the question of what the national unemployment rate is at the time of the election, the share of Haters answering correctly was the lowest, but it was within one percentage point of the other groups. It seems reasonable to consider this result a three-way tie. If we do, that would mean there was only one question where Haters performed worse than the other groups and seven questions where Haters performed better.[5]

The question that Haters flubbed was about the relative size of different parts of the federal budget. Respondents had to choose whether the federal government spent the least on foreign aid, Medicare, national defense, or Social Security. About 1 percent of the federal budget goes to foreign aid, but on average the public assumes that about 28 percent of the budget does.[6] Overall, only a third (33.3 percent) of ANES respondents could identify foreign aid as the smallest budget item. Haters underperformed this average slightly, with 28.8 percent identifying foreign aid as the smallest part of the federal budget.[7]

Surprisingly, Haters are more likely than Conservatives and Moderates-Liberals to believe that national defense is the smallest budget item (22.5 percent for Haters, vs. 10.4 percent for Conservatives, and 8.6 percent for Moderates-Liberals).[8] The United States is the only remaining military superpower, and the United States has recently been involved simultaneously in two wars in Iraq and Afghanistan. It is not possible for the United States to be so dominant militarily without a large military budget. In 2011 (remember the ANES respondents were surveyed in 2012), defense made up 20 percent of the federal budget. It tied for second place with Social Security, behind the health insurance programs (21 percent), Medicare, Medicaid, and the Children's Health Insurance Program.[9] For these reasons, it is a bit surprising that Haters would be so likely to think that national defense is the smallest budget item.

Obama Haters generally are a bit more knowledgeable than average about basic political facts. They seem to be able to retain new facts well. They basically tied with the other two groups in the share of correct answers on the question about the current unemployment rate. They were the most likely to correctly identify the secretary of the Treasury.[10] These are answers that one could not have simply remembered from when one learned civics in school. It is not a general lack of political interest and knowledge or an inability to retain new information that explains why Obama Haters can be so factually incorrect about Obama.

If it is not a lack of political interest that leads to Obama Haters' misinformation about Obama, then maybe it is a susceptibility to conspiracy theories. The ANES asks respondents a series of questions to gauge a person's willingness to accept "non-mainstream beliefs." We have already encountered two of the non-mainstream beliefs questions. One is about Obama's place of birth. Nearly two-thirds of Obama Haters (65.1 percent) believe that Obama was definitely or probably born in another country. Only about a third (30.9 percent) of Conservatives and a seventh of Moderates-Liberals (14.0 percent) believe the same.[11] The other question that we have already encountered is about whether the Obama administration favors blacks over whites. Nearly two-thirds (65.4 percent) of Obama Haters said that the administration does favor blacks over whites. Only about a third (35.1 percent) of Conservatives and an eighth (12.5 percent) of Moderates-Liberals feel the same.[12] A third "Obama-conspiracy-theory" question, for lack of a better term, yields similar results. Nearly three-quarters (72.4 percent) of Haters believe that the ACA definitely or probably authorizes government panels to make end-of-life decisions (i.e., has "death panels") for people on Medicare. About half (49.2 percent) of Conservatives and more than a quarter of Moderates-Liberals (29.1 percent) share this belief.[13]

When it comes to conspiracy theories about Obama, Obama Haters seem to be eager to believe what they hear. Not only do they think he is not Christian, but also they think he is foreign-born, they think he favors blacks over whites, and they think Obamacare has "death panels." But maybe this is just because they are drawn to conspiracy theories. Two of the conspiracy theories in the ANES relate to the George W. Bush administration. These two questions will allow us to see if Obama Haters are inclined to believe conspiracy theories generally or just conspiracy theories about Obama.

When asked if senior government officials knew about the terrorist attacks on September 11, 2001, before they happened, a majority of Obama Haters reject the idea. Two-thirds (65.8 percent) indicate that the government definitely or probably did *not* know about the attacks in advance. On this question Obama Haters look like Conservatives. About two-thirds (69.1 percent) of Conservatives agree that the government definitely or probably did not know about 9/11 in advance. A majority of Moderates-Liberals feel the same, but a smaller majority (56.4 percent) than for Haters and Conservatives.[14]

Another question is whether, during Hurricane Katrina in 2005, the federal government intentionally breached the levees so that they would flood poor neighborhoods in order to save middle-class neighborhoods. On this question also, Haters' responses match Conservatives. For both of these groups, about 9 in 10 (90.2 percent for Haters and 86.5 percent for Conservatives) said that the federal government definitely or probably did *not* do this. Eight in ten (80.5 percent) Moderates-Liberals said the same.[15]

Obama Haters reject conspiracy theories that reflect negatively on the Bush administration, but they accept conspiracy theories that are connected to the Obama administration. This pattern is not due to Haters being ill-informed or disinterested in politics. It appears that because of their hatred of Obama, any negative stories about him are seductive and believable to them.

HATERS' EXTREME VIEW OF OBAMA'S LIBERALISM

Haters differ greatly with Conservatives in how liberal they see Obama, but they are fairly similar to Conservatives in how conservative they see Romney. Haters are more than twice as likely as Conservatives to see Obama as "extremely liberal." Nearly 9 in 10 (85.0 percent) Haters see Obama this way compared to 4 in 10 (40.5 percent) of Conservatives. Only about a tenth (11.2 percent) of Moderates-Liberals feel the same.[16]

Haters differ less from Conservatives in their assessment of Romney. A little more than half (53.4 percent) of Haters characterize Romney as just "conservative" as opposed to "slightly conservative" or "extremely conservative." More than two-fifths (42.6 percent) of Conservatives see Romney as "conservative." While Haters are more likely than the Conservative group to see Romney as "conservative," the difference here is not nearly as great as in the view of Obama as "extremely liberal."[17] Haters are twice as likely as Conservatives to see Obama as "extremely liberal."

Asked to assess Obama's orientation with regard to whether the government should provide more services even if it means an increase in spending or fewer services to reduce spending, again Haters have the most extreme view of Obama. Haters are nearly twice as likely as Conservatives to believe that Obama wants the government to provide many more services (76.5 percent vs. 39.6 percent).[18]

When asked the same question of Romney, a plurality of about three-tenths (31.6 percent) of Haters place Romney in the slightly conservative position of reducing government services a little. Conservatives' distribution in their assessment of Romney is statistically the same as the Haters' distribution. As with Haters, three tenths (31.3 percent), also the plurality, of Conservatives see Romney as favoring reducing government services a little.[19]

The general pattern is repeated in the question of whether the candidate wants to increase or reduce defense spending. Haters are nearly three times as likely as Conservatives to see Obama as pushing strongly for defense cuts.[20]

And, again, Haters only differ a little from Conservatives in their views of Romney's desires for defense spending.[21]

On every question examined assessing the liberalism of Obama, Haters are the most likely to see Obama as extremely liberal. Except for the question of defense spending, a majority of Haters put Obama in the most extreme liberal position. Haters are about twice as likely as Conservatives to see Obama as extremely liberal. In contrast, on Romney, Haters and Conservatives have similar views. Both groups see Romney as slightly conservative or conservative but not extremely conservative. Moderates-Liberals are more likely to put Romney in the extreme conservative position than Haters, but the degree to which they do this is much less than the degree to which Haters put Obama in the extreme liberal position.

HATERS' POLICY PRIORITIES

In terms of big policy priorities, Obama Haters only seem to be strongly committed to reducing welfare programs and increasing defense spending. When given a menu[22] of the different categories of federal spending, Haters provide the strongest support for decreasing spending on welfare programs. More than four-fifths (82.3 percent) of Haters want to see welfare spending decrease. On the other hand, a smaller share—only half (49.1 percent)—say that they want to decrease federal spending on aid to the poor.[23] This is a bit confusing because welfare is aid for the poor. It is not clear where "aid to the poor" ends and "welfare programs" begin.[24]

The difference in the level of support may be due to a stigma attached to the word "welfare" and to the influence of antiblack bias in people's thinking about welfare. The political scientist Martin Gilens found that whites are supportive of programs for the poor, but they oppose welfare because they tend to believe the stereotype that welfare is a program that benefits supposedly lazy blacks.[25] The stronger support for decreasing welfare may be due to this racial stereotype and antiblack bias.

The pattern of greater support for reducing spending on welfare than on spending for the poor also applies to Conservatives and Moderates-Liberals. Among Conservatives, more than three-fifths (62.3 percent) want to see a decrease in spending on welfare, but a bit less than a third (29.1 percent) want to see a decrease in spending on the poor. About a third (32.8 percent) of Moderates-Liberals want a decrease in welfare spending, but about an eighth (11.7 percent) want a decrease in spending on the poor.[26]

Haters approach 50 percent support for reducing federal spending on child care and on the environment. Nearly half (47.4 percent) of Haters favor cutting spending for child care in comparison to about a third (30.4 percent) of Conservatives and an eighth (12.8 percent) of Moderates-Liberals. Nearly half (45.0 percent) of Haters want to reduce spending for the environment while a little less than a third (29.6 percent) of Conservatives and less than a tenth (7.3 percent) of Moderates-Liberals feel the same.[27]

After reducing spending on welfare programs, Haters express the strongest support for increasing defense spending. A slight majority (53.6 percent) of Haters want to see defense spending increase. Less than a third (30.3 percent) of Conservatives and only a fifth (20.6 percent) of Moderates-Liberals feel the same.[28]

Haters indicate significant support, but not majority support, for increasing two other areas of federal spending. About half (49.4 percent) indicate that they would support increased spending to deal with crime. This level of support is about the same for Conservatives (47.2 percent) and Moderates-Liberals (50.7 percent). The only other budget item that receives more than two-fifths (42.0 percent) support for increased spending from Haters is Social Security. A similar level (38.7 percent) of Conservatives feel the same, but about half (51.3 percent) of Moderates-Liberals express support for increased Social Security spending.[29]

Haters want welfare spending decreased, and they express significant support for cutting spending for the poor, child care, and the environment. Relative to Conservatives, they generally take the more fiscally conservative position of expressing greater support for reducing spending. The three exceptions are for spending on defense, crime, and Social Security. On defense, a greater share of Haters than Conservatives are willing to increase spending. This is not so surprising when one recalls that Haters are the most likely to believe that defense is the smallest item on the federal budget. On crime and Social Security, Haters express significant levels of support for increasing spending at rates similar to that expressed by Conservatives.

SUMMARY

Obama Haters are very conservative fiscally, and they are strongly biased against Barack Obama. What Haters want most strongly is to reduce government spending on welfare and to increase government spending on defense. A few Haters even believe, very incorrectly, that defense spending is the smallest item in the federal budget.

On questions relating to President George W. Bush or to the presidential candidate Mitt Romney, Haters' responses are very similar to Conservatives' responses. There is no sign of a strong bias for or against these men relative to the views of Conservatives. On questions relating to President Barack Obama, they differ strongly from Conservatives. In Haters' eyes, Obama is far more radical and far more sinister than in the eyes of Conservatives. This difference is likely driven by the Haters' hatred of Obama, which arises from xenophobia, Islamophobia, and racism.

CHAPTER 9

The Future of Hate

President Obama has been plagued by hatred stemming from xenophobia, Islamophobia, and racism. He is American, but he is hated for supposedly being an immigrant. He is Christian, but he is hated for supposedly being Muslim. He is a centrist, but he is hated for supposedly being a left-wing radical. He is an aggressive compromiser, but he is hated for supposedly being a tyrant. He *is* black, and he is hated for that too.

These hatreds combined with increasingly partisan politics, at the time of this writing, have effectively blocked President Obama from signing any major legislation in his second term. Nonetheless, one can argue that he is still a very lucky man. He is wealthy and successful. He has had a hard time in office, but he will survive it, and he will likely continue to do well after his tenure as president.

The larger issue raised by the analysis of the Obama Haters is the fate of black people and other people of color not named Barack Obama. As we saw with much of the intellectual commentary after the 2008 election, many Americans are eager to claim that we have transcended race, that we have put race behind us, that we are colorblind, that we are post-racial. We have been making this type of claim repeatedly—and wrongly—since at least as early as the 1960s.[1] The fact that a black man raised by a white mother and white grandparents, with two degrees from Ivy League universities, and who is "articulate and bright and clean and a nice-looking guy"[2] can still be subject to virulent racial hatred should make us definitively reject claims of post-racialism.

Obama has the cultural background, the academic credentials, the self-presentation, and the temperament that conservative pundits tell blacks are the keys to black success.[3] And yet, he is still seen as unqualified, lazy, and lacking in self-control by a segment of the American population. He is still called a nigger by some.[4] Obama was much luckier than the average African American in that the non-haters were able to overwhelm the haters in deciding if he would obtain the job of presidency. For blacks applying for other jobs, if they are unlucky enough to stumble upon an employer with strong antiblack prejudice, there is no group of non-haters to overrule that employer. If Obama, nearly the perfect black man according to conventional conservative thinking, can be harmed by racial hatred, all blacks can be affected. If Obama experiences race-based challenges, average blacks, who lack his many advantages, likely experience more.

America may be on a dangerous path in terms of racial relations. Nearly a third of whites express anxiety about the idea of whites not being the numerical majority.[5] As a racial minority group grows in size relative to the majority group, a body of sociological research predicts more racial conflict.[6] This is the demographic challenge to racial relations that we face as a country.

The second challenge for racial relations is due to increasing economic inequality. Since the late 1970s, the share of the country's income and wealth going to the very rich has steadily grown while maintaining living standards has become harder for everyone else.[7] Unfortunately, there does not appear to be any forces to halt this trend in the near future. Part of the white-victimhood mentality is likely the result of middle- and working-class whites directing their economic frustrations at racial and ethnic minorities.[8] Of course, if anything, increasing economic inequality disproportionately hurts racial and ethnic minorities who are overrepresented among the lower classes.

Unless we intervene positively, it is reasonable to expect that racial anxiety, beliefs in white victimization, and outright hostility will increase in American society. One way we can begin to address this problem is to use the Obama Haters to help craft an anti-prejudice agenda.

HATE ISN'T LIMITED TO THE OBAMA HATERS

While the concentration of negative racial and ethnic attitudes is stronger among Obama Haters than among Non-Haters, no hateful attitude is unique to Haters. Nearly half (46.7 percent) of Obama Haters rate blacks as significantly lazier than whites, but a quarter (26.4 percent) of all Non-Haters feel the same.[9] Six in ten (60.3 percent) Haters feel a high level of racial resentment toward blacks, but a quarter (27.1 percent) of Non-Haters feel the same.[10] When Haters and Non-Haters are combined, one finds that about 3 in 10 American adults view blacks as relatively lazy (28.7 percent) and 3 in 10 have strong feelings of racial resentment toward blacks (30.7 percent).[11] This means that in day-to-day life perhaps as many as 3 of every

10 individuals a black person interacts with has a significant degree of anti-black bias. Perhaps as many as 3 of every 10 black job applications end up on the desk of someone not inclined to hire blacks.

There is explicit bias that individuals may be conscious of, and there is implicit bias that taps into individuals' unconscious associations. American culture contains many negative images and stereotypes of black people. Individuals living in American culture cannot help being exposed to these negative ideas. Even individuals who are true believers in racial equality can be affected subconsciously by these antiblack aspects of American culture. The famous writer Malcolm Gladwell spoke about his results after taking an implicit measure of antiblack bias.

> It told me that I had a moderate preference for White people. . . . I was biased—slightly biased—against Black people, toward White people, which horrified me because my mom's Jamaican. . . . The person in my life who I love more than almost anyone else is Black, and here I was taking a test, which said, frankly, I wasn't too crazy about Black people.[12]

The research on implicit bias suggests that three-quarters of Americans are subconsciously biased against blacks.[13]

The survey data on racial attitudes and the implicit-bias research provides a sense of the challenges faced by blacks in day-to-day interpersonal interactions. It is important to recognize that these are measures of prejudice and bias, not indications that a person desires to join a white-supremacist hate group. Sometimes people think of racial prejudice and discrimination only in extreme terms, and in doing so they completely miss the day-to-day challenges faced by blacks. In day-to-day life, these attitudes and biases are most likely to be manifest in individuals showing a preference in favor of whites over blacks, not in hate-crime violence. For example, an individual may have fairly good relations with blacks but still assume that a white candidate is better than a black candidate for a job *before looking at the applications* because the individual assumes that whites have a better work ethic than blacks. The individual may still come to hire the black candidate *if the black candidate is twice as good as the white candidate*. If the black candidate were only a little better than the white candidate, then the white candidate may get the job because of the individuals' bias against blacks. In this situation, like in the cases of the "racists-for-Obama" voters (discussed in Chapter 2), the specific details about the situation matter in determining how the bias affects behavior. But overall, the fairly widespread bias against blacks means that blacks end up losing opportunities and access to resources more than they should, given their abilities.

While interpersonal interactions are important, the institutional aspects of racial relations are even more important. Institutional discrimination, the denial of opportunities and resources that results from the routine policies and procedures of organizations and institutions, plays a more significant role in racial inequality than interpersonal discrimination. For example, we can look at our educational system. From our preschools to our high schools, our schools remain largely racially separate and unequal. In the South, the peak year for integration was 1988 when 44 percent of black students attended majority white schools. Today, only about 20 percent of black students in the South attend integrated schools.[14] Nationally only about a quarter of black students attend racially integrated schools.[15]

We still have a great deal of racial segregation in our educational system, and that matters because racially separate schools still produce racially unequal schools. The economist David T. Burkam presents his assessment of elementary schools:

> Black, Hispanic, and lower-SES children begin school at kindergarten in systematically lower-quality elementary schools than their more advantaged and white counterparts. Whether defined by less favorable social contexts, larger kindergarten classes, less outreach to smooth the transition to first grade, less well prepared and experienced teachers, less positive attitudes among teachers, fewer school resources, or poor neighborhood and school conditions, the least advantaged U.S. children begin their formal schooling in consistently lower-quality schools.[16]

The picture at other levels of grade school is largely the same. The Civil Rights Project states, "Racially and socioeconomically isolated schools are strongly related to an array of factors that limit educational opportunities and outcomes."[17] Our educational system in its day-to-day policies and procedures systematically disadvantage black children.

The forces that maintain separate and unequal schools are not the result of a handful of individuals consciously trying to produce racial inequality. Much of the work maintaining our unequal school system is done by routine, supposedly race-neutral policies and procedures. If we wish to produce a school system that provides the average black and Latino students with the same educational opportunities as the average white student, we need to unmask the ways in which the "race-neutral" policies and procedures for funding schools and allocating teachers systematically disadvantage black and Latino students. The problem of institutional discrimination is not limited to education. We could also look at housing, health care, criminal justice, the labor market, and so on and find, to varying degrees, institutional discrimination that touches the lives of the majority of African Americans.

Prejudice and Discrimination against Latinos, Immigrants, and Muslims

The preceding discussion focused on prejudice and discrimination against African Americans, but, of course, other groups face prejudice and discrimination in America. I will briefly discuss attitudes toward Latinos, immigrants, and Muslims. For all of these groups also, it would be a mistake to assume that negative attitudes can be found only among the Obama Haters. The negative views are more common and perhaps more intense among Haters, but they are not limited to Haters.

Nationally, about 10 to 20 percent of Americans express anti-Hispanic attitudes. About a tenth (11.7 percent) of Americans think Hispanics are lazier than whites. On the other hand, an equivalent share (11.6 percent) think Hispanics are more hardworking than whites.[18] "Positive" stereotyping can sometimes be as dangerous as negative stereotyping. Asians and Jews have been stereotyped as very intelligent, but this "positive" stereotype has supported the view of them as evilly devious.[19] Americans who see Hispanics as more hardworking than whites could also have negative attitudes toward Hispanics. They may view them as people to be feared because they aim to "steal" jobs from non-Hispanics. A simpler-to-interpret measure is warmth or coldness toward Hispanics. A fifth of Americans (19.3 percent) are cold toward Hispanics.[20] Thus, depending on the measure, about 10 to 20 percent of Americans appear to have biases against Hispanics.

There has been less research on implicit bias against Latinos than against blacks. Researchers do find that unconscious biases against Latinos do exist.[21] However, there is no estimate of the prevalence of these anti-Latino implicit biases, but one would expect their prevalence to be much greater than that for the more explicit measures.

Latinos, too, are subject to institutional discrimination across all of the major institutions in American society. In terms of school segregation, Latino children are even more segregated than black children. Only about a fifth of Latino children attend integrated schools compared to about a quarter of blacks.[22] The worst regions for Latino students are the West and the South. In 2011, in the West, 84 percent of Latinos attended majority minority schools. In the South, 81 percent did.[23] And again, these schools tend to be of lower quality than the average majority white school on all measures. Thus, the educational system creates a widespread disadvantage for Latino students.

About a fifth (21.6 percent) of American adults possess a high level anti-immigrant attitudes,[24] and a fifth (20.0 percent) possess strong anti-undocumented-immigrant attitudes. There is, however, about a fifth of Americans (21.0 percent) who strongly support assisting undocumented immigrants.[25]

Islamophobic attitudes appear to be freely expressed and fairly widespread. While Americans are often reluctant to reveal their racial and ethnic prejudices, they seem fairly comfortable expressing negative attitudes about Muslims to interviewers.[26] Two-fifths (41.4 percent) of Americans are cold toward Muslims.[27] This is more than double the share of Americans cold toward Hispanics, and 10 percentage points higher than the share of Americans registering high in antiblack racial resentment.

We have to face the fact that some Americans are prejudiced against racial and ethnic minorities and are religiously intolerant. Before we declare again that America is post-racial, we need to examine the evidence from the research on racial attitudes, implicit racial bias, and institutional discrimination. Anyone looking at this research in 2008 would have seen absolutely no basis for claiming that the country is post-racial. Any person claiming that the country is post-racial, colorblind, and so on who cannot demonstrate this with findings from racial-attitude, implicit-bias, *and* institutional-discrimination studies should not be taken seriously.

RESPONDING TO THE WORRISOME WHITE-VICTIMHOOD MENTALITY

Most of you want to play the race card for Mr. Obama in sympathy. Well that is a crock. I'm a white male that was born and raised in this country, and my parents were, and their parents, etc. I cannot find a job I'm qualified for, nor can I get a free education because someone else's accent or skin tone needs to be addressed before mine and other whites like myself. And the funny part is that I'm the minority now, not Mr. Obama and other non-Caucasian racial people of this country. Caucasians have passed laws and rules that try to be fair to every other race in the country which is more than okay with me, but we excluded ourselves.[28]

—online newspaper comment

It's completely crazy. The inmates are running the asylum. They're completely in power, and they get anything they want. And us regular, normal white guys—we're like nothing. We don't count for shit anymore.[29]

—an "angry white male"

In Chapter 4, the white-victimhood mentality is discussed. This is the false—but believed—idea that whites are an oppressed minority group being dominated by powerful African Americans and Hispanics. Two-fifths of Americans believe that whites face as much or more discrimination than blacks and Latinos.[30] Nearly one in seven Americans believe that blacks and Latinos have too much influence in U.S. politics.[31] Individuals with these views are likely to resist attempts to address institutional discrimination to ensure equal opportunity for these minority groups. Further, these individuals may support attempts to restrict the rights and opportunities available to people of color. If one feels blacks have too much political power, then one may think that it is a good idea to find ways to block blacks' exercise of their voting rights, for example.

As is also discussed in Chapter 4, this mentality is quite surprising because on all economic measures, on average, whites are significantly better off than blacks and Latinos. Politically, as the majority racial group, whites are also collectively more powerful than blacks and Latinos. They significantly outnumber nonwhites in votes and also occupy 90 percent of all elected offices. Nonetheless, decades of misleading political rhetoric has led many to see whites as racial victims of minority groups.

Part of the reason for the popularity of the false idea that whites are victims of minorities is that about half of Americans believe that the country has already done enough to provide African Americans with equal opportunities.[32] Also, about half of Americans believe incorrectly that blacks are as well off financially as whites, if not better off than whites.[33] For individuals with these views, any programs or policies aimed at providing opportunities for blacks appear to be programs aimed at achieving black superiority, not black equality.

Another problem is the fact that many Americans overestimate the size of racial minority groups. For example, one Obama Hater states that one of the most important problems facing the United States is "the fact that the English-speaking, white-skinned people in America are the minority,"[34] although whites are, in fact, still solidly the majority racial group. Nearly three-quarters of Americans significantly overestimate the size of the black American population.

In 2010, non-Hispanic blacks made up 12 percent of the population, Hispanics made up 16 percent of the population, and non-Hispanic whites made up 64 percent of the population.[35] In 2008, about a third of Americans believed that blacks make up between 20 and 30 percent of the population. Another third believed that blacks make up 30 to 50 percent. Nearly a tenth believed that the United States is more than 50 percent black.[36] In fact, blacks and Hispanics combined were still less than half the size of the white population. It is easier to maintain the belief that one is being dominated by a group if one greatly overestimates the size of the group and its political and economic power. We should remember that the classic pattern for anti-Semitism is for groups to greatly exaggerate the influence and power of Jews and then use these exaggerations as a rationale for harming Jews.[37]

A more just and harmonious America will require reducing the spread of the white-victimhood mentality. To do this, racial-justice advocates will need to be more effective at communicating to the public the relative social, political, economic, and demographic status of whites and nonwhites. Advocates should take every opportunity to ground the public in basic facts. It is a mistake to assume that people know that the white population is more than five times the size of the black population. It is a mistake to assume that people know that blacks have a poverty rate about three times that of whites.[38] It is a mistake to assume that people know that more than 60 years after the *Brown v. Board of Education* decision, America's schools are still mainly racially separate and unequal. It is a mistake to assume that there is knowledge of the basic facts.

End the Presentation of Civil Rights Fairytales

One opportunity racial-justice advocates have to challenge the white-victimhood mentality is the discussion of civil rights history. Every year around Martin Luther King Jr. Day and also often during black history month, this history is revisited. Typically, however, people discuss the civil rights movement as if it were an unmitigated success. If people believe incorrectly that the civil rights movement achieved all of its goals then one can see how they may come to believe that the country has done all that is necessary to achieve equal opportunity for people of color.

The fact of the matter is that most of what civil rights activists wanted has *not* been achieved. *Brown v. Board of Education* was the first major legal victory of the civil rights movement. But, with regard to schooling, it was a victory mainly on paper. As discussed earlier, while we have made some progress (and have experienced reversals), at no point in America's history could we say that we provided integrated and equal education for all—or even most—black children. Despite the fact that about 75 percent of black children and about 80 percent of Latino children attend majority minority schools, many people, even Barack Obama,[39] talk about the *Brown* decision as if it desegregated America's schools. It did not.

How we talk about the *Brown* decision is not the only truth about our civil rights record that we misrepresent. At the 1963 March on Washington for Jobs and Freedom, the march where Martin Luther King Jr. gave his famous "I Have a Dream" speech, there were seven rallying demands. They were for (1) decent housing, (2) equal access to public accommodations, (3) adequate and integrated education, (4) the right to vote, (5) a federal full-employment jobs program for all, (6) legislation ending racial discrimination in employment, and (7) a living wage.[40] We have achieved only three of these goals.

We have achieved equal access to public accommodations. Blacks are no longer subject to the back of the bus, racially segregated bathrooms, and other similar Jim Crow practices. Blacks, for the most part, have the right to vote. And there is legislation ending racial discrimination in employment.[41] While the right to vote and the antidiscrimination legislation are successes, they are qualified successes.[42]

While one can argue that equal access to public accommodations, voting rights, and legislation banning racial discrimination in the labor market have been achieved, the other demands have not. These other demands, one should note, are more grounded in economics. African Americans are still mainly housed in segregated neighborhoods with high rates of poverty, which indicates a failure to achieve the first demand. As discussed earlier, black students' education is still largely separate and unequal, failing to achieve the third demand. From the 1960s to today, the black unemployment rate has ranged from about 2 times to 2.5 times the white rate, failing to achieve the fifth demand.[43] Jobs are essential, but it is also important that the jobs are at wages that can support a family. In 1963, the organizers of the March for Jobs and Freedom called for a $2.00 an hour minimum wage. In 2013, after adjusting for inflation that wage would be worth more than $13.00 an hour. In 2013, the federal minimum wage was $7.25 an hour—about $2.00 *less* than it was worth in 1968 when one adjusts for inflation. This indicates a failure to achieve the seventh demand.[44]

When one acknowledges that we have achieved only three of the seven key goals of civil rights activists, we cannot say that the movement was a complete success. On Martin Luther King Jr. Day, rather than engaging in generic community service, we should be engaging in activism to fully realize the goals of the movement. At minimum, we should use King Day and other similar occasions to speak about what has *not* been achieved. It will be harder for individuals to believe that we are a post-racial society or that the country has already done enough to achieve equal rights for blacks after receiving this information.

Advocates for People of Color Need to Talk More about Their Vision for White People

Some people believe that whites are already being dominated by nonwhites, and some fear that whites may be dominated by nonwhites as the nonwhite population grows. One can see this fear in the following remarks by a white man from Ohio:

> The first thing that I thought [after the 2008 election of Barack Obama] was that the African Americans, the colored community, was going to take over. . . . I got the picture that the next time that I walk in McDonald's or something, I would hear "white boy, you get down and wash the dishes. You go do this. We rule the country now." . . . Is what we've done to them coming back to haunt us? . . . Do you see that happening

whenever you go . . . do the Coloreds overrule the Whites? Are they puffing their chests out to say "We are the kings now. We have a man in the Big House"?[45]

Or we can consider the views of this white, Pennsylvania woman, a lifelong Democrat: "[If Obama won the presidency] I was worried I would have to go to the back of the bus."[46] Similar feelings were expressed by a white woman in Nevada: "I've never been around a lot of black people before. I just worry that they're nice to your face but then when they get around their own people you just have to worry about what they're going to do to you."[47] For racial-justice advocates, these fears are absurd. The desire to end prejudice and discrimination against nonwhites is not a desire to oppress whites.

But just as many do not know the size of the black population, many know nothing about the goals of racial-justice advocates. Racial-justice advocates need to be more explicit about their vision for whites. In part, because racial-justice advocates have been primarily concerned about the more disadvantaged populations, they have said little about whites explicitly. Unfortunately, some whites have let their wildest fears fill this void. And some hatemongers are eager to cultivate false beliefs that racial-justice advocates are waging a "war on whites."[48]

It may be helpful for racial-justice advocates to be more explicit about how their policy goals will benefit whites because many of the goals do. Policies aimed at assisting low-income minorities, more often than not, also help low-income whites. When A. Philip Randolph called for a federal program for full employment, he was explicit that this program should benefit *all* of the unemployed, not just the black unemployed.[49]

A minimum living wage too would benefit a significant share of the white population. For example, an evaluation of a proposed federal minimum-wage increase found that 54.1 percent of the workers who would benefit were white.[50] Hispanics would obtain the greatest disproportionate benefit, because they are overrepresented in very low-wage work,[51] but the majority of workers benefiting would be white.

The War on Drugs has been devastating to African American communities.[52] While ending this war will bring tremendous benefit to blacks, it will also bring significant benefit to whites. From 1980 to 2009, the arrest rate for drug possession for whites doubled. (It tripled from a much higher starting rate for blacks.)[53] Less punitive and more rehabilitative drug policies are not only about improving life for many blacks. It will also keep significant numbers of whites out of the criminal justice system.

There are broad social and economic benefits to the society when people of color are able to participate fully as workers and as citizens. Because of the current mechanisms of institutional discrimination, a disproportionate share of people of color end up undereducated, unemployed, and incarcerated. We would all benefit if these individuals were employed and working at their full potential. Research shows that firms with more racially and ethnically diverse leadership are more likely to have above-average financial performance.[54] Other recent economic research suggests that policies of equity and inclusion can lead to stronger economic growth for the society as a whole.[55] Closing the racial gaps in academic achievement is predicted to increase the U.S. economy by nearly 6 percent by 2050.[56] The racial-justice vision yields a society that is more socially harmonious, more economically productive, and more globally competitive. Americans of all races, ethnicities, and religions can benefit.

THE FUTURE OF ANTI-IMMIGRANT AND ANTI-MUSLIM SENTIMENTS

After the tenure of our first African American president, while some of the antiblack anger of the Obama Haters may subside, they will likely still be directing their hate at immigrants and Muslims. Democracy Corps, a liberal political research firm, finds that anti-immigrant attitudes are a key component of current Republican thinking. More than 9 in 10 Obama Haters are Republicans, and more than half of them identify as strong Republicans. Democracy Corps reports, "The Republicans, led by the Tea Party, are about as hostile to 'undocumented' immigrants in the U.S. as they are to Obamacare. . . . On the topic of immigration, Republicans speak literally and in graphic terms of being invaded."[57] At the time of this writing, there does not appear to be any long-term and comprehensive resolution to the problem of unauthorized immigration forthcoming. The strength of the opposition to comprehensive immigration reform is not moderating. If anything, the Tea Party Republicans are forcing the rest of the Republican Party to take a harder line against reform.[58]

The hopeful news about anti-immigrant sentiment in America is that the fears are largely fictional fantasies. The legal scholar Ian Haney López provides a nice summary:

> On the more fundamental question of assimilation, scholars recognize that today's immigrants from Latin America (and also from Asia), no different from generations of European immigrants before them, are "being successfully incorporated into American society"; indeed, studies find "great continuities between the experiences of earlier European immigrants and current, predominantly non-European immigrants." Moreover, the notion that crossing the border without authorization generates a pervasive disdain for the law is demonstrably false. Research

shows that undocumented immigrants from Latin America commit far fewer depredations, not far more, than citizens. Evidence shows too that undocumented immigrants are far less likely than others to use expensive social services, including hospital emergency rooms. Indeed, unauthorized immigrants pay considerably more in taxes—typically through payroll withholding—than they receive in social services.[59]

There is reason to hope that effective communication about the facts can lead to support for comprehensive immigration reform.

Another important point to challenge is the too-simple idea that immigrants take away jobs from the native born. Some people believe that if we remove immigrant workers from the United States, we would automatically open up all jobs formerly held by immigrants to the U.S.-born unemployed. The flaw in this thinking rests upon this point: "In the economy as a whole . . . income and spending are interdependent: my spending is your income, and your spending is my income."[60] Immigrants are not simply workers; they are also consumers. Immigrants buy milk. They buy school supplies. Immigrants, like everyone else in the country, have to buy food, buy clothing, pay for shelter, pay utilities, and so on to live in the United States. Their spending pays the salaries of lots of workers. The loss of this spending would mean the loss of millions of jobs.[61]

Immigrants also create jobs more directly by being entrepreneurs. It appears that they are slightly more likely to be entrepreneurs than the native-born. Deporting immigrants would also disrupt job creation in the United States by removing many hundreds of thousands of entrepreneurs.[62]

The way to protect U.S.-born workers and immigrant workers is through comprehensive immigration reform. If we continue to allow unauthorized workers to be exploited with illegal lower-than-minimum wages and substandard working conditions,[63] then they are harmed and U.S.-born workers are harmed by the degradation of standards. Better immigration policies and stronger enforcement of labor laws can improve conditions for immigrants and for U.S.-born workers without depriving our economy of the benefits that immigrants can bring.

Islamophobic attitudes show no sign of dissipating. They may be spreading. The Council on American-Islamic Relations of California saw a 9 percent increase in anti-Islamic civil rights complaints from 2013 to 2014.[64] A poll by the Arab American Institute finds that "favorable" views of Muslims declined from 35 percent in 2010 to 27 percent in 2014. The share of "favorable" views for Muslims is less than half that of the Christian groups in the survey.[65] Even if the favorability of Muslims were to increase, it is likely that it would take several years to reach the level of the Christian groups.

The good news regarding Islamophobia is that individuals who know a Muslim are more likely to have favorable views of Muslims.[66] This suggests that providing people with information about the lives of average American Muslims could help dispel fears. Creatively done educational and media campaigns may be able to reduce Islamophobia.

CONCLUSION

The first step in solving a problem is admitting that one has a problem. The alacrity with which individuals declared that Obama's election signified that America is post-racial shows that many Americans do not wish to admit that we have a problem. In fact, they are eager to engage in denial about prejudice and discrimination in America.

We do have a problem. Looking just at the fairly overt and conscious attitudes, significant shares of Americans are antiblack, anti-Latino, anti-immigrant, and anti-Muslim. Much of this hatred in based on misinformation and unfounded fears. These attitudes interfere with the American ideals of equal opportunity for all.

The good news is that there is also a solution. It's not an easy solution, but it is a solution. Since much of the hatred is based on misinformation and unfounded fears, effective education and communication strategies can counteract them. These negative images and false ideas were not created overnight. In most cases, they are the results of many decades of anti-minority communication and action. Counteracting these images and ideas will also require many decades of accurate and compelling counter-speech and effective organizing and action. A good time to begin this effort is now. The longer we wait, the more the irrational fears about a nation without a white numerical majority will likely grow.

Afterword

OBAMA UNLEASHED IN THE SECOND TERM?

In 2014, President Barack Obama announced several major executive actions that appeared to come from out of the blue and in rapid succession. Some on the left thought that the more aggressive, left-leaning Obama that they had been hoping for had finally appeared. For Obama's opponents, his actions were seen as more evidence that Obama is a far-left-leaning tyrant. But when one looks more carefully at the issues and the context around them, they do not challenge the image of him as a centrist politician.

One runs for president because one wants to do things to make the country better. President Barack Obama has had to govern while working with possibly the most recalcitrant Congresses in U.S. history. The 112th Congress which served from 2011 to 2012 was the least productive since records have been kept. The 113th Congress, serving from 2013 to 2014, was the second least productive.[1] These Congresses have been determined to see that president Obama accomplishes nothing. In fact, they have set a goal to undo his achievements including his major policy success, the Affordable Care Act.[2] President Obama could either let Congress essentially nullify his presidency or use the full extent of his executive powers to govern. In 2014, he chose the latter.

It is important to be aware that as of November 2014, President Obama had used executive orders at a lower rate than any president in the twentieth or twenty-first century.[3] This suggests that Obama prefers to work with Congress. But when Congress simply refuses to act on what he considers to be important issues, Obama has to choose whether he will let a hostile Congress destroy his agenda or whether he will act using his executive powers. President Obama campaigned vowing to address climate change, to reform the immigration system, and to improve relations with Cuba. These are long-standing issues for the country. Given that he was nearing the end of his presidency and given that Congress showed no signs of acting on these issues, it was not surprising that he chose to take executive action to accomplish them.

The My Brother's Keeper Initiative

One issue that was not a campaign promise is the My Brother's Keeper initiative. President Obama has received strong criticism from black racial-justice advocates for doing too little to help African Americans.[4] In February 2014, he announced the My Brother's Keeper initiative, which may have been in response to those criticisms. The initiative aims "to address persistent opportunity gaps faced by boys and young men of color and ensure that all young people can reach their full potential."[5] The initiative is not exclusively focused on African American males. Latino and Native American males are also among its primary foci.[6]

Since the My Brother's Keeper initiative to help boys and young men of color has received a good bit of discussion and debate,[7] people may think that this is a major government program. In fact, it is a relatively small initiative composed of the activities of private foundations and other charitable organizations, and of state and local governments accepting the My Brother's Keeper Community Challenge.[8] The White House has received $318 million in commitments from several organizations. Of this amount, $14 million came from federal funds.[9] It is not a "federal program" since the vast majority of the funds are nonfederal, and the vast majority of the activities are not run by the federal government.

It is also not major in terms of the amount of spending. The $318 million will be spent over multiple years. Different organizations have specified three-year and five-year commitments. Other organizations have not specified a number of years, but the projects proposed are likely multiyear projects.[10] A fair estimate is that the initiative will provide about $100 million a year to address the challenges facing boys and young men of color over the next three years. While this effort is laudable, it is still a small amount when one considers the scale of the problem. For example, America's foundations provided over $4 *billion* for children and youth in 2012.[11] Even if we assume that only half of that amount went to boys—$2 billion—the My Brother's Keeper initiative is still a relatively small amount. The amount $100 million is only 5 percent of $2 billion.

Perhaps a better assessment would take into account the share of Latino, black, and Native American male youth who are at risk. If one uses impoverishment[12] as a proxy for at risk, then for males under 25 about half are Latino, black, and Native American.[13] If one assumes that all foundation dollars goes to this at-risk population, then the initiative would be increasing the available dollars for at-risk boys and young men of color by about 10 percent for three years. This increased support should not be dismissed. It will help improve the lives of many, but it is not enough to address all of the needs. Also, these dollar figures and estimates do not count the value of the state and local initiatives.

Even after considering the My Brother's Keeper initiative, it is still correct to say that as of 2014 there have been no major federal policies targeted specifically to help blacks by the Obama administration.

Taking Action on Climate Change

Most Americans recognize climate change as a serious problem facing the country. There is a global scientific consensus that the world needs to reduce carbon pollution sooner rather than later to prevent severe harm to people and ecosystems.[14] President Obama has been "[f]aced with a Congress that has shut down his attempts to push through an environmental agenda," the *New York Times* reports.[15] This situation has forced Obama to act on his own. Among his executive actions in 2014 was one placing limits on emissions from power plants and one reaching an agreement with China to limit carbon dioxide emissions.

In June 2014, the Environmental Protection Agency (EPA), at the direction of President Obama, issued a Clean Power Plan proposal to reduce carbon emissions from power plants. While the EPA sets the guidelines, states would have flexibility in how they achieve their goals.[16] Christine Todd Whitman, the former Republican governor of New Jersey and the former head of the EPA under the Republican president George W. Bush, sees the proposal as "strik[ing] the important balance between a national standard for reduced emissions and state flexibility to achieve that end." She also believes that the proposal could be "the most significant environmental accomplishment of President Obama's administration."[17]

In November 2014, after nine months of negotiations, President Obama and President Xi Jinping of China announced a historic agreement to curb carbon emissions. Because the United States and China are the world's number one and number two carbon polluters, respectively, this agreement is an important first step in addressing the global problem. Many environmental activists and analysts agree with Angela Ledford Anderson of the Union of Concerned Scientists that "[t]he significance of the U.S.-China climate deal cannot be underestimated."[18]

Even if one disagrees with Obama's actions to address climate change, one has to acknowledge that these actions are not arbitrary and self-serving. They are in line with the desires of the majority of the American people and in accord with the scientific consensus about what is needed to protect the United States and the planet. The Clean Power Plan also continues Obama's pattern of crafting policy so that it is potentially appealing to Republicans who are not hyper-partisan. The flexibility in the plan should be appealing to those Republicans who want more authority left at the state level.

Executive Action for Immigration Reform

In November 2014, President Obama announced three executive actions to reform our immigration system. He summarized the actions in this manner:

> First, we'll build on our progress at the border with additional resources for our law enforcement personnel so that they can stem the flow of illegal crossings, and speed the return of those who do cross over.
>
> Second, I'll make it easier and faster for high-skilled immigrants, graduates, and entrepreneurs to stay and contribute to our economy, as so many business leaders have proposed.
>
> Third, we'll take steps to deal responsibly with the millions of undocumented immigrants who already live in our country.[19]

We should note that these first two actions should be highly appealing to conservatives. Obama is, in the first, again increasing border security, and, in the second, he is providing high-skilled labor for growing businesses. Although Obama initiated three actions, it is only the third one which provided deferred action on deportation that is controversial. And it is only the third one that has received significant media discussion. This has been the dynamic for the Obama administration generally. His conservative policies are generally ignored, and his liberal policies are loudly attacked.

All presidents since President Eisenhower have used executive action to protect unauthorized immigrants from deportation. Prior to President Obama's executive order, President George H. W. Bush took the most dramatic action. In 1990, he protected over 40 percent of the unauthorized immigrant population from deportation.[20] Obama's third action would make available temporary relief from deportation to approximately 35 percent of unauthorized immigrants.[21]

There is general agreement that the immigration system in the United States needs reform, and a solid majority of the American public supports President Obama's deferred action on deportation.[22] It is understood that it is not possible to deport 11 million unauthorized immigrants dispersed throughout the country without spending a very large amount of money and without making the United States into a police state. Increased border security and a path to legal status for the unauthorized is broadly seen as the way to address the unauthorized immigrant problem. Even the Tea Party Republican senator Marco Rubio agrees with this basic approach.[23]

While campaigning in 2008, Obama indicated that reforms that would bring unauthorized immigrants "out of the shadows" would be one of his top priorities.[24] Prior to his 2014 executive order, his critics had continually reminded him that he had failed to deliver on his campaign promise. The head of the nation's largest Latino advocacy organization called him the "deportation president"[25] because while he had put more agents on the border and had removed more unauthorized immigrants than any other president in history,[26] he had done little to bring long-term unauthorized immigrants out of the shadows.

In June 2013, the Senate passed an immigration reform bill that Obama has been waiting to sign into law. The leaders of the House of Representatives, however, have not allowed the bill to be voted on there.[27] Obama has improved border security, and he has waited six years for Congress to implement the additional measures to reform our broken immigration system. Unfortunately, the House of Representatives has blocked movement on immigration reform. This inaction by the House of Representatives is the reason why President Obama has proceeded with immigration reforms through executive action.

Normalizing the United States' Relations with Cuba

In December 2014, President Obama restored diplomatic relations with Cuba. He had indicated his interest in doing this while he was campaigning for president in 2008.[28] In 2009, he began to change the United States' relationship with Cuba by loosening travel and remittance restrictions for Cuban Americans.[29] His moves toward normalizing relations were halted with the arrest of Alan P. Gross, a contractor for the United States Agency for International Development. With the aid of Pope Francis, after a year and a half of negotiations, Obama was able to obtain the release of Gross. The United States also agreed to release three Cuban agents.[30] Obama can reestablish diplomatic relations with Cuba, but the full lifting of the embargo will require an act of Congress.

In this action, President Obama is in accord with the majority of the American people. Polls show that a majority of Americans, including the conservative U.S. Chamber of Commerce, support reestablishing diplomatic relations with Cuba.[31] Cuban Americans are about evenly divided in favor and against.[32] There is every indication that were Hillary Clinton the president, she too would have normalized relations with Cuba.[33]

Obama Keeping His Promises and Responding to Criticism

If one steps back and examines Obama's executive actions in 2014, one sees that they are the Obama administration's attempt to address long-standing problems and campaign promises under the constraint of a Congress that has refused to work with the administration on these issues. Obama's low rate of use of executive orders is a sign that he prefers to work with Congress. It is also important to note that these actions were not actions that were planned to occur at any specific time. The agreement with China was the result of many months of negotiations.[34] The agreement with Cuba was the result of over a year of negotiations.[35] Either of these agreements could have occurred sooner, later, or not at all. It is just by coincidence that they were finalized so close together. When one considers these things and the fact that Obama's actions reflect majority opinion or is seen generally as on the reasonable path, he does not seem like an emerging "secret lefty" or a left-wing dictator.

The only action that was not a campaign promise is the My Brother's Keeper initiative. There are numerous statistics that can be cited to show the challenges faced by black men and boys. African Americans as American citizens who suffer from past and present forms of institutional discrimination have a right to have their concerns addressed by their government. The political scientist Fredrick C. Harris illustrates that American politics is routinely about addressing the needs of specific groups:

> Obama, for instance, met several times during the campaign with Jewish leaders and voters to clarify his positions on Middle East policy. He talked to Latino voters about immigration policy and to gay and lesbian voters about his position on gay marriage and the military's "don't ask, don't tell" policy. The candidate also met with Cuban-American leaders about the United States opening dialogue with Cuba and with feminist groups about the importance of protecting abortion rights and of ensuring equal pay for equal work for women. But again, when Obama spoke before black audiences in 2008, he talked mostly about universal policies and the need for greater personal responsibility on behalf of blacks.[36]

It is important to recognize that catering to specific constituencies is not unique to Obama or to Democrats. There are many tax policies, trade policies, rules, and regulations that have been championed by Republicans because they benefit specific constituency groups.[37]

Politically, African Americans are an important Democratic constituency; however, a case can be made that they have had much less influence on the Obama administration than other constituencies. After receiving continued criticism from black racial-justice advocates, it appears that the Obama administration has responded with a relatively small and centrist program that is not focused exclusively on African Americans.

Appendix

Unless otherwise indicated, the data source for the tables is the 2012 American National Election Study, Vincent Hutchings, Gary Segura, Simon Jackman, and Ted Brader, principal investigators (Arbor, MI, and Palo Alto, CA: the University of Michigan and Stanford University, 2013). Tables are created by the author.

Introduction Table 1 Gallup Overall Presidential Approval Ratings and Republican Presidential Approval Ratings on Selected Days within the First Term for Selected Democratic Presidents

		Republicans					
	Overall Average (%)	Day 14 (%)	Day 352 (%)	Day 716 (%)	Day 1,066 (%)	Day 1,414 (%)	Average of the Selected Days (%)
Obama[a]	48	34	15	13	10	11	17
Clinton	55	24	28	19	17	26	23
Carter	46	49	34	33	40	14	34
Johnson	55	78	47	46	23	23	43
Kennedy[b]	70	52	59	53	na	na	55
Truman[c]	45	na	na	na	26	32	29

Source: Author's analysis of data from Gallup Presidential Job Approval Center, 2015. Available at http://www.gallup.com/poll/124922/Presidential-Approval-Center.aspx.
Note: The dates were selected to obtain five points at roughly equal intervals from the beginning to the end of the first term.
na: not available.
a To February 24, 2015.
b President Kennedy was assassinated before the end of his first term on November 22, 1963.
c President Truman assumed office after President Franklin Delano Roosevelt died. Thus, he was not elected into the presidency, and he served fewer days in office than the other presidents by day 1,414.

Table 2.1 Vote Choice of High-Racial-Resentment Voters, 2008 and 2012

	Barack Obama (%)	Republican Candidate (%)	Other (%)	Unweighted N
2008	29.5*	66.7	3.8	1,164
2012 (intended)	25.2*	69.8	5.0	1,133

Note: A high level of antiblack racial resentment is defined as more than one standard deviation (0.25) above the neutral value (0.50). See Michael Tesler and David O. Sears, *Obama's Race: The 2008 Election and the Dream of a Post-Racial America* (Chicago: The University of Chicago Press, 2010), Chapter 1, "The Theory of Symbolic Racism" section, for more information on the measure.
* Significantly different from the Republican Candidate and Other shares at the p < .05 level.

Table 3.1 Correlations and Cronbach's Alpha for Obama-Hater Construct

	Angry at Obama	Afraid of Obama	Cold toward Obama[a]
Angry at Obama	1	0.75	0.72
Afraid of Obama	0.75	1	0.65
Cold toward Obama[a]	0.72	0.65	1
Cronbach's alpha	0.88		
Valid cases	5,823		

Note: If Obama has never made the respondent angry, the ANGRY_AT_OBAMA value is 0. If Obama always makes the respondent angry, the ANGRY_AT_OBAMA value is 4. The coding is the same for AFRAID_OF_OBAMA.
COLD_TOWARD_OBAMA is the relative Obama–Romney feeling thermometer rating. The middle value, 50, indicates the respondent rates Obama and Romney equally. The higher the rating above 50, the warmer the respondent is toward Obama and the colder toward Romney. The lower the value below 50, the colder the respondent is toward Obama and the warmer toward Romney.
a Sign of correlations reversed for this variable.

Table 3.2 Basic Demographic Characteristics of Obama Haters, Conservative Non-Haters, and Moderate and Liberal Non-Haters

	Obama Haters (%)	Conservative Non-Haters (%)	Moderate-Liberal Non-Haters (%)	All (%)	Unweighted N
Under 35 years old	16.8[a]	24.3	32.2	28.1	5,217
Over 64 years old	29.3[b]	20.0	16.8	19.2	5,217
Female	50.3	46.5	54.4	51.5	5,259
White, not Hispanic	88.7[b]	78.1	66.2	72.3	5,238

	Obama Haters (%)	Conservative Non-Haters (%)	Moderate-Liberal Non-Haters (%)	All (%)	Unweighted N
Has bachelor's and no higher degree	22.6	23.1	18.3	20.2	5,215
Family income $55,000 or above	51.8[a]	52.2	43.2	47.0	4,905
Owns home	86.5[b]	75.4	68.7	72.8	5,243
Has invested in the stock market	55.9[a]	51.2	37.7	43.8	5,159

a Obama Haters statistically different from Moderate-Liberal Non-Haters and All at the $p < .05$ level.
b Obama Haters statistically different from other categories at the $p < .05$ level.

Table 3.3 Political Ideology and Party Identification of Obama Haters, Conservative Non-Haters, and Moderate and Liberal Non-Haters

	Obama Haters (%)	Conservative Non-Haters (%)	Moderate-Liberal Non-Haters (%)	All (%)	Unweighted N
Slightly to extremely conservative	82.3*	100.0	0.0	39.6	5,253
Extremely conservative	16.5*	9.3	0.0	4.7	5,253
Independent-Republican[a] to strong Republican	92.7*	70.0	16.0	41.0	5,249
Strong Republican	56.5*	26.2	2.6	15.8	5,249
Lean toward supporting to strong support for the Tea Party	70.3*	44.1	9.3	26.9	5,016
Strong support for the Tea Party	43.7*	19.6	2.3	12.3	5,016

a Independent-Republicans are considered to lean Republican.
* Obama Haters statistically different from other categories at the $p < .05$ level.

Table 3.4 Political Engagement of Obama Haters, Conservative Non-Haters, and Moderate and Liberal Non-Haters

	Obama Haters (%)	Conservative Non-Haters (%)	Moderate-Liberal Non-Haters (%)	All (%)	Unweighted N
Pays attention to politics always or most of the time	71.5*	50.7	45.3	49.9	5,258
Voted in a presidential primary or caucus	53.2*	38.5	30.7	35.6	5,229
Have contacted U.S. representative or senator in the past four years	31.1*	21.9	18.4	20.9	4,900
Have contributed money to a candidate's campaign	17.1*	9.8	11.8	11.8	4,901
Were contacted by a political party about the 2012 campaign	51.3*	43.7	42.5	43.9	4,904

* Obama Haters statistically different from other categories at the p < .05 level.

Table 4.1 Effect of Barack Obama's Race on 2012 Vote Choice by Hater Group

	Obama Haters (%)	Conservative Non-Haters (%)	Moderate and Liberal Non-Haters (%)	All (%)
Voted for Obama	0.1	4.5	11.2	7.9
Voted for Romney	14.9	6.8	3.1	5.5
Made no difference	85.0	88.7	85.7	86.6

Unweighted N = 4,884.
Rao-Scott-P = 0.00.

Table 4.2 Mean and Share with the Highest Antiblack Racial Resentment Score by Hater Group

	Obama Haters	Conservative Non-Haters	Moderate and Liberal Non-Haters
Mean	0.81*	0.70	0.57
Percentage with 1.0 score	26.2%*	11.4%	7.0%

Unweighted N = 4,171.
Note: This analysis is limited to individuals who said Obama's race made no difference in their 2012 vote choice. See Michael Tesler and David O. Sears, *Obama's Race: The 2008 Election and the Dream of a Post-Racial America* (Chicago: The University of Chicago Press, 2010), Chapter 1, "The Theory of Symbolic Racism" section, for more information on the measure.

* Obama Haters statistically different from other categories at the p < .05 level.

Table 4.3 Mean Relative Feeling Thermometer Rating for Blacks, Hispanics, and Asians by Hater Group

	Obama Haters	Conservative Non-Haters	Moderate and Liberal Non-Haters	All	Unweighted N
Blacks	43.53[a]	45.19	47.75	46.48	4,169
Hispanics	43.43[a]	45.08	46.94	45.96	4,168
Asians	45.63[b]	46.25	47.16	46.71	4,170

Note: This analysis is limited to individuals who said Obama's race made no difference in their 2012 vote choice.
The groups are measured relative to the white rating. The middle value, 50, indicates the respondent rates the minority group and whites equally. The higher the rating above 50, the warmer the respondent is toward the minority group and the colder toward whites. The lower the value below 50, the colder the respondent is toward the minority group and the warmer toward whites.
a Obama Haters statistically different from other categories at the $p < .05$ level.
b Obama Haters statistically different from Moderate and Liberal Non-Haters at the $p < .05$ level.

Table 4.4 Mean Rating of Whether Blacks, Hispanics, and Asians Are Lazy or Hardworking Relative to Whites by Hater Group

	Obama Haters	Conservative Non-Haters	Moderate and Liberal Non-Haters	All	Unweighted N
Blacks	0.38	0.41	0.44*	0.43	4,182
Hispanics	0.48	0.50	0.51	0.50	4,182
Asians	0.53	0.53	0.53	0.53	4,180

Note: This analysis is limited to individuals who said Obama's race made no difference in their 2012 vote choice. A value of 0.50 indicates that the group is seen as being as hardworking as whites. A value of 0.0 indicates that the group is seen as lazy and whites as hardworking. A value of 1.0 indicates that the group is seen as hardworking and whites as lazy.
* Statistically higher than the Obama Hater value at the $p < .05$ level.

Table 4.5 Percentage Saying Whites, Blacks, and Hispanics Experience a "Great Deal" or "A Lot" of Discrimination by Hater Group

	Obama Haters (%)	Conservative Non-Haters (%)	Moderate and Liberal Non-Haters (%)	All (%)	Unweighted N	Rao-Scott-P
Whites	12.8	7.3	5.1	6.6	4,188	0.00
Blacks	13.9	20.2	36.4	29.1	4,187	0.00
Hispanics	15.7	24.2	38.8	31.7	4,185	0.00

Note: This analysis is limited to individuals who said Obama's race made no difference in their 2012 vote choice.

Table 4.6 Percentage Rating Whites as Experiencing As Much or More Discrimination Than Blacks and Hispanics

	Obama Haters (%)	Conservative Non-Haters (%)	Moderate and Liberal Non-Haters (%)	All	Unweighted N	Rao-Scott-P
Whites discriminated against as much or more than blacks	66.4	55.2	30.7	41.4	4,188	0.00
Whites discriminated against as much or more than Hispanics	64.3	46.7	29.9	38.9	4,183	0.00

Note: This analysis is limited to individuals who said Obama's race made no difference in their 2012 vote choice.

Table 4.7 Percentage Saying Whites Have Too Little Influence in U.S. Politics by Hater Group

Obama Haters	Conservative Non-Haters	Moderate and Liberal Non-Haters	All	Unweighted N	Rao-Scott-P
19.9%	11.0%	5.0%	8.5%	4,186	0.00

Note: This analysis is limited to individuals who said Obama's race made no difference in their 2012 vote choice.

Table 4.8 Percentage Saying Blacks and Hispanics Have Too Much Influence in U.S. Politics by Hater Group

	Obama Haters (%)	Conservative Non-Haters (%)	Moderate and Liberal Non-Haters (%)	All (%)	Unweighted N	Rao-Scott-P
Blacks	33.7	17.5	6.9	13.2	4,182	0.00
Hispanics	29.2	17.1	8.3	13.4	4,184	0.00

Note: This analysis is limited to individuals who said Obama's race made no difference in their 2012 vote choice.

Table 4.9 Percentage Believing That the Obama Administration Favors Blacks over Whites by Hater Group

	Obama Haters (%)	Conservative Non-Haters (%)	Moderate and Liberal Non-Haters (%)	All (%)	Unweighted N	Rao-Scott-P
Excluding individuals who said race affected their vote choice	61.6	33.0	11.4	23.7	4,150	0.00
Entire sample	65.4	35.1	12.5	25.3	4,844	0.00

Table 4.10 Logistic Regression Analyses of Relative Black–White Feeling Thermometer Ratings as a Predictor for Being an Obama Hater and a Romney Hater

	Obama Hater	Obama Hater	Romney Hater	Romney Hater
Black–White Relative Feeling Thermometer	−0.020*** (0.003)	−0.020*** (0.004)	0.002 (0.005)	0.000 (0.005)
Political Ideology	0.291*** (0.059)	0.230** (0.075)	−0.307*** (0.033)	−0.325*** (0.035)
Party Identification	0.563*** (0.030)	0.539*** (0.029)	−0.438*** (0.031)	−0.458*** (0.031)
Tea Party support	2.146*** (0.236)	2.116*** (0.223)	−1.605*** (0.289)	−1.555*** (0.304)
Male		0.045 (0.161)		−0.012 (0.058)
Age		0.073*** (0.018)		0.029** (0.011)
Black, Non-Hispanic		−1.854 (7.517)		−0.092 (0.113)
Hispanic		−0.371** (0.106)		−0.381** (0.123)
Other, Non-Hispanic		0.758*** (0.166)		0.051 (0.523)
Religiosity		0.004 (0.036)		0.023 (0.031)
Education		−0.096* (0.038)		−0.023 (0.049)

(Continued)

Table **4.10** (Continued)

	Obama Hater	Obama Hater	Romney Hater	Romney Hater
Income		0.001		–0.015
		(0.012)		(0.019)
Owns Home		0.523*		–0.134
		(0.219)		(0.139)
Has Invested in Stocks		–0.033		–0.099
		(0.153)		(0.194)
Southern Residence		0.243		–0.187*
		(0.301)		(0.074)
Intercept	–6.087**	–7.173***	0.478*	0.939**
	(0.384)	(0.651)	(0.225)	(0.311)
Log likelihood	–1,140.08	–1,024.311	–1,174.21	–1,065.40
Pseudo R sq	0.316	0.329	0.213	0.223
Unweighted N	4,618	4,237	4,618	4,237

Note: Standard errors in parentheses.
Notes on the coding of the variables:
Black–White Relative Feeling Thermometer: This measure is created by subtracting the black feeling thermometer from the white and rescaling it to 100. The high value indicates pro-black/antiwhite feelings; the low value indicates antiblack/pro-white feelings.
Political Ideology: The high value indicates "extremely conservative," and the low value indicates "extremely liberal."
Party Identification: The high value indicates "strong Republican," and the low value indicates "strong Democrat."
Tea Party support: The high value indicates "strong support" for the Tea Party, and the low value "strong opposition."
Religiosity: This variable is a composite of how often the respondent prays and how often the respondent attends religious services. The high value indicates that the respondent prays several times a day and attends religious services every week. The low value indicates that the respondent never does these things.
* $p < .05$; **$p < .01$; ***$p < .001$.

Table **4.11** Logistic Regression Analyses of Antiblack Racial Resentment as a Predictor for Being an Obama Hater and a Romney Hater

	Obama Hater	Obama Hater	Romney Hater	Romney Hater
Antiblack Racial Resentment	2.260***	2.400***	0.048	0.025
	(0.557)	(0.473)	(0.491)	(0.576)
Political Ideology	0.261***	0.203*	–0.310***	–0.321***
	(0.059)	(0.086)	(0.036)	(0.037)
Party Identification	0.533***	0.521***	–0.447***	–0.461***
	(0.024)	(0.030)	(0.033)	(0.035)
Tea Party support	1.936***	1.803***	–1.601***	–1.555**
	(0.236)	(0.218)	(0.415)	(0.441)

	Obama Hater	Obama Hater	Romney Hater	Romney Hater
Male		0.033		−0.018
		(0.153)		(0.061)
Age		0.071***		0.027*
		(0.019)		(0.011)
Black,		−1.594		−0.080
Non-Hispanic		(7.556)		(0.138)
Hispanic		−0.295**		−0.372**
		(0.101)		(0.125)
Other,		0.683***		0.051
Non-Hispanic		(0.126)		(0.543)
Religiosity		0.029		0.022
		(0.040)		(0.032)
Education		−0.038		−0.019
		(0.035)		(0.066)
Income		−0.003		−0.016
		(0.012)		(0.019)
Owns Home		0.519*		−0.118
		(0.205)		(0.119)
Has Invested in		0.016		−0.088
Stocks		(0.152)		(0.209)
Southern		0.132		−0.182**
Residence		(0.288)		(0.067)
Intercept	−8.948***	−9.570***	0.557***	0.930**
	(0.280)	(0.454)	(0.125)	(0.341)
Log likelihood	−1,121.74	−1,004.91	−1,179.35	−1,068.07
Pseudo R sq	0.324	0.337	0.213	0.221
Unweighted N	4,634	4,247	4,634	4,247

Note: Standard errors in parentheses.
Notes on the coding of the variables:
Antiblack Racial Resentment: A value of 1.0 indicated a high level of resentment toward blacks. A value of 0 indicates strong racially liberal attitudes toward blacks.
Political Ideology: The high value indicates "extremely conservative," and the low value indicates "extremely liberal."
Party Identification: The high value indicates "strong Republican," and the low value indicates "strong Democrat."
Tea Party support: The high value indicates "strong support" for the Tea Party, and the low value "strong opposition."
Religiosity: This variable is a composite of how often the respondent prays and how often the respondent attends religious services. The high value indicates that the respondent prays several times a day and attends religious services every week. The low value indicates that the respondent never does these things.
* $p < .05$; **$p < .01$; ***$p < .001$.

Table 5.1 Percentage Believing That President Obama Is Foreign-Born and Muslim by Level of Antiblack Racial Resentment

	Low Resentment (%)	Moderate Resentment (%)	High Resentment (%)	All (%)	Unweighted N	Rao-Scott-P
Obama definitely or probably born in another country	4.0	18.4	43.6	25.1	5,256	0.00
Obama is Muslim	2.7	18.5	46.7	26.2	4,685	0.00

Note: A high level of antiblack racial resentment is defined as more than one standard deviation (0.25) above the neutral value (0.50). See Michael Tesler and David O. Sears, *Obama's Race: The 2008 Election and the Dream of a Post-Racial America* (Chicago: The University of Chicago Press, 2010), Chapter 1, "The Theory of Symbolic Racism" section, for more information on the measure.

Table 5.2 Logistic Regression Analyses of Antiblack Racial Resentment as a Predictor for Believing Obama Is Foreign-Born or Muslim

	Foreign-Born	Muslim
Antiblack Racial Resentment	1.937*** (0.202)	2.338*** (0.456)
Political Ideology	0.037 (0.044)	−0.020 (0.065)
Party Identification	0.276*** (0.022)	0.176*** (0.035)
Tea Party support	1.171** (0.336)	0.782*** (0.145)
Male	−0.161 (0.151)	−0.133^ (0.067)
Age	0.024 (0.016)	0.011 (0.008)
Black, Non-Hispanic	0.476*** (0.121)	−0.713*** (0.141)
Hispanic	0.434 (0.513)	−0.436** (0.128)
Other, Non-Hispanic	0.730 (0.441)	0.122 (0.416)
Religiosity	0.112** (0.041)	−0.007 (0.029)
Education	−0.223*** (0.048)	−0.215** (0.070)
Income	−0.019** (0.006)	−0.011 (0.010)

	Foreign-Born	Muslim
Owns Home	−0.124	0.279
	(0.107)	(0.202)
Has Invested in Stocks	−0.060	−0.243**
	(0.085)	(0.072)
Southern Residence	0.335***	−0.003
	(0.067)	(0.153)
Anti-immigrant	1.333***	
	(0.144)	
Anti-unauthorized-immigrant	1.314***	
	(0.193)	
Christian-Muslim Relative Feeling Thermometer		0.031***
		(0.005)
Intercept	−5.546***	−5.048***
	(0.382)	(0.334)
Log likelihood	−1,745.87	−1,756.85
Pseudo R sq	0.263	0.229
Unweighted N	4,153	3,912

Note: Standard errors in parentheses.

Notes on the coding of the variables:

Foreign-Born: "Foreign-Born" means that the respondent thinks that President Obama was definitely or probably born in another country.

Antiblack Racial Resentment: A value of 1.0 indicates a high level of resentment toward blacks. A value of 0 indicates strong racially liberal attitudes toward blacks.

Political Ideology: The high value indicates "extremely conservative," and the low value indicates "extremely liberal."

Party Identification: The high value indicates "strong Republican," and the low value indicates "strong Democrat."

Tea Party support: The high value indicates "strong support" for the Tea Party, and the low value "strong opposition."

Religiosity: This variable is a composite of how often the respondent prays and how often the respondent attends religious services. The high value indicates that the respondent prays several times a day and attends religious services every week. The low value indicates that the respondent never does these things.

Anti-immigrant: This variable is a composite of respondents' desires for the level of immigration and their beliefs about whether immigrants take away jobs from people already here. The high value indicates that respondents believe the level of immigration should be decreased a lot and that it is extremely likely that immigration will take away jobs.

Anti-unauthorized-immigrant: This variable is a composite of respondents' feelings about police checking the status of individuals they suspect to be unauthorized, about allowing children brought into the country illegally to obtain citizenship, and about the goals of U.S. policy toward unauthorized immigrants more generally. The high value indicates that the respondent favors police checking the status of individuals, opposes granting citizenship to children brought to the country illegally, and favors deporting all unauthorized immigrants.

Christian-Muslim Relative Feeling Thermometer: This variable is constructed by subtracting the Christian feeling thermometer rating from the Muslim rating. The high value indicates favorable feelings toward Christians and negative feelings toward Muslims. The low value indicates the reverse.

$^\wedge p = .05$; $^*p < .05$; $^{**}p < .01$; $^{***}p < .001$.

Table 5.3 Percentage Believing President Obama to Be Foreign-Born by Hater Group

	Obama Haters	Conservative Non-Haters	Moderate and Liberal Non-Haters	All	Unweighted N	Rao-Scott-P
Obama definitely or probably born in another country	65.1%	30.9%	14.0%	24.8%	4,780	0.00

Table 5.4 Employment-to-Population Ratios for Individuals Born in Selected Countries, 2013

United States	Mexico	Central America	Canada	China	Germany	Unweighted N	Rao-Scott-P
56.7%	63.8%	69.8%	54.4%	56.6%	57.2%	2,335,679	0.00

Source: Author's analysis of 2013 American Community Survey data from Steven Ruggles, J. Trent Alexander, Katie Genadek, Ronald Goeken, Matthew B. Schroeder, and Matthew Sobek, Integrated Public Use Microdata Series: Version 5.0 (Machine-Readable Database) (Minneapolis: University of Minnesota, 2015).

Table 5.5 Percentage Believing That It Is Likely That Immigration Will Take Jobs Away from People Already Here

	Obama Haters	Conservative Non-Haters	Moderate and Liberal Non-Haters	All	Unweighted N	Rao-Scott-P
Extremely or Very Likely	58.4%	43.2%	32.2%	38.5%	4,869	0.00

Table 5.6 Percentage Believing That the Immigration Level Should Be Decreased by Hater Group

	Obama Haters	Conservative Non-Haters	Moderate and Liberal Non-Haters	All	Unweighted N	Rao-Scott-P
Decreased a little or a lot	61.5%	46.1%	40.0%	44.3%	4,829	0.00

Table 5.7 Percentage Favoring the Police Stopping and Checking the Legal Status of People Suspected of Being Undocumented Immigrants by Hater Group

Obama Haters	Conservative Non-Haters	Moderate and Liberal Non-Haters	All	Unweighted N	Rao-Scott-P
88.2%	65.4%	40.2%	53.2%	5,230	0.00

Questionnaire text: "Some states have passed a law that will require state and local police to determine the immigration status of a person if they find that there is a reasonable suspicion he or she is an undocumented immigrant. Those found to be in the U.S. without permission will have broken state law. From what you have heard, do you favor, oppose, or neither favor nor oppose these immigration laws?"

Table 5.8 Percentage Favoring Children Brought to the United States Illegally to Obtain Legal Status by Hater Group

Obama Haters	Conservative Non-Haters	Moderate and Liberal Non-Haters	All	Unweighted N	Rao-Scott-P
34.0%	50.0%	59.7%	53.9%	5,243	0.00

Questionnaire text: "There is a proposal to allow people who were illegally brought into the U.S. as children to become permanent U.S. residents under some circumstances. Specifically, citizens of other countries who illegally entered the U.S. before age 16, who have lived in the U.S. 5 years or longer, and who graduated high school would be allowed to stay in the U.S. as permanent residents if they attend college or serve in the military. From what you have heard, do you favor, oppose, or neither favor nor oppose this proposal?"

Table 5.9 Percentage Favoring Making Unauthorized Immigrants Felons and Deporting Them All by Hater Group

Obama Haters	Conservative Non-Haters	Moderate and Liberal Non-Haters	All	Unweighted N	Rao-Scott-P
36.4%	19.1%	16.3%	17.0%	5,235	0.00

Table 5.10 Illegal Immigrant-White Relative Feeling Thermometer Means by Hater Group

Obama Haters	Conservative Non-Haters	Moderate and Liberal Non-Haters	All	Unweighted N
22.13*	30.89	36.03	32.89	4,859

Note: The rating for "illegal immigrants" is relative to the rating given whites. The middle value, 50, indicates the respondent rates illegal immigrants and whites equally. The higher the rating above 50, the warmer the respondent is toward illegal immigrants and the colder toward whites. The lower the value below 50, the colder the respondent is toward illegal immigrants and the warmer toward whites.
* Statistically lower than the other categories at the $p < .05$ level.

Table 5.11 Logistic Regression Analyses of Xenophobia and Islamophobia as Predictors for Being an Obama Hater

	Obama Hater
Anti-immigrant	0.999***
	(0.229)
Anti-unauthorized-immigrant	0.773**
	(0.253)
Christian-Muslim Relative Feeling Thermometer	0.017***
	(0.003)
Antiblack Racial Resentment	1.431**
	(0.431)
Political Ideology	0.192**
	(0.063)
Party Identification	0.494***
	(0.029)
Tea Party support	1.659***
	(0.242)
Male	0.032
	(0.194)
Age	0.072***
	(0.013)
Black, Non-Hispanic	–1.54
	(7.643)
Hispanic	–0.062
	(0.179)
Other, Non-Hispanic	0.762***
	(0.130)
Religiosity	0.009
	(0.043)
Education	0.034
	(0.048)
Income	0.004
	(0.014)
Owns Home	0.487*
	(0.219)
Has Invested in Stocks	0.048
	(0.156)
Southern Residence	0.096
	(0.296)
Constant	–11.187***
	(0.415)

	Obama Hater
Log likelihood	−950.835
Pseudo R sq	0.36
Unweighted N	4,148

Note: Standard errors in parentheses.

Notes on the coding of the variables:

Antiblack Racial Resentment: A value of 1.0 indicates a high level of resentment toward blacks. A value of 0 indicates strong racially liberal attitudes toward blacks.

Political Ideology: The high value indicates "extremely conservative," and the low value indicates "extremely liberal."

Party Identification: The high value indicates "strong Republican," and the low value indicates "strong Democrat."

Tea Party support: The high value indicates "strong support" for the Tea Party, and the low value indicates "strong opposition."

Religiosity: This variable is a composite of how often the respondent prays and how often the respondent attends religious services. The high value indicates that the respondent prays several times a day and attends religious services every week. The low value indicates that the respondent never does these things.

Anti-immigrant: This variable is a composite of respondents' desires for the level of immigration and their beliefs about whether immigrants take away jobs from people already here. The high value indicates that respondents believe the level of immigration should be decreased a lot and that it is extremely likely that immigration will take away jobs.

Anti-unauthorized-immigrant: This variable is a composite of respondents' feelings about police checking the status of individuals they suspect to be unauthorized, about allowing children brought into the country illegally to obtain citizenship, and about the goals of U.S. policy toward unauthorized immigrants more generally. The high value indicates that the respondent favors police checking the status of individuals, opposes granting citizenship to children brought to the country illegally, and favors deporting all unauthorized immigrants.

Christian-Muslim Relative Feeling Thermometer: This variable is constructed by subtracting the Christian feeling thermometer rating from the Muslim rating. The high value indicates favorable feelings toward Christians and negative feelings toward Muslims. The low value indicates the reverse.

* $p < .05$; **$p < .01$; ***$p < .001$.

Table 6.1 Percentage Believing That President Obama Is Christian and Muslim, and Percentage Believing Mitt Romney Is Mormon by Hater Group

	Obama Haters (%)	Conservative Non-Haters (%)	Moderate and Liberal Non-Haters (%)	All (%)	Unweighted N	Rao-Scott-P
Obama is Christian	13.6	41.6	63.8	51.0		
Obama is Muslim	62.4	31.6	16.4	26.6	4,716	0.00
Mitt Romney is Mormon	90.2	79.7	71.7	76.3	4,895	0.00

Table 6.2 Mean Muslim-Christian and Mormon-Christian Relative Feeling Thermometer Rating by Hater Group

	Obama Haters	Conservative Non-Haters	Moderate and Liberal Non-Haters	All	Unweighted N
Muslim	22.69*	32.39	40.62	36.08	4,832
Mormon	38.98	38.78	40.16	39.61	4,834

Note: The rating for Mormons is relative to the rating given Christians. The middle value, 50, indicates the respondent rates Mormons and Christians equally. The higher the rating above 50, the warmer the respondent is toward Mormons and the colder toward Christians. The lower the value below 50, the colder the respondent is toward Mormons and the warmer toward Christians.
* Statistically lower than the other categories at the $p < .05$ level.

Table 6.3 Percentage Saying Most Muslims Are Not At All Patriotic by Hater Group

Obama Haters	Conservative Non-Haters	Moderate and Liberal Non-Haters	All	Unweighted N	Rao-Scott-P
56.7%	38.3%	32.8%	37.3%	3,506	0.00

Table 6.4 Percentage Saying That "Violent" Describes Most Muslims Well by Hater Group

	Obama Haters (%)	Conservative Non-Haters (%)	Moderate and Liberal Non-Haters (%)	All (%)	Unweighted N	Rao-Scott-P
Moderately to Extremely Well	67.4	47.4	39.1	45.0	3,510	0.01
Extremely Well	20.4	7.0	7.2	8.8	3,510	0.00

Table 7.1 Mean and Highest Antiblack Racial Resentment Score for Tea Party Supporters and Non-Tea-Party Conservatives

	Tea Party Supporters	Non-Tea-Party Conservatives
Mean	0.77	0.67*
Percentage with 1.0 score	19.8%	9.1%*
Unweighted N	1,258	872

Note: Tea Party supporters include liberals and moderates. For more information on the racial resentment measure, see Michael Tesler and David O. Sears, *Obama's Race: The 2008 Election and the Dream of a Post-Racial America* (Chicago: The University of Chicago Press, 2010), Chapter 1, "The Theory of Symbolic Racism" section.
* Different from Tea Party supporters at the $p < .05$ level.

Table 7.2 Percentage of Tea Party Supporters and Non-Tea-Party Conservatives Rating Whites as Experiencing As Much or More Discrimination Than Blacks and Hispanics

	Tea Party Supporters (%)	Non-Tea-Party Conservatives (%)	Tea-Party Unweighted N	Non-Tea-Party-Conservatives Unweighted N
Whites discriminated against as much or more than blacks	63.9	42.8*	1,258	870
Whites discriminated against as much or more than Hispanics	60.3	38.6*	1,258	869

Note: Tea Party supporters include liberals and moderates.
* Different from Tea Party supporters at the p < .05 level.

Table 7.3 Percentage of Tea Party Supporters and Non-Tea-Party Conservatives Believing That the Obama Administration Favors Blacks over Whites

	Tea Party Supporters	Non-Tea-Party Conservatives
	48.9%	30.1%*
Unweighted N	1,246	863

Note: Tea Party supporters include liberals and moderates.
* Different from Tea Party supporters at the p < .05 level.

Table 7.4 Percentage of Tea Party Supporters and Non-Tea-Party Conservatives Believing That the Immigration Level Should Be Decreased

	Tea Party Supporters	Non-Tea-Party Conservatives
Decreased a little or a lot	51.7%	49.3%
Unweighted N	1,247	869

Note: Tea Party supporters include liberals and moderates.

Table 7.5 Percentage of Tea Party Supporters and Non-Tea-Party Conservatives Favoring Making Unauthorized Immigrants Felons and Deporting Them All

	Tea Party Supporters	Non-Tea-Party Conservatives
	27.2%	17.4%*
Unweighted N	1,359	929

Note: Tea Party supporters include liberals and moderates.
* Different from Tea Party supporters at the p < .05 level.

Table 7.6 Illegal Immigrant-White Relative Feeling Thermometer Means for Tea Party Supporters and Non-Tea-Party Conservatives

	Tea Party Supporters	Non-Tea-Party Conservatives
	27.03	31.75*
N	1,339	918

Note: Tea Party supporters include liberals and moderates.
The rating for "illegal immigrants" is relative to the rating given whites. The middle value, 50, indicates the respondent rates illegal immigrants and whites equally. The higher the rating above 50, the warmer the respondent is toward illegal immigrants and the colder toward whites. The lower the value below 50, the colder the respondent is toward illegal immigrants and the warmer toward whites.
* Different from Tea Party supporters at the p < .05 level.

Table 7.7 Mean Muslim-Christian Relative Feeling Thermometer Rating for Tea Party Supporters and Non-Tea-Party Conservatives

	Tea Party Supporters	Non-Tea-Party Conservatives
	28.62	33.91*
N	1,346	909

Note: Tea Party supporters include liberals and moderates.
The rating for Muslims is relative to the rating given Christians. The middle value, 50, indicates the respondent rates Muslims and Christians equally. The higher the rating above 50, the warmer the respondent is toward Muslims and the colder toward Christians. The lower the value below 50, the colder the respondent is toward Muslims and the warmer toward Christians.
* Different from Tea Party supporters at the p < .05 level.

Table 7.8 Percentage of Tea Party Supporters and Non-Tea-Party Conservatives Saying That "Violent" Describes Most Muslims Well

	Tea Party Supporters	Non-Tea-Party Conservatives
Moderately to Extremely Well	56.9%	45.5%*
Unweighted N	906	649

Note: Tea Party supporters include liberals and moderates.
* Different from Tea Party supporters at the p < .05 level.

Table 7.9 Percentage of Tea Party Supporters and Non-Tea-Party Obama Haters Saying Most Muslims Are Not At All Patriotic

	Tea Party Supporters	Non-Tea-Party Conservatives
	44.9%	38.6%
Unweighted N	905	645

Note: Tea Party supporters include liberals and moderates.

Table 7.10 Political Ideology and Party Identification of Tea-Party Obama Haters, Non-Tea-Party Obama Haters, and Tea-Party Non-Haters

	Tea-Party Obama Haters (%)	Non-Tea-Party Obama Haters (%)	Tea-Party Non-Haters (%)	Obama Haters Rao-Scott-P	Tea Party Rao-Scott-P	Unweighted Obama Haters N	Unweighted Tea Party N
Slightly to Extremely Conservative	91.8	58.9	71.0	0.00	0.00	572	1,290
Extremely Conservative	20.6	7.5	8.3	0.00	0.00	572	1,290
Independent-Republican to Strong Republican	96.2	84.3	75.4	0.00	0.00	576	1,292
Strong Republican	60.9	44.7	28.0	0.00	0.00	576	1,292

Note: Independent-Republicans are considered to lean Republican. Individuals who "lean toward supporting" the Tea Party are treated as Tea Party supporters.

Table 7.11 Share of Tea-Party Obama Haters, Non-Tea-Party Obama Haters, and Tea-Party Non-Haters Wanting to Decrease Government Spending on the Poor

Tea-Party Obama Haters	Non-Tea-Party Obama Haters	Tea-Party Non-Haters	Obama Haters Rao-Scott-P	Tea Party Rao-Scott-P	Unweighted Obama Haters N	Unweighted Tea Party N
55.2%	32.1%	34.3%	0.00	0.00	571	1,288

Table 7.12 Political Engagement of Tea-Party Obama Haters, Non-Tea-Party Obama Haters, and Tea-Party Non-Haters

	Tea-Party Obama Haters (%)	Non-Tea-Party Obama Haters (%)	Tea-Party Non-Haters (%)	Obama Haters Rao-Scott-P	Tea Party Rao-Scott-P	Unweighted Obama Haters N	Unweighted Tea Party N
Voted in a presidential primary or caucus	.60.5	35.3	44.1	0.00	0.00	572	1,285
Have contacted U.S. representative or senator in the past four years	37.4	17.9	25.5	0.00	0.01	538	1,194
Have contributed money to a candidate's campaign	22.1	6.2	13.4	0.00	0.00	538	1,195

Table 7.13 Mean and Highest Antiblack Racial Resentment Score for Tea-Party Obama Haters, Non-Tea-Party Obama Haters, and Tea-Party Non-Haters

	Tea-Party Obama Haters	Non-Tea-Party Obama Haters	Tea-Party Non-Haters	Obama Haters Rao-Scott-P	Tea Party Rao-Scott-P	Unweighted Obama Haters N	Unweighted Tea Party N
Mean	0.83	0.77	0.74*	na	na	532	1,188
Percentage with 1.0 score	33.5%	19.5%	13.8%	0.0	0.0	532	1,188

Note: For more information on the racial resentment measure, see Michael Tesler and David O. Sears, *Obama's Race: The 2008 Election and the Dream of a Post-Racial America* (Chicago: The University of Chicago Press, 2010), Chapter 1, "The Theory of Symbolic Racism" section.
na: not applicable.
* Statistically lower than the Tea-Party Obama Haters at the $p < .05$ level.

Table 7.14 Percentage of Tea-Party Obama Haters, Non-Tea-Party Obama Haters, and Tea-Party Non-Haters Rating Whites as Experiencing As Much or More Discrimination Than Blacks and Hispanics

	Tea-Party Obama Haters (%)	Non-Tea-Party Obama Haters (%)	Tea-Party Non-Haters (%)	Obama Haters Rao-Scott-P	Tea Party Rao-Scott-P	Unweighted Obama Haters N	Unweighted Tea Party N
Whites discriminated against as much or more than blacks	69.5	59.0	63.4	0.03	0.09	535	1,190
Whites discriminated against as much or more than Hispanics	68.1	53.0	58.9	0.01	0.02	536	1,190

Table 7.15 Percentage of Tea-Party Obama Haters, Non-Tea-Party Obama Haters, and Tea-Party Non-Haters Believing That the Obama Administration Favors Blacks over Whites

Tea-Party Obama Haters	Non-Tea-Party Obama Haters	Tea-Party Non-Haters	Obama Haters Rao-Scott-P	Tea Party Rao-Scott-P	Unweighted Obama Haters N	Unweighted Tea Party N
65.8%	62.9%	42.3%	0.55	0.00	533	1,181

Table 7.16 Percentage of Tea-Party Obama Haters, Non-Tea-Party Obama Haters, and Tea-Party Non-Haters Believing President Obama to Be Foreign-Born

	Tea-Party Obama Haters	Non-Tea-Party Obama Haters	Tea-Party Non-Haters	Obama Haters Rao-Scott-P	Tea Party Rao-Scott-P	Unweighted Obama Haters N	Unweighted Tea Party N
Obama definitely or probably born in another country	64.6%	69.6%	37.3%	0.61	0.00	525	1,158

Table 7.17 Percentage of Tea-Party Obama Haters, Non-Tea-Party Obama Haters, and Tea-Party Non-Haters Believing That the Immigration Level Should Be Decreased

	Tea-Party Obama Haters	Non-Tea-Party Obama Haters	Tea-Party Non-Haters	Obama Haters Rao-Scott-P	Tea Party Rao-Scott-P	Unweighted Obama Haters N	Unweighted Tea Party N
Decreased a little or a lot	59.1%	66.8%	48.9%	0.30	0.00	532	1,180

Table 7.18 Percentage of Tea-Party Obama Haters, Non-Tea-Party Obama Haters, and Tea-Party Non-Haters Favoring Making Unauthorized Immigrants Felons and Deporting Them All

Tea-Party Obama Haters	Non-Tea-Party Obama Haters	Tea-Party Non-Haters	Obama Haters Rao-Scott-P	Tea Party Rao-Scott-P	Unweighted Obama Haters N	Unweighted Tea Party N
39.2%	29.3%	22.2%	0.27	0.00	575	1,289

Table 7.19 Illegal Immigrant-White Relative Feeling Thermometer Means for Tea-Party Obama Haters, Non-Tea-Party Obama Haters, and Tea-Party Non-Haters

Tea-Party Obama Haters	Non-Tea-Party Obama Haters	Tea-Party Non-Haters	Unweighted Obama Haters N	Unweighted Tea Party N
21.60	23.35	29.12*	534	1,183

Note: The rating for "illegal immigrants" is relative to the rating given whites. The middle value, 50, indicates the respondent rates illegal immigrants and whites equally. The higher the rating above 50, the warmer the respondent is toward illegal immigrants and the colder toward whites. The lower the value below 50, the colder the respondent is toward illegal immigrants and the warmer toward whites.
* Statistically higher than the Tea-Party Obama Haters at the $p < .05$ level.

Table 7.20 Percentage of Tea-Party Obama Haters, Non-Tea-Party Obama Haters, and Tea-Party Non-Haters Believing That President Obama Is Muslim

Tea-Party Obama Haters	Non-Tea-Party Obama Haters	Tea-Party Non-Haters	Obama Haters Rao-Scott-P	Tea Party Rao-Scott-P	Unweighted Obama Haters N	Unweighted Tea Party N
63.6%	60.9%	35.4%	0.43	0.00	562	1,211

Table 7.21 Mean Muslim-Christian Relative Feeling Thermometer Rating for Tea-Party Obama Haters, Non-Tea-Party Obama Haters, and Tea-Party Non-Haters

Tea-Party Obama Haters	Non-Tea-Party Obama Haters	Tea-Party Non-Haters	Unweighted Obama Haters N	Unweighted Tea Party N
21.43	25.82[a]	31.10[b]	533	1,183

Note: The rating for Muslims is relative to the rating given Christians. The middle value, 50, indicates the respondent rates Muslims and Christians equally. The higher the rating above 50, the warmer the respondent is toward Muslims and the colder toward Christians. The lower the value below 50, the colder the respondent is toward Muslims and the warmer toward Christians.
a Statistically higher than the Tea-Party Obama Haters at the p < .05 level.
b Statistically higher than the Tea-Party and Non-Tea-Party Obama Haters at the p < .05 level.

Table 7.22 Percentage of Tea-Party Obama Haters, Non-Tea-Party Obama Haters, and Tea-Party Non-Haters Saying That "Violent" Describes Most Muslims Well

	Tea-Party Obama Haters	Non-Tea-Party Obama Haters	Tea-Party Non-Haters	Obama Haters Rao-Scott-P	Tea Party Rao-Scott-P	Unweighted Obama Haters N	Unweighted Tea Party N
Moderately to Extremely Well	70.9%	58.0%	50.7%	0.36	0.04	448	902

Table 7.23 Percentage of Tea-Party Obama Haters, Non-Tea-Party Obama Haters, and Tea-Party Non-Haters Saying Most Muslims Are Not At All Patriotic

Tea-Party Obama Haters	Non-Tea-Party Obama Haters	Tea-Party Non-Haters	Obama Haters Rao-Scott-P	Tea Party Rao-Scott-P	Unweighted Obama Haters N	Unweighted Tea Party N
60.7%	47.4%	37.5%	0.26	0.02	450	901

Table 8.1 Percentage of Correct Answers to Selected Political Knowledge Questions by Hater Group

	Obama Haters (%)	Conservative Non-Haters (%)	Moderate and Liberal Non-Haters (%)	All (%)	Unweighted N
Number of times can an individual be elected president?	94.5	93.0	90.6	91.8	5,222
Relative size of the U.S. federal budget deficit?	97.6[a]	89.0	83.5	86.8	5,238

(Continued)

Table 8.1 (Continued)

	Obama Haters (%)	Conservative Non-Haters (%)	Moderate and Liberal Non-Haters (%)	All (%)	Unweighted N
Length of a full U.S. Senate term?	41.7[b]	38.6	33.7	36.1	5,169
What is Medicare?	88.4[b]	81.9	79.3	81.1	5,235
Which is the smallest federal government program?	28.8[c]	35.4	33.1	33.3	5,225
Who is the secretary of the treasury?	69.0[a]	58.3	55.7	58.1	4,269
What is the current unemployment rate?	67.2	67.5	68.1	67.8	4,618
Which political party came in second in U.S. House of Representative seats won?	73.0[a]	66.5	65.0	66.4	4,449
Who is the current secretary general of the United Nations?	36.3	31.8	35.4	34.5	3,828
Average	66.3	62.4	60.5	61.8	

a Obama Haters statistically higher than all other categories at the p < .05 level.
b Obama Haters statistically higher than Moderate and Liberal Non-Haters and All categories at the p < .05 level.
c Obama Haters statistically lower than Conservative Non-Haters at the p < .05 level.

Table 8.2 Percentage of Obama Haters, Conservative Non-Haters, and Moderate and Liberal Non-Haters Identifying Different Government Programs as Receiving the Least Spending

	Obama Haters (%)	Conservative Non-Haters (%)	Moderate and Liberal Non-Haters (%)	All (%)	Unweighted N	Rao-Scott-P
Foreign aid	28.8	35.4	33.1	33.3	5,225	0.00
Medicare	19.4	22.5	23.4	22.7		
National defense	22.5	10.4	8.6	10.7		
Social Security	29.3	31.7	35.0	33.4		

Table 8.3 Percentage Believing That the Affordable Care Act Authorizes Government Panels to Make End-of-Life Decisions by Hater Group

	Obama Haters	Conservative Non-Haters	Moderate and Liberal Non-Haters	All	Rao-Scott-P	Unweighted N
Definitely or probably	72.4%	49.2%	29.1%	40.3%	0.00	4,580

Table 8.4 Percentage Believing That Senior Federal Government Officials Did Not Know about the Terrorist Attacks on September 11, 2001, before They Happened by Hater Group

	Obama Haters	Conservative Non-Haters	Moderate and Liberal Non-Haters	All	Rao-Scott-P	Unweighted N
Definitely or probably did not know	65.8%	69.1%	56.4%	61.4%	0.00	4,836

Table 8.5 Percentage Rejecting the Idea That the Federal Government Intentionally Breached Flood Levees in Poor New Orleans Neighborhoods by Hater Group

	Obama Haters	Conservative Non-Haters	Moderate and Liberal Non-Haters	All	Rao-Scott-P	Unweighted N
Definitely or probably did not flood poor neighborhoods	90.2%	86.5%	80.5%	83.4%	0.00	4,807

Table 8.6 Percentage Seeing Obama as Extremely Liberal by Hater Group

Obama Haters	Conservative Non-Haters	Moderate and Liberal Non-Haters	All	Rao-Scott-P	Unweighted N
85.0%	40.5%	11.2%	28.6%	0.00	5,171

Table 8.7 Views of Mitt Romney's Conservatism by Hater Group

	Obama Haters (%)	Conservative Non-Haters (%)	Moderate and Liberal Non-Haters (%)	All (%)	Rao-Scott-P	Unweighted N
Slightly Conservative	22.2	20.0	10.9	15.0	0.00	5,130
Conservative	53.4	42.6	34.7	39.3		
Extremely Conservative	6.0	9.3	26.0	18.6		
Slightly to Extremely Conservative	81.6	71.9	71.6	72.9	0.00	

Table 8.8 Percentage Thinking Barack Obama Desires to Provide Many More Government Services by Hater Group

Obama Haters	Conservative Non-Haters	Moderate and Liberal Non-Haters	All	Rao-Scott-P	Unweighted N
76.5%	39.6%	12.2%	27.8%	0.00	5,213

Table 8.9 Respondents' Beliefs about Whether Mitt Romney Wishes to Provide Many More or Many Fewer Government Services by Hater Group

	Obama Haters (%)	Conservative Non-Haters (%)	Moderate and Liberal Non-Haters (%)	All (%)	Rao-Scott-P	Unweighted N
1: Government should provide many fewer services	11.3	14.0	30.2	23.1	0.00	5,170
2	30.3	26.5	27.3	27.4		
3	31.6	31.3	15.4	22.1		
4	18.5	17.0	15.1	16.1		
5	5.3	6.4	5.7	5.9		
6	1.2	2.1	3.1	2.6		

	Obama Haters (%)	Conservative Non-Haters (%)	Moderate and Liberal Non-Haters (%)	All (%)	Rao-Scott-P	Unweighted N
7: Government should provide many more services	1.8	2.8	3.1	2.9		

Obama Haters-Conservative Non-Haters Rao-Scott-P	Unweighted N
0.64	2,067

Table 8.10 Percentage Thinking Barack Obama Desires to Decrease Defense Spending[a] by Hater Group

Obama Haters	Conservative Non-Haters	Moderate and Liberal Non-Haters	All	Rao-Scott-P	Unweighted N
43.3%	15.7%	4.5%	12.3%	0.00	5,165

a These responses are for only the most extreme liberal response.

Table 8.11 Respondents Beliefs about Whether Mitt Romney Wishes to Increase or Decrease Defense Spending by Hater Group

	Obama Haters (%)	Conservative Non-Haters (%)	Moderate and Liberal Non-Haters (%)	All (%)	Rao-Scott-P	Unweighted N
1: Government should spend much less on defense	1.4	2.1	4.0	3.1	0.00	5,085
2	3.1	5.2	6.6	5.8		
3	4.8	7.7	8.6	7.9		
4	20.8	25.2	19.0	21.1		
5	28.0	28.8	19.5	23.3		
6	29.2	22.1	21.2	22.4		
7: Government should spend much more on defense	12.7	8.9	21.0	16.4		
Sum: 5–7	69.9	59.8	61.7	62.1		

Table 8.12 Share of Respondents Wanting to Increase or Decrease Government Spending on Selected Items by Hater Group

	Increase Spending on			Decrease Spending on			
	Obama Haters (%)	Conservative Non-Haters (%)	Moderate and Liberal Non-Haters (%)	Obama Haters (%)	Conservative Non-Haters (%)	Moderate and Liberal Non-Haters (%)	Unweighted N
Protecting the environment	13.1[a]	26.8	50.6	45.0[a]	29.6	7.3	5,246
Aid to the poor	11.6[a]	23.1	43.7	49.1[a]	29.1	11.7	5,232
Child care	8.3[a]	23.6	39.6	47.4[a]	30.4	12.8	5,222
Welfare programs	2.8[b]	7.1	17.9	82.3[a]	62.3	32.8	5,226
Dealing with crime	49.4	47.2	50.7	11.1	10.7	7.7	5,232
Science and technology	33.9[a]	43.2	50.9	22.2[a]	15.1	10.1	5,234
Public schools	34.2[a]	50.5	72.8	32.4[a]	15.2	4.3	5,243
Social Security	42.0	38.7	51.3	9.6	10.1	4.9	5,216
Defense	53.6[a]	30.3	20.6	11.7[a]	24.3	38.8	4,878

a Obama Haters different from other categories at the p < .05 level.
b Obama Haters different from Moderate and Liberal Non-Haters at the p < .05 level.

Table 9.1 Percentage of Obama Haters and Non-Haters Seeing Blacks as Lazy or Hard-working Relative to Whites

	Obama Haters (%)	All Non-Haters (%)	All (%)	Rao-Scott-P	Unweighted N
Blacks are lazier	46.7	26.4	28.7	0.00	4,875
Blacks are about the same	51.8	69.1	67.1		
Blacks are more hardworking	1.5	4.5	4.2		

Note: This measure is constructed by subtracting the rating for whites from the rating for blacks. The value 0.50 indicates that the respondent views blacks and whites as equally hardworking or lazy. Values greater than one standard deviation (0.14) above indicate that blacks are seen as more hardworking than whites. Values less than one standard deviation lower indicate that blacks are seen as lazier than whites.

Table 9.2 Percentage of Obama Haters and Non-Haters with a High Level of Antiblack Racial Resentment

Obama Haters	All Non-Haters	All	Rao-Scott-P	Unweighted N
60.3%	27.1%	30.7%	0.00	4,867

Note: A high level of antiblack racial resentment is defined as more than one standard deviation (0.25) above the neutral value (0.50). See Michael Tesler and David O. Sears, *Obama's Race: The 2008 Election and the Dream of a Post-Racial America* (Chicago: The University of Chicago Press, 2010), Chapter 1, "The Theory of Symbolic Racism" section, for more information on the measure.

Table 9.3 Percentage of Obama Haters and Non-Haters Seeing Hispanics as Lazy or Hardworking Relative to Whites

	Obama Haters (%)	All Non-Haters (%)	All (%)	Rao-Scott-P	Unweighted N
Hispanics are lazier	20.7	10.6	11.7	0.00	4,875
Hispanics are about the same	72.5	77.2	76.7		
Hispanics are more hardworking	6.8	12.2	11.6		

Note: This measure is constructed by subtracting the rating for whites from the rating for Hispanics. The value 0.50 indicates that the respondent views Hispanics and whites as equally hardworking or lazy. Values greater than one standard deviation (0.13) above indicates that Hispanics are seen as more hardworking than whites. Values less than one standard deviation lower indicates that Hispanics are seen as lazier than whites.

Table 9.4 Obama Haters and Non-Haters Degree of Feelings of Relative Warmth or Coldness toward Hispanics Relative to Whites

	Obama Haters (%)	All Non-Haters (%)	All (%)	Rao-Scott-P	Unweighted N
Very Cold/Unfavorable	30.4	17.9	19.3	0.00	4,860
Neither Very Warm or Cold	68.2	77.5	76.5		
Very Warm/Favorable	1.4	4.6	4.2		

Note: This measure is constructed from the feeling thermometers for Hispanics and whites. The value 50.0 indicates that the respondent views Hispanics and whites equally. More than one standard deviation (11.17 "degrees") above 50.0 indicates that the respondent is "warmer" or more favorable toward Hispanics than to whites. More than one standard deviation lower than 50.0 indicates that the respondent is "cooler" or less favorable toward Hispanics than to whites.

Table 9.5 Obama Haters and Non-Haters Level of Support for Immigration

	Obama Haters (%)	All Non-Haters (%)	All (%)	Rao-Scott-P	Unweighted N
Immigration costs jobs and should be reduced	38.4	19.5	21.6	0.00	4,818
Not strongly for or against immigration	59.7	73.3	71.8		
There should be more immigration	1.9	7.2	6.6		

Note: This measure is constructed from two questions about the desired immigration level and whether immigration will take away jobs. The median value is 0.50. More than one standard deviation (0.27) above the median value is taken to indicate strong negative views toward immigration. More than one standard deviation below the median is taken to indicate positive views toward immigration. See the following for more details about the coding of the individual variables.
IMMIGPO_JOBS: How likely is it that immigration will take away jobs.
   Not at all = 1; Somewhat= 2; Very = 4; Extremely = 5
IMMIGPO_LEVEL: What should immigration levels be.
   Increased a lot = 1; Decreased a lot = 5
Cronbach's alpha = 0.64.

Table 9.6 Obama Haters and Non-Haters Level of Support for Policies against Unauthorized Immigrants

	Obama Haters (%)	All Non-Haters (%)	All (%)	Rao-Scott-P	Unweighted N
Strong support for policies against unauthorized immigrants	44.7	16.9	20.0	0.00	5,195
No strong feelings on unauthorized immigrants	53.4	59.7	59.0		
Strong opposition to polices against unauthorized immigrants	1.9	23.3	21.0		

Note: This measure is constructed from the questions about immigration status checks, about allowing children brought to the country illegally to obtain legal residency, and about U.S. policy toward unauthorized immigrants. The median value is 0.50. More than one standard deviation (0.26) above the median value is taken to indicate strong negative views toward unauthorized immigrants. More than one standard deviation below the median is taken to indicate positive views toward unauthorized immigrants. See the following for more details about the coding of the individual variables.
IMMIG_CHECKS: Opinion on laws to allow immigration status checks on suspects
    Favor = 3; Neither favor or oppose = 2; Oppose = 1
IMMIG_CITIZEN: Opinion on proposal to allow citizenship to children brought to the country illegally
    Oppose = 3; Neither favor or oppose = 2; Favor = 1
IMMIG_POLICY: U.S. government policy toward unauthorized immigrants should be . . .
    Send them back home = 3; guest worker program = 2; allow them to remain with requirements = 2; allow them to remain without penalties = 1
Cronbach's alpha = 0.59.

Table 9.7 Obama Haters and Non-Haters Degree of Feelings of Warmth or Coldness toward Muslims Relative to Whites

	Obama Haters (%)	All Non-Haters (%)	All (%)	Rao-Scott-P	Unweighted N
Very Cold/Unfavorable	74.0	37.3	41.4	0.00	4,832
Neither Very Warm or Cold	26.0	60.6	56.7		
Very Warm/Favorable	0.0	2.1	1.9		

Note: This measure is constructed from the feeling thermometers for Christians and Muslims. The value 50.0 indicates that the respondent views Muslims and Christians equally. One standard deviation (15.92 "degrees") or higher above 50.0 indicates that the respondent is "hotter" or more favorable toward Christians than to Muslims. One standard deviation or more lower than 50.0 indicates that the respondent is "cooler" or less favorable toward Muslims than to Christians.

Table 9.8 Percentage Rating Whites as Experiencing As Much or More Discrimination Than Blacks and Hispanics

	Whites Discriminated against As Much As or More Than Blacks	Whites Discriminated against As Much As or More Than Hispanics
	41.4%	39.5%
Unweighted N	5,462	5,459

Table 9.9 Percentage Saying Blacks and Hispanics Have Too Much Influence in U.S. Politics

	Blacks	Hispanics
	13.8%	14.0%
Unweighted N	5,470	5,473

Notes

Preface

1. Xuan Thai and Ted Barrett, "Biden's Description of Obama Draws Scrutiny," CNN.com, February 9, 2007.

Introduction

1. This quotation was from a quick, off-the-cuff, e-mail with a noted presidential historian. Because of the causal nature of the communication, I have chosen to keep the author confidential. For similar remarks about the names presidents have been called, see John Avlon, *Wingnuts: How the Lunatic Fringe Is Hijacking America* (New York: Beast Books, 2010), 8.

2. Gary C. Jacobson, "Presidents, Partisans, and Polarized Politics," in *Can We Talk?: The Rise of Rude, Nasty, Stubborn Politics*, Daniel M. Shea and Morris P. Fiorina, eds. (New York: Pearson, 2012), 111.

3. Paul Waldman, "Republicans Are Beginning to Act as though Barack Obama Isn't Even the President," *The Plum Line* blog, *Washington Post*, March 9, 2015.

4. Appendix, Introduction Table 1. For a similar analysis with the same conclusion, see Jacobson, "Presidents, Partisans, and Polarized Politics," Figures 8.2–8.6.

5. Robert Farley, "Fact Check: Obama on the 'Fiscal Cliff' Deal," *USA Today*, January 5, 2013.

6. Quoted in David Kravets, "Former CIA Chief: Obama's War on Terror Same as Bush's, but with More Killing," *Wired.com*, September 10, 2012.

7. Paul Krugman, "Conservative Origins of Obamacare," *The Conscience of a Liberal* blog, *New York Times*, July 27, 2011; John Aravosis, "Original 1989 Document Where Heritage Foundation Created Obamacare's Individual Mandate," *Americablog*, October 24, 2013, http://americablog.com/2013/10/original-198 9-document-heritage-foundation-created-obamacares-individual-mandate.html.

8. Reid J. Epstein, "National Council of La Raza Leader Calls Barack Obama 'Deporter-in-Chief,'" *Politico.com*, March 4, 2014. Others have also called Obama the "deportation president." For example, see Katie McDonough, "The Deportation

President: Obama Has Banished Nearly 1.6 Million People for Minor Offenses like Traffic Violations," *Alternet.org*, April 8, 2014.

9. U.S. Department of Homeland Security, "Border Security Results," November 1, 2013, http://www.dhs.gov/border-security-results; Louis Jacobson, "Barack Obama Touts Record High Border Agents, Lowest Immigration from Mexico in 40 Years," *Politifact.com*, October 17, 2012.

10. Changes in policy and terminology and push and pull factors on immigrants make it impossible to accurately compare different administrations' deportation statistics. However, the Obama administration has achieved a record number for "removals." Nora Caplan-Bricker, "Who's the Real Deporter-in-Chief: Bush or Obama?" *NewRepublic.com*, April 17, 2014.

11. Barack Obama, *The Audacity of Hope: Thoughts on Reclaiming the American Dream* (New York: Three Rivers Press, 2006), 255–256. See Chapter 1 for more discussion of this point.

12. See Michael D. Shear, "Obama Budget Is Dismissed by G.O.P. and Attacked by Left," *New York Times*, April 5, 2013.

13. See Sharon O'Brien, "Why Is Social Security Called the Third Rail of American Politics?" *SeniorLiving.About.com*, http://seniorliving.about.com/od/social security101/a/socialsecurity.htm.

14. See Chapter 1 for further discussion of this point.

15. The researchers found a similar result with Obama's Deferred Action for Childhood Arrivals policy. Public Religion Research Institute, "Roughly Three-Quarters of Americans Favor Goals of Obama's Immigration Action" (Washington, DC: Public Religion Research Institute, 2015).

16. Michael Tesler and David O. Sears, *Obama's Race: The 2008 Election and the Dream of a Post-racial America* (Chicago: The University of Chicago Press, 2010), Chapter 8, "The Spillover of Racialization into the Obama Administration's Policies" section.

17. Daniel M. Shea, and Morris P. Fiorina, *Can We Talk?: The Rise of Rude, Nasty, Stubborn Politics* (New York: Pearson, 2012).

18. Hater 558. Verbatim text: "He's Muslim and the proof is all over the place, but people refuse to see it. Whether out of ignorance (lazy) or blind loyalty doesn't matter. Evidence is there. Straight from the jackasses mouth: If he has to choose between American and Muslim, he will side with his Muslim brethren. I could give example after example. He has apologized and kowtowed to every nation in the world that we should be watching like a hawk. Showing weakness and subservience is no". The text was truncated in the database.

19. Xuan Thai and Ted Barrett, "Biden's Description of Obama Draws Scrutiny," *CNN.com*, February 9, 2007.

20. Robert P. Jones et al., *Citizenship, Values, and Cultural Concerns: What Americans Want from Immigration Reform* (Washington, DC: Public Religion Research Institute, Inc.; Governance Studies at Brookings, 2013), 20.

21. Cindy Brooks Dollar, "Racial Threat Theory: Assessing the Evidence, Requesting Redesign," *Journal of Criminology*, vol. 2014, Article ID 983026 (2014): 7 pages; Chris Mooney, "The Troubling Reason Why Whites in Some States May

Show More Hidden Racial Bias," *Washington Post*, December 19, 2014; Maureen A. Craig and Jennifer A. Richeson, "More Diverse Yet Less Tolerant? How the Increasingly Diverse Racial Landscape Affects White Americans' Racial Attitudes," *Personality and Social Psychology Bulletin*, 40, no. 6 (June 2014): 750–761.

Chapter 1

1. Edward Schumacher-Matos, "NPR's Ombudsman on Diversity, Controversy and Leadership," *The Kojo Nnamdi Show* (Washington, DC: WAMU, June 4, 2014).

2. Bill Press, *The Obama Hate Machine: The Lies, Distortions, and Personal Attacks on the President—and Who Is behind Them* (New York: St. Martin's Press, 2012).

3. Jodi Kantor, "In Law School, Obama Found Political Voice," *New York Times*, January 28, 2007.

4. Charles Ogletree, "Foreword," in *The Obamas and a (Post) Racial America?*, Gregory S. Parks and Matthew W. Hughey, eds. (New York: Oxford University Press, 2011).

5. Ezra Klein, "Obama Revealed: A Moderate Republican," *Washington Post*, April 25, 2011.

6. Bruce Bartlett, "Barack Obama: The Democrats' Richard Nixon?" *The Fiscal Times*, July 22, 2011.

7. Jordan Fabian, "Obama: More Moderate Republican Than Socialist," *ABCNews.com*, December 14, 2012.

8. Laura L. Finley and Luigi Esposito, "Conclusion: Obama and the Future of Progressivism in the United States," in *Grading the 44th President: A Report Card on Barack Obama's First Term as a Progressive Leader*, Luigi Esposito and Laura L. Finley, eds. (Santa Barbara, CA: Praeger, 2012), 241.

9. P. Tom Semm and Christina Sanchez-Weston, "Waiting for Change: Obama and the LGBT Community," in *Grading the 44th President: A Report Card on Barack Obama's First Term as a Progressive Leader*, Luigi Esposito and Laura L. Finley, eds. (Santa Barbara, CA: Praeger, 2012), 215.

10. Ibid.

11. Lisa Keen, "White House: New Federal Contractor EO Coming," *WindyCityMediaGroup.com*, June 18, 2014.

12. Gautam Raghavan, "Obama Administration Statements on the Supreme Court's DOMA Ruling," *The White House* blog, June 27, 2013.

13. GLAAD, "Frequently Asked Questions: Defense of Marriage Act (DOMA)," glaad.org (n.d.), http://www.glaad.org/marriage/doma.

14. Alejandro Mayorkas, "Deferred Action for Childhood Arrivals: Who Can Be Considered?" *The White House* blog, August 15, 2012.

15. August Swanenberg, *Macroeconomics Demystified* (New York: McGraw-Hill, 2005), 228–229; Investopedia, "Keynesian Economics," Investopedia.com; Alan S. Blinder, "Keynesian Economics," *The Concise Encyclopedia of Economics*, David R. Henderson, ed. (Library of Economics and Liberty [Online], Liberty Fund, Inc., 2008), http://www.econlib.org/library/Enc/KeynesianEconomics.html.

16. Paul Krugman, "Conservative Origins of Obamacare," *The Conscience of a Liberal* blog, *New York Times*, July 27, 2011; John Aravosis, "Original 1989 Document Where Heritage Foundation Created Obamacare's Individual Mandate," *Americablog*, October 24, 2013, http://americablog.com/2013/10/original-1989-document-heritage-foundation-created-obamacares-individual-mandate.html.

17. Henry J. Kaiser Family Foundation, "Massachusetts Health Care Reform: Six Years Later," *Focus on Health Reform* (Washington, DC: Henry J. Kaiser Family Foundation, May 2012), 7–8.

18. Senator Jim DeMint quoted in Michael Grunwald, *The New New Deal: The Hidden Story of Change in the Obama Era* (New York: Simon & Schuster, 2012), 218.

19. Josh Bivens, "Abandoning What Works (and Most Other Things, Too): Expansionary Fiscal Policy Is Still the Best Tool for Boosting Jobs," *EPI Briefing Paper #304* (Economic Policy Institute, 2011), Figure C.

20. Justin Wolfers, "What Debate? Economists Agree the Stimulus Lifted the Economy," *The New York Times*, July 29, 2014.

21. Bivens, "Abandoning What Works," Figure C.

22. Grunwald, *The New New Deal*, 214.

23. Semm and Sanchez-Weston, "Waiting for Change: Obama and the LGBT Community."

24. Grunwald, *The New New Deal*, 218–226.

25. Mark Lisheron, "Texas Stimulus Opponents Later Sought Stimulus Funds for Their Districts," TexasWatchdog.org, October 18, 2010; John Solomon and Aaron Mehta, "Stimulating Hypocrisy: Scores of Recovery Act Opponents Sought Money out of Public View" (Washington, DC: The Center for Public Integrity, October 19, 2010).

26. Michael Linden and Michael Ettlinger, "Obama vs. Bush: Who's the Bigger Tax Cutter? Different Cuts Reflect Different Philosophies" (Washington, DC: Center for American Progress, September 13, 2011).

27. Recovery.gov, "Overview of the Funding," http://www.recovery.gov/arra/Transparency/fundingoverview/Pages/fundingbreakdown.aspx.

28. David M. Herszenhorn, "Congress Sends $801 Billion Tax Cut Bill to Obama," *New York Times*, December 16, 2010; Richard Rubin, "Obama Delivers on Tax Cut Promises," *Bloomberg.com*, April 17, 2012.

29. Robert Farley, "Fact Check: Obama on the 'Fiscal Cliff' Deal," *USA Today*, January 5, 2013.

30. Chuck Marr and Nathaniel Frentz, "Federal Income Taxes on Middle-Income Families Remain Near Historic Lows" (Washington, DC: Center on Budget and Policy Priorities, April 15, 2014).

31. Jake Tapper, "The Terrorist Notches on Obama's Belt," *ABCNews.com*, September 30, 2011.

32. Kevin Gosztola, "More Killing in Obama's 'War on Terror' Than Bush's 'War,'" *Firedoglake.com*, September 11, 2012.

33. Quoted in David Kravets, "Former CIA Chief: Obama's War on Terror Same as Bush's, But with More Killing," *Wired.com*, September 10, 2012.

34. U.S. Department of Homeland Security, "Border Security Results," November 1, 2013, http://www.dhs.gov/border-security-results.

35. Quoted in Louis Jacobson, "Barack Obama Touts Record High Border Agents, Lowest Immigration from Mexico in 40 Years," *Politifact.com*, October 17, 2012, http://www.politifact.com/truth-o-meter/statements/2012/oct/17/barack-obama/ barack-obama-touts-record-high-border-agents-lowes/.

36. Ibid.

37. Changes in policy and terminology and push and pull factors on immigrants make it impossible to accurately compare different administration's deportation statistics. However, the Obama administration has achieved a record number for "removals." Nora Caplan-Bricker, "Who's the Real Deporter-in-Chief: Bush or Obama?" *NewRepublic.com*, April 17, 2014.

38. Julia Preston, "Report Finds Deportations Focus on Criminal Records," *New York Times*, April 29, 2014.

39. Barack Obama, *The Audacity of Hope: Thoughts on Reclaiming the American Dream* (New York: Three Rivers Press, 2006), 255–256.

40. Barack Obama, Text of Obama's Fatherhood Speech, *Politico.com*, June 15, 2008.

41. Barack Obama, "Remarks by the President at Morehouse College Commencement Ceremony" (Washington, DC: The White House, Office of the Press Secretary, May 19, 2013), http://www.whitehouse.gov/the-press-office/2013/05/19/ remarks-president-morehouse-college-commencement-ceremony.

42. Paul N. Van de Water, "Health Reform Essential for Reducing Deficit and Slowing Health Care Costs" (Washington, DC: Center on Budget and Policy Priorities, 2010).

43. Henry J. Kaiser Family Foundation, "Snapshots: Health Care Spending in the United States & Selected OECD Countries" (Washington, DC: Henry J. Kaiser Family Foundation, April 12, 2011); New York State Department of Health, "Foreign Countries with Universal Health Care" (Albany, NY: NY.gov, April 2011), http://www.health.ny.gov/regulations/hcra/univ_hlth_care.htm.

44. Healthcare—NOW!, "What Is Single-Payer Healthcare?" (Philadelphia: Healthcare—NOW! n.d.), http://www.healthcare-now.org/whats-single-payer.

45. Krugman, "Conservative Origins of Obamacare"; Aravosis, "Original 1989 Document Where Heritage Foundation Created Obamacare's Individual Mandate."

46. Scott Horsley, "Obama Sticks with 'No Ransom' Strategy, Comes Out Ahead," NPR, October 17, 2013.

47. Grunwald, *The New New Deal*, 214.

48. Ibid.

49. Paul Krugman, "The Boehnerization of Barack Obama," *New York Times*, October 16, 2010.

50. Grunwald, *The New New Deal*, 334–335.

51. Ibid., 342.

52. Michael D. Shear, "Obama Budget Is Dismissed by G.O.P. and Attacked by Left," *New York Times*, April 5, 2013.

53. See Sharon O'Brien, "Why Is Social Security Called the Third Rail of American Politics?" *SeniorLiving.About.com*, http://seniorliving.about.com/od/socialsecurity 101/a/socialsecurity.htm; Paul Krugman, "Orwell and Social Security," *Conscience of a Liberal* blog, *New York Times*, August 24, 2010; William A. Galston, "Why the 2005

Social Security Initiative Failed, and What It Means for the Future" (Washington, DC: Brookings, September 21, 2007).

54. See David Cooper, "By the Numbers: Income and Poverty, 2013," *Working Economics* blog (Washington, DC: Economic Policy Institute, September 16, 2014).

55. See Maya M. Rockeymoore and Meizhu Lui, *Plan for a New Future: The Impact of Social Security Reform on People of Color* (Washington, DC: Commission to Modernize Social Security, 2011); Michael Lind, "Elizabeth Warren vs. the Neo-liberals: The Battle over Americans' Retirement Security," *Salon.com*, February 12, 2014.

56. Appendix Introduction Table 1.

Chapter 2

1. Ian Haney López discusses the rise of "color blindness" in law, politics, and social science as a rationale to deny racial discrimination and to block efforts at integration in Chapter 4 of *Dog Whistle Politics: How Coded Racial Appeals Have Reinvented Racism and Wrecked the Middle Class* (New York: Oxford University Press, 2014). López sees the social scientists Nathan Glazer and Daniel Patrick Moynihan in the 1960s as downplaying the significance of racial discrimination. Fred L. Pincus in *Reverse Discrimination: Dismantling the Myth* (Boulder, CO: Lynne Rienner, 2003, 52) finds that "[r]ather than seeing black inequality as caused by discrimination, [Glazer in a 1971 publication] argues that there is simply a lack of supply of educated, skilled black workers." Since the 1970s, Thomas Sowell has argued that cultural traits are the primary explanation of differences in the economic status of racial groups. See his *Race and Economics* (New York: D. McKay Co., 1975).

2. See Bill Cosby and Alvin F. Poussaint, MD, *Come On, People: On the Path from Victims to Victors* (Nashville, TN: Thomas Nelson, 2007); Juan Williams, *Enough: The Phony Leaders, Dead-End Movements, and Culture of Failure That Are Undermining Black America—and What We Can Do about It* (New York: Crown Publishers, 2006); Orlando Patterson, "A Poverty of the Mind," *New York Times*, March 26, 2006.

3. Barack Obama, *The Audacity of Hope: Thoughts on Reclaiming the American Dream* (New York: Three Rivers Press, 2006), 255–256.

4. Daniel Schorr, "A New, 'Post-Racial' Political Era in America," *All Things Considered*, NPR, January 28, 2008.

5. Henry Louis Gates, Jr., "Introduction," in *Barack Obama: A Pocket Biography of Our 44th President*, Steven J. Niven, ed. (New York: Oxford University Press, 2009), 2.

6. Jonetta Rose Barras, "He Leapt the Tallest Barrier. What Does It Mean for Black America?" *Washington Post*, November 9, 2008.

7. Mark P. Orbe, *Communication Realities in a "Post-Racial" Society: What the U.S. Public Really Thinks about Barack Obama* (Lanham, MD: Lexington Books, 2011), Chapter 6, "Barack Obama Transcends Race" section.

8. One way this manifested itself was in the argument that blacks now had "no excuses" for not being successful. Barras, "He Leapt the Tallest Barrier," is an example

of this argument. Wornie L. Reed and Bertin M. Louis, Jr., "'No More Excuses': Problematic Responses to Barack Obama's Election," *Journal of African American Studies*, 13 (2009): 97–109; Enid Logan, "*At This Defining Moment*": *Barack Obama's Presidential Candidacy and the New Politics of Race* (New York: NYU Press, 2011), Chapter 2, "No More Excuses" section.

9. Mark Berman, "Americans Increasingly Say Race Is the Country's Most Important Issue," *Washington Post*, December 19, 2014.

10. Since my concern is about individuals who have the potential to discriminate against blacks, the voting-age population as opposed to the voting-eligible population is the better reference.

11. Michael McDonald's "2008 General Election Turnout Rates," *United States Election Project*, http://www.electproject.org/2008g.

12. Author's calculations from "2008 General Election Turnout Rates," *United States Election Project* and *ElectionCenter2008*, *CNN.com*, http://www.cnn.com/ELECTION/2008/results/president/.

13. Mia Love and others have treated the election as evidence that Utahans are either antiracist or colorblind. See Justin Moyer, "Meet Mia Love. You'll Be Seeing a Lot More of the Republicans' First Black Congresswoman," *Washington Post*, November 5, 2014; Ryan Grenoble, "CNN's Interview with Mia Love Was One Big Communication Breakdown," *Huffington Post*, November 5, 2014.

14. Author's calculation of the voting-age population turnout rate from data from the U.S. Census Bureau's *My Congressional District*, http://www.census.gov/mycd/, and Utah.gov's *Utah Election Preliminary Results*, "US Congressional District 4," http://electionresults.utah.gov/elections/uscongress/4. Michael McDonald's estimate for the entire state is 27.5 percent. "2014 November General Election Turnout Rates," *United States Election Project*, http://www.electproject.org/2014g.

15. Real Clear Politics, "Utah 4th District—Love vs. Owens," http://www.realclearpolitics.com/epolls/2014/house/ut/utah_4th_district_love_vs_owens-5130.html.

16. See Grenoble, "CNN's Interview with Mia Love."

17. Philip Bump, "The Chart Summarizing the 2014 Election That We Never Intended For You to See," *Washington Post*, December 8, 2014.

18. Richard T. Schaefer, *Racial and Ethnic Groups*, 8th ed. (Upper Saddle River, NJ: Prentice Hall, 2000), 55.

19. The radio program *This American Life* provides an example of a white man who works amicably with blacks but is upset that his children has black friends, and he refuses to vote for Obama because of his race. "Act three: Union halls," *Ground Game*, Episode 367 (radio broadcast) (Chicago: Chicago Public Radio, October 24, 2008).

20. Andrew Grant-Thomas, "Does Barack Obama's Victory Herald a Post-Racial America?" *Colorlines.com*, December 5, 2008.

21. Michael Powell, "Democrats in Steel Country See Color, and Beyond It," *New York Times*, October 26, 2008.

22. *This American Life*, "Act Three: Union Halls," *Ground Game*, Episode 367 (radio broadcast) (Chicago: Chicago Public Radio, October 24, 2008).

23. Ben Smith, "Racists for Obama?" *Politico.com*, October 18, 2008.

24. Appendix, Table 2.1.

25. Lester Feder, "Dreams of My . . . Grandparents? Obama's Campaign Ad Omits All Mention of His Father," *Huffington Post*, June 28, 2008; Jennifer Steinhauer, "Volunteers for Obama Face a Complex Issue," *New York Times*, October 14, 2008; Shankar Vendantham, *The Hidden Brain: How Our Unconscious Minds Elect Presidents, Control Markets, Wage Wars, and Save Our Lives* (New York: Spiegel & Grau, 2010), 220–221.

26. Sam Roberts and Peter Baker, "Asked to Declare His Race, Obama Checks 'Black,'" *New York Times*, April 2, 2010.

27. F. James Davis, *Who Is Black?: One Nation's Definition* (University Park, PA: Pennsylvania State University Press, 1991).

28. Kerry Ann Rockquemore and David L. Brunsma, *Beyond Black: Biracial Identity in America* (Thousand Oaks, CA: Sage Publications, Inc., 2002).

29. Davis, *Who Is Black?*

30. Quoted in Vendantham, *The Hidden Brain*, 214.

31. Steinhauer, "Volunteers for Obama Face a Complex Issue."

32. Ibid.

33. Pew Social and Demographic Trends, *Blacks Upbeat about Black Progress, Prospects: A Year after Obama's Election* (Washington, DC: Pew Research Center, 2010).

34. Samuel Sinyangwe, "The Significance of Mixed-Race: Public Perceptions of Barack Obama's Race and Its Effect on His Favorability," *Stanford Undergraduate Research Journal*, 11 (Spring 2012): 87–94.

35. Quoted in Vendantham, *The Hidden Brain*, 229.

36. See, for example, Mark E. Hill, "Color Differences in the Socioeconomic Status of African American Men: Results of a Longitudinal Study," *Social Forces* 78, no. 4 (2000): 1437–1460; Arthur H. Goldsmith, Darrick Hamilton, and William Darity, Jr., "From Dark to Light: Skin Color and Wages among African-Americans," *Journal of Human Resources*, XLII, no. 4 (2007): 701–738.

37. Orbe, *Communication Realities*, Chapter 6, "Barack Obama Transcends Race" section.

38. See the discussion in Algernon Austin, "The Unfinished March: An Overview" (Washington, DC: Economic Policy Institute, 2013).

39. Ezekiel Edwards, Will Bunting, and Lynda Garcia, *The War on Marijuana in Black and White: Billions of Dollars Wasted in Racially-Biased Arrests* (New York: American Civil Liberties Union, 2013); Michelle Alexander, *The New Jim Crow: Mass Incarceration in the Age of Colorblindness*, rev. ed. (New York: The New Press, 2012); A. Rafik Mohamed and Erik D. Fritsvold, *Dorm Room Dealers: Drugs and the Privileges of Race and Class* (Boulder, CO: Lynne Rienner Publishers, 2011).

40. The Obama administration did reduce—but did not eliminate—the crack-versus-cocaine sentencing disparity in the federal criminal justice system. There are also disparities at the state level. Nicole D. Porter and Valerie Wright, "Cracked Justice" (Washington, DC: The Sentencing Project, 2011). More important, institutional discrimination in the criminal justice system encompasses much more than just this disparity in sentencing.

41. Vincent L. Hutchings, "Change or More of the Same? Evaluating Racial Attitudes in the Obama Era," *Public Opinion Quarterly*, 73, no. 5 (2009), 917–942.

42. Suzi Parker, "In Arkansas, Racism Cuts against Obama," *Washington Post,* May 25, 2012.

43. Ibid.

44. Kevin Merida, "Racist Incidents Give Some Obama Campaigners Pause," *Washington Post,* May 13, 2008; Martin A. Parlett, *Demonizing a President: The "Foreignization" of Barack Obama* (Santa Barbara, CA: Praeger, 2014), ix–xii; Tim Wise, *Between Barack and a Hard Place: Racism and White Denial in the Age of Obama* (San Francisco, CA: City Lights Books, 2009), 150n2.

45. Ibid.

46. Nadia Y. Kim, "Campaigning for Obama and the Politics of Race: The Case of California, Texas, and Beyond," *Research in Race and Ethnic Relations,* 16 (2010): 247–266.

47. Parlett, *Demonizing a President,* xi.

48. *This American Life,* "Act Three: Union Halls."

49. Ibid.

50. Merida, "Racist Incidents Rattle Obama Backers."

51. Michael Tesler and David O. Sears, *Obama's Race: The 2008 Election and the Dream of a Post-Racial America* (Chicago: The University of Chicago Press, 2010).

52. Ibid., Chapter 8, "Concluding Remarks" section.

53. John Amato and David Neiwert, *Over the Cliff: How Obama's Election Drove the American Right Insane* (Sausalito, CA: PoliPointPress, 2010), 4–5.

54. Ibid., 1–2; Orbe, *Communication Realities,* "Black Perceptions of White Opposition to President Obama" section; Larry Keller, "Racist Backlash Greets New U.S. President," *Intelligence Report,* Spring 2009, Issue Number: 133.

55. Quoted in Amato and Neiwert, *Over the Cliff,* 2.

56. Quoted in Orbe, *Communication Realities,* Chapter 8, "Black Perceptions of White Opposition to President Obama" section.

57. Ibid.

58. Quoted in Vendantham, *The Hidden Brain,* 214.

59. Merida, "Racist Incidents Give Some Obama Campaigners Pause"; Parlett, *Demonizing a President,* ix–xii.

60. Quoted in Tesler and Sears, *Obama's Race,* Chapter 3, "Race in the General Election Campaign," section, emphasis in the original text.

61. Bill Bishop, *The Big Sort: Why the Clustering of Like-Minded America Is Tearing Us Apart* (New York: Houghton Mifflin Harcourt, 2008).

62. The campaign workers Martin A. Parlett (*Demonizing a President*) and Nadia Y. Kim ("Campaigning for Obama") turned to academic publishing to tell their and their coworkers' stories. Others e-mailed the antiracism activist Tim Wise. Wise, *Between Barack and a Hard Place,* 150n2.

63. Others have discussed this issue in different ways. Gunnar Myrdal does so directly in *An American Dilemma: The Negro Problem and Modern Democracy* (New York: Harper & Brothers Publishers, 1944). Ezra Klein notes that research shows that people often use their reasoning ability to support erroneous ideas that conform to their biases. There is no reason to think that this process would not exist around biases related to racial issues. "How Politics Makes Us Stupid," *Vox.com,* April 6, 2014.

64. Jay Smooth, "TEDxHampshireCollege—How I Learned to Stop Worrying and Love Discussing Race [video]," November 15, 2011, https://www.youtube.com/watch?v=MbdxeFcQtaU.

65. A specifically racial slavery began in approximately 1660. Winthrop D. Jordan, *White over Black: American Attitudes toward the Negro, 1550–1812* (New York: Norton, 1977).

Chapter 3

1. Verbatim text: "He's a Muslim radical set to destroy the country, replace the constitution with Shariha law, and become dictator. He is an illegal sitting as president and should be on trial for treason with the senile democratic leadership."

2. James A. Stimson, *Tides of Consent: How Public Opinion Shapes American Politics* (New York: Cambridge University Press, 2004), Chapter 5: Between the Campaigns, "The National Economy" section.

3. Vincent Hutchings, Gary Segura, Simon Jackman, and Ted Brader (principal investigators), *American National Election Study 2012* (electronic data file), (Arbor, MI, and Palo Alto, CA: the University of Michigan and Stanford University, 2013), accessed via *SDA: Survey Documentation and Analysis* (Berkeley: University of California, Berkeley, 2014).

4. Correlations and the Cronbach's alpha for these elements can be found in Appendix, Table 3.1.

5. There was a change in the response categories for the ANGRY and AFRAID survey questions from the 2004 to the 2012 ANES. If one uses the "cold" feeling-thermometer level only to define *Haters*, one also finds equivalent levels of *Bush Haters* and *Obama Haters*.

6. Appendix, Introduction Table 1.

7. A total of 22.6 percent of *Haters* had a bachelor's degree as their highest level of education compared to 20.2 percent for the entire sample; 25.3 percent of *Haters* had a high school diploma as their highest level of education compared to 28.4 percent for the sample overall.

8. Appendix, Table 3.3.

9. Appendix, Table 3.4.

10. **Obama Hater 370**.

11. Verbatim text: "He cannot tell the truth, hates any business that is successful, passes regulations that strangle our economy, tramples on our constitution, illegally bypasses congress, and seems to want to bring down our country so that it is not the greatest country in the world anymore. He is not a proud American, he is a Globalist. The horrible economy in the US can be directly laid at his and his appointee's feet."

12. Verbatim text: "He's a communist dictator wanna-be who has no respect for God, our history, our constitution, our freedoms, our culture, our borders, our military, or our tax money, or for Israel or the truth. Also, he's a pro-terrorist Muslim anti-colonialist with an animus toward Whites in general and American Whites in particular. He has no love for this country or its people. He's also narcissistic

and will say anything or do anything to get his way . . . a man to be feared not respected."

13. Verbatim text: "I think he HATES this country. Everything has gone the wrong way ever since he became president. I do not like the way he is always apologizing for our country. He is very bad for our country and it seems he is doing everything he can to ruin our country."

14. Stimson, *Tides of Consent*, Chapter 5: Between the Campaigns, "The National Economy" section.

15. Verbatim text: "badly mishandling finances resulting in astronomical budget deficits and continuing weak economy. He also seems totally ideological and has not adjusted policies despite past clear cut failures."

16. Verbatim text: "Everything; He's taken us into bankruptcy, our whole country; he's raised our debt and we have almost no chance of getting out of it// he has made us a laughing stock//he's made us a weak country//he has disgraced our military; took away our space program//I mean there's no good things he's done.//"

17. Verbatim text: "Rule by Executive Order rather than by legislation. 2) Out of control spending. 3) Excessive regulations by EPA and other agencies."

18. Verbatim text: "He did not improve the economy, he made it worse."

19. Verbatim text: "I do not trust him and he has made a lot of really bad changes that are hurting our economy."

20. Verbatim text: "The fact that he hasnt done anything in the past 4 years; lies about unemployment rate; lies about money he spent; lies that he is a Christian.//"

21. Verbatim text: "lyar lyar pants on fire. He kept no promises and is hurting the economy and tax payers. If you are on the dole, he is your guy. He is a marxist. He embaresses our country by being week and appolgizing for the USA prosperity. He is too week on crime. His cabinet is full of corrupt politicians. Erik Holder is a lyer."

22. Verbatim text: "he said he would be transparent—he lied he said things would get better for America—he lied we are not in a better place—he has spent money we do not have, he has given money to people without a payback plan, he, I feel, is destroying the America I grew up knowing. and believing in. . . ."

23. Verbatim text: "He lies, he abuses the constitution, he doesn't do his job, and he had led this country down a path that is hell. He is more interested in smoozing with movie stars than in attending necessary briefings, and he surrounds himself with Chicago Mafia—and look what has happened to some of them. They don't tell the truth either."

24. Verbatim text: "Acts like a used car salesman, doesnt produce what he says// has lied to american people.// something fishy about birth certificate, dont think he is an american citizen//more for self thn american people//takes money from medicare to support obamacare//not that he is black, even worse than carter.//no."

25. Verbatim text: "4 years of nothing but debt and obamacare. the man has done nothing but travel and play. i dont think he really knows what's going on."

26. Verbatim text: "He is leading this country into financial disaster. I would vote for any one that is qualified before voting for (I hope) our current Pres."

27. Verbatim text: "I work very hard for my income, 60 to 70 hours a week. I currently make less then half of what I made 4 years ago before he was elected plus all my expenses went up. He is an amateur and has no idea what he is doing. Everything he

has tried has failed, the companies he has backed etc. and yet he still wants to take what I have and give it to people that don't want to work at all."

28. Verbatim text: "COMUNISTA/SOCIALISTA/ATEO/DISCIPULO DE SOL ALINSKY."

29. Verbatim text: "Big government—socialist—large deficits—out of control spending and regulation—not focused on the economy—not focused on jobs—will sacrifice the common good of people just to stay elected."

30. Verbatim text: "He has done a very poor job of running the country. He has created the highest debt America has ever been in. He is a socialist liberal that only does to suit himself and not the american people. He was not born in the USA!"

31. Verbatim text: "His love of huge government, communism, and his undying support of the muslim faith. So, pretty much everything he is for."

32. Verbatim text: "marxist anticolonist, he is destroying the country with the other progressives."

33. This analysis basically fits the party typologies presented by Matt Grossman and David A. Hopkins in "More Proof That Republicans Are from Mars and Democrats Are from Venus," *Monkey Cage* blog, *Washington Post*, March 10, 2015.

34. Associated Press, "Palin: Obama Pals around with Terrorists," *USA Today*, October 4, 2008.

35. Jim Rutenberg and Ashley Parker, "Romney Says Remarks on Voters Help Clarify Position," *New York Times*, September 18, 2012. There are many things he was wrong about regarding "the 47 percent." They pay no federal income taxes, but many of them do pay payroll taxes, sales taxes, property taxes, and other taxes. In fact, many of them pay a larger share of their income in taxes than Mitt Romney. Contrary to Romney's statement they are probably more likely to vote Republican than Democratic. For more errors, see Juliet Lapidos, "The 47 Percent," *Taking Note* blog, *New York Times*, September 18, 2012.

36. *The Ed Show*, "Romney Tells Students to Borrow Money 'From Your Parents,'" *MSNBC.com*, April 27, 2012.

37. Nicholas Kristof, "How Romney Would Treat Women," *New York Times*, November 3, 2012.

38. See the mention in Ed O'Keefe and Robert Costa, "Jeb Bush, Scott Walker Emerging as Front-Runners for GOP Nod—and Rivals," *Washington Post*, March 10, 2015.

39. David Morgan, Roberta Rampton, and Susan Cornwell, "House Votes to Repeal and Eventually Replace Obamacare," *Reuters*, February 3, 2015.

40. Thomas Edsall, "The Anti-Entitlement Strategy," *Campaign Stops* blog, *New York Times*, December 25, 2011; Mitt Romney, "Why I'd Repeal Obamacare," *USA Today*, March 22, 2012.

41. Appendix, Table 5.3.

Chapter 4

1. Quoted in Christopher S. Parker and Matt A. Barreto, *Change They Can't Believe In: The Tea Party and Reactionary Politics in America* (Princeton, NJ: Princeton

University Press, 2013), Conclusion, "Postscript: The 2012 Election" section. Verbatim text: "How dare you state that Republicans are criticizing Barrack Obama because he is black? What evidence do you have of that? We judge him by the content of his character, not the color of his skin. We criticize him because his ignorance, incompetence, and arrogance is destroying this country, the greatest one on earth."

2. Melinda Deslatte, "Sen. Landrieu's Remarks on Race Anger Republicans," *Yahoo! News*, October 30, 2014.

3. Verbatim text: "His track record.//Fast and Furious.//Benghazi.//Lack of leadership in that the Democrats have not passed a budget in 3 years.//The stimulus.//Healthcare.//His disengenuous nature.//Use of czars to by-pass congress.//While Rome was burning Obama was playing golf.//He was and still is unqualified for the office of President of the United States// no."

4. Verbatim text: "4 years of nothing but debt and obamacare. the man has done nothing but travel and play. i dont think he really knows what's going on."

5. Verbatim text: "he prefers to play golf and go on talk shows and play basketball with friends-than take care of business. He prefers to spend his time with movie stars and not pay attention to world affairs. His wife and him are on vacation all the time."

6. Appendix, Table 4.1.

7. Ibid.

8. Appendix, Table 4.2.

9. An online comment to a *New York Times* article quoted in Sheryll Cashin, *Place, Not Race: A New Vision of Opportunity in America* (Boston: Beacon Press, 2014), 11–12.

10. Appendix, Table 4.5.

11. Appendix, Table 4.6.

12. See the discussion in Algernon Austin, "The Unfinished March: An Overview" (Washington, DC: Economic Policy Institute), June 18, 2013, http://www.epi.org/publication/unfinished-march-overview/; Valerie E. Lee, and David T. Burkam, *Inequality at the Starting Gate: Social Background Differences in Achievement as Children Begin School* (Washington, DC: Economic Policy Institute, 2002); Karen J. DeAngelis, Bradford R. White, and Jennifer B. Presley, "The Changing Distribution of Teacher Qualifications across Schools: A Statewide Perspective Post-NCLB," *Education Policy Analysis Archives* 18, no. 28 (November 2010): 1–34; Jennifer Y. Cheng, "At Home and in School: Racial and Ethnic Gaps in Educational Preparedness," *California Counts: Population Trends and Profiles* 3, no. 2 (2001) (San Francisco: Public Policy Institute of California).

13. Marianne Bertrand and Sendhil Mullainathan, "Are Emily and Greg More Employable Than Lakisha and Jamal: A Field Experiment on Labor Market Discrimination," *American Economic Review* 94, no. 4: 991–1013. See also Devah Pager, Bruce Western, and Bart Bonikowski, "Discrimination in a Low-Wage Labor Market: A Field Experiment," *American Sociological Review*, 74 (October 2009): 777–799.

14. See the discussion in Algernon Austin, "The Unfinished March: An Overview" (Washington, DC: Economic Policy Institute), June 18, 2013, http://www.epi.org/publication/unfinished-march-overview/.

15. Ezekiel Edwards, Will Bunting, and Lynda Garcia, *The War on Marijuana in Black and White: Billions of Dollars Wasted in Racially Biased Arrests* (New York: American Civil Liberties Union, 2013).

16. Marc Mauer, *Race to Incarcerate* (New York: The New Press, 2006).

17. Author's calculations based on Federal Bureau of Investigation, "Table 1. Incidents, Offenses, Victims, and Known Offenders by Bias Motivation, 2012," *2012 Hate Crime Statistics* (Washington, DC: U.S. Department of Justice, 2013), and 2012 American Community Survey race and ethnicity data from Steven Ruggles, J. Trent Alexander, Katie Genadek, Ronald Goeken, Matthew B. Schroeder, and Matthew Sobek, *Integrated Public Use Microdata Series: Version 5.0* (Machine-readable database) (Minneapolis: University of Minnesota, 2014). If everyone were equally likely of being subject to a hate crime, the distribution of hate-crime incidents by race and ethnicity would be the same as the population distribution. Since blacks made up 12 percent of the population in 2012, they would have been victims in 12 percent of the hate-crime incidents. Instead, blacks were victims in 52 percent of the total of all of the racial and ethnicity hate-crime incidents. Blacks were victimized 4.2 times what one would expect if hate crimes were equal-opportunity crimes, but whites were victimized 0.3 times what one would expect. This black rate of victimization is 14 times the white rate.

18. For example, in a community in Long Island, New York, where Latino immigrants were regularly harassed and assaulted, the immigrants told the *New York Times* that they "never report such incidents because they do not trust the police and fear deportation." Kirk Semple, "A Killing in a Town Where Latinos Sense Hate," *New York Times*, November 13, 2008.

19. Appendix, Table 4.7.

20. Appendix, Table 4.8.

21. Hispanic Trends Project, "Table 1. Population, by Race and Ethnicity: 2000 and 2012," (Washington, DC: Pew Research Center), http://www.pewhispanic.org/2014/04/29/statistical-portrait-of-hispanics-in-the-united-states-2012/.

22. Jennifer E. Manning, *Membership of the 112th Congress: A Profile* (Washington, DC: Congressional Research Service, 2012). There is some contradictory information about the Hispanic number due to the different definitions who is Hispanic. See Suzanne Gamboa, "How Many Latinos Are in the House of Representatives?" *Huffington Post*, February 5, 2013.

23. *Who Leads US?* http://wholeads.us, a project of the Reflective Democracy Campaign of the Women Donors Network (San Francisco, CA: WDN, 2014).

24. Author's analysis of the 2013 American Community Survey data from Steven Ruggles, J. Trent Alexander, Katie Genadek, Ronald Goeken, Matthew B. Schroeder, and Matthew Sobek, *Integrated Public Use Microdata Series: Version 5.0* (Machine-readable database) (Minneapolis: University of Minnesota, 2014).

25. Tom File, "The Diversifying Electorate—Voting Rates by Race and Hispanic Origin in 2012 (and Other Recent Elections)," *Population Characteristics: Current Population Survey*, (Washington, DC: U.S. Census Bureau, 2013), 5.

26. Sentencing Project, "Felony Disenfranchisement" (Washington, DC: Sentencing Project, n.d.), http://www.sentencingproject.org/template/page.cfm?id=133.

27. The 2012 election was the only recent election where the black turnout rate exceeded the white rate. The Hispanic rate remained much lower than the white rate. File, "The Diversifying Electorate."

28. Carmen DeNavas-Walt and Bernadette D. Proctor, "Table A-1. Households by Total Money Income, Race, and Hispanic Origin of Householder: 1967 to 2013," in *Income and Poverty in the United States: 2013*, U.S. Census Bureau, Current Population Reports, P60-249 (Washington, DC: U.S. Government Printing Office, 2014).

29. Rakesh Kochhar and Richard Fry, "Wealth Inequality Has Widened along Racial, Ethnic Lines since End of Great Recession" (Washington, DC: Pew Research Center, December 12, 2014), http://www.pewresearch.org/fact-tank/2014/12/12/racial-wealth-gaps-great-recession/.

30. Appendix, Table 4.9.

31. Zerlina Maxwell, "Obama Says He's Not 'President of Black America'—Turns Out He's Right," *The Grio*, August 8, 2012.

32. Paul Glastris, "Introduction: Race, History, and Obama's Second Term," *Washington Monthly*, January/February 2013.

33. The American Recovery and Reinvestment Act, for example, contained several provisions for businesses. Katherine Lim and Roberton Williams of the Tax Policy Center discuss some of them in "Economic Stimulus: What Does the American Recovery and Reinvestment Act Do for Businesses?," *Tax Policy Briefing Book* (Washington, DC: Urban Institute; Brookings Institution, 2009), http://www.taxpolicycenter.org/briefing-book/background/stimulus/ARRA_business.cfm.

34. Appendix, Tables 4.10 and 4.11.

35. Ibid.

Chapter 5

1. The more common and explicitly racist terms were prohibited from the site. Adam Murphree and Deirdre A. Royster, "Race Threads and Race Threats: How Obama/Race-Discourse among Conservatives Changed through the 2008 Presidential Campaign," *Research in Race and Ethnic Relations*, 16 (2010): 287 and 291.

2. Quotations from Murphree and Royster, "Race Threads and Race Threats," 285.

3. Enid Logan, *"At This Defining Moment": Barack Obama's Presidential Candidacy and the New Politics of Race* (New York: NYU Press, 2011), Chapter 7, "Who Is the Real Barack Obama?"

4. Nadia Y. Kim, "Campaigning for Obama and the Politics of Race: The Case of California, Texas, and Beyond," *Research in Race and Ethnic Relations*, 16 (2010): 259 and 263.

5. Quoted in Michael Tesler and David O. Sears, *Obama's Race: The 2008 Election and the Dream of a Post-Racial America* (Chicago: The University of Chicago Press, 2010), Chapter 7, Introduction.

6. Quoted in Tesler and Sears, *Obama's Race*, Chapter 7, "Concluding Remarks: Obama as 'Other.'"

7. Logan, *"At This Defining Moment*," Chapter 7, "Who Is the Real Barack Obama?"

8. Michael Dobbs, "John McCain's Birthplace," *Washington Post*, May 20, 2008.

9. Mark Hosenball, "Romney's Birth Certificate Evokes His Father's Controversy," *Reuters*, May 29, 2012.

10. There have been minor challenges to George Romney's, Mitt Romney's, and John McCain's eligibility to run for office, but there has not been attacks and opposition on the scale that Obama has received. We can get a sense of the difference in the challenges to Obama and McCain in the Google Trends for the searches "Obama birth certificate" and "McCain birth certificate." From January 2007 to January 2009, the Obama search averages a score of five but the McCain search averages a score of zero. Both searches peak the week of November 2 to November 8, 2008, but the Obama search peaks at 100 and the McCain search peaks at five.

11. Derald Sue and Michel Martin, "Microaggressions: Be Careful What You Say," *Tell Me More, NPR*, April 3, 2014.

12. Eric Sorensen, "Asian Groups Attack MSNBC Headline Referring to Kwan—News Web Site Apologizes for Controversial Wording," *Seattle Times*, March 3, 1998.

13. Mike Fancher, "Times Won't Forget Readers' Reminder on Kwan Headline," *Seattle Times*, March 3, 2002.

14. Shankar Vedantam, "Does Your Subconscious Think Obama Is Foreign?" *Washington Post*, October 13, 2008.

15. Ibid.

16. Ibid.

17. Appendix, Table 5.1.

18. Ibid.

19. See Appendix, Table 5.2, for full regression results. Angie Maxwell, Pearl Ford Dowe, and Todd Shields found the same relationship between racial resentment and the belief that Obama is Muslim. Angie Maxwell, Pearl Ford Dowe, and Todd Shields, "The Next Link in the Chain Reaction: Symbolic Racism and Obama's Religious Affiliation," *Social Science Quarterly* 94, no. 2 (June 2012): 321–343.

20. Anand Giridharadas, "Immigrants, Nationhood and the U.S.," *New York Times*, May 26, 2014.

21. Megan Burke, Maureen Cavanaugh, and Peter Schrag, "The Long View on American Attitudes toward Immigration," *KPBS.org*, May 10, 2011.

22. Burke, Cavanaugh, and Schrag, "The Long View on American Attitudes toward Immigration"; Richard T. Schaefer, *Racial and Ethnic Groups*, 8th ed. (Upper Saddle River, NJ: Prentice Hall, 2000), 108–113.

23. Matthew Frye Jacobson, *Whiteness of a Different Color: European Immigrants and the Alchemy of Race* (Cambridge: Harvard University Press, 1998); Karen Brodkin, *How Jews Became White Folks and What That Says about Race in America* (New Brunswick, NJ: Rutgers University Press, 1998).

24. Office of the Historian, "Milestones: 1921–1936: The Immigration Act of 1924 (The Johnson-Reed Act)" (Washington, DC: U.S. Department of State, n.d.), http://history.state.gov/milestones/1921–1936/immigration-act; Jacobson, *Whiteness of a Different Color*; Schaefer, *Racial and Ethnic Groups*, 108–113.

25. Robert P. Jones et al., *What Americans Want from Immigration Reform in 2014: Findings from the PRRI/Brookings Religion, Values, and Immigration Reform Survey, Panel Call Back* (Washington, DC: Public Religion Research Institute; The Brookings Institution, 2014).

26. Appendix, Table 5.3.

27. For example, the following author who is anti-Obama is pro-Cruz-for-president: razshafer, "It's Time to Draft Ted Cruz for President," *RedState.com*, March 19, 2014. As of March 2015, Ted Cruz does not appear to have any major unusual negatives among Republican voters. A total of 40 percent of Republican primary voters—a group that would likely include a significant amount of Obama Haters—could see supporting him. This places him in the middle of a crowded field. *Washington Wire* blog, "Where Ted Cruz Stands in Early GOP Polls," *Wall Street Journal*, March 23, 2015.

28. Chris Gentilviso, "Arnold Schwarzenegger 2016? Former Governor Mulls Rule Change Push to Run for President," *The Huffington Post*, October 19, 2013.

29. The very end of the response was cut off after the "a" in "a[ll." This is my guess as to the final words based on the U.S. Army oath. "Oaths of Enlistment and Oaths of Office," U.S. Army Center of Military History, http://www.history.army.mil/html/faq/oaths.html. Verbatim text: "Besides everything he has done so far, I don't believe he is an American. I think he is a terrorist sympathizer. Also the fact that he pulled our Marines out of the embassy in Egypt. He pulled those Marines out and made it so our embassy would be over run and the Taliban would take over without blood shed. He is selling us out. We are going to have a revolution in this country. Right now there are veterans and we have all fought for our flag; we took a oath to protect our country against a."

30. Verbatim text: "He is not from the UNITED STATE OF AMERICA, and not for the people of this country. Obamacare."

31. Verbatim text: "He is not from the united states, he has lied for years about a false birth certificate, and he is running our country in the ground."

32. Verbatim text: "He's not an American, he lies, he disrespect America and Americans."

33. Verbatim text: "I don't trust him and I don't think he has our best interest for the United States. I don't think he was born in the states."

34. Verbatim text: "wetbacks people from other countries that slipped in."

35. Verbatim text: ". . . the mexicans in the US."

36. Verbatim text: "immigration, get them out."

37. **Hater MIP3 138.**

38. **Hater MIP2 20.** Verbatim text: "Concerned about freedom in the near future, free speech, right to bare arms, islam growth, illegal imagriants getting financial aid from the government!!!!!!!!!!!"

39. **Hater MIP2 394.**

40. **Hater MIP2 273.** Verbatim text: "our welfare intitiative is getting out of hand. we are not adressing it, just giving out more and to people who aren't even citizens who are not paying into the system."

41. Jeffrey S. Passel, D'Vera Cohn, and Ana Gonzalez-Barrera, "Population Decline of Unauthorized Immigrants Stalls, May Have Reversed: New Estimate: 11.7 Million in 2012" (Washington, DC: Pew Hispanic Center, 2013).

42. Passel, Cohn, and Gonzalez-Barrera, "Population Decline of Unauthorized Immigrants Stalls, May Have Reversed"; Daniel Costa, David Cooper, and Heidi Shierholz, "Facts about Immigration and the U.S. Economy: Answers to Frequently Asked Questions" (Washington, DC: Economic Policy Institute, 2014).

43. Appendix, Table 5.4.

44. Appendix, Table 3.3.

45. Appendix, Table 5.11.

Chapter 6

1. Quoted in Peter Wallsten, "Frank Talk of Obama and Race in Virginia," *Los Angeles Times*, October 8, 2008.

2. *CNN.com*, "CNN Debunks False Report about Obama," January 23, 2007.

3. James Barron, "9 Jewish Leaders Say E-Mail Spread Lies about Obama," *New York Times*, January 16, 2008.

4. Enid Logan, *"At This Defining Moment": Barack Obama's Presidential Candidacy and the New Politics of Race* (New York: NYU Press, 2011), Chapter 7, "Anti-American Obama."

5. Journalism Project Staff, *The Media, Religion and the 2012 Campaign for President* (Washington, DC: Pew Research Center, 2012), 3.

6. J. Bennett Guess, "Barack Obama, Candidate for President, Is 'UCC,'" UCC. org, February 8, 2007, http://www.ucc.org/barack-obama-candidate.

7. See the discussion in Charles M. Blow, "A Blacklash?" *New York Times*, May 3, 2008; Lisa Miller, "Cover Story: Barack Obama's Christian Journey," *Newsweek*, July 11, 2008. It is interesting to note that potentially offensive statements made by the pastors of John McCain and Sarah Palin never developed into controversies. See Shankar Vendantham, *The Hidden Brain: How Our Unconscious Minds Elect Presidents, Control Markets, Wage Wars, and Save Our Lives* (New York: Spiegel & Grau, 2010), 218.

8. Tricia Sartor and Dana Page, "Obama Rumors Get More Press," Journalism Project (Washington, DC: Pew Research Center, July 17, 2008).

9. Lisa Miller, "Cover Story: Barack Obama's Christian Journey," *Newsweek*, July 11, 2008.

10. Laurie Goodstein, "Without a Pastor of His Own, Obama Turns to Five," *New York Times*, March 14, 2009.

11. Religion and Public Life Project, *Little Voter Discomfort with Romney's Mormon Religion* (Washington, DC: Pew Research Center, 2012).

12. Appendix, Table 6.1.

13. Council on American-Islamic Relations—California, *The Status of Muslim Civil Rights in California, 2014* (Anaheim, CA: Council on American-Islamic Relations—California, 2014), 18.

14. Ibid. Verbatim text: "I do not approve of this, this is America!"

15. Council on American-Islamic Relations-California, *Growing in Faith: California Muslim Youth Experiences with Bullying, Harassment, and Religious Accommodation in Schools* (Anaheim, CA: Council on American-Islamic Relations-California, 2014).

16. See the discussion in Michael Charles Grillo, "The Social Psychology of Leadership and Followership in Symbolic Politics Theory: The Case of Islamophobia in American Politics" (Ph.D. diss., University of Delaware, 2011), 15–57. Only 14 percent of Americans say that they know a lot about Islam. Robert P. Jones et al., *What It Means to Be American: Attitudes in an Increasingly Diverse America Ten Years after 9/11* (Washington, DC: Public Religion Research Institute, Inc.; Governance Studies at Brookings, 2011), 10.

17. Grillo, "The Social Psychology of Leadership and Followership," 34–36.

18. Pew Center for the People and the Press, "After Boston, Little Change in Views of Islam and Violence: 45% Say Muslim Americans Face 'A Lot' of Discrimination" (Washington, DC: Pew Research Center, 2013).

19. Jones et al., *What It Means to Be American*, 10–11.

20. Arab American Institute, "American Attitudes toward Arabs and Muslims" (Washington, DC, 2014), 9.

21. Verbatim text: "You want the top 10 or the whole list? He's Muslim and the proof is all over the place, but people refuse to see it. Whether out of ignorance (lazy) or blind loyalty doesn't matter. Evidence is there. Straight from the jackasses mouth: If he has to choose between American and Muslim, he will side with his Muslim brethren. I could give example after example. He has apologized and kowtowed to every nation in the world that we should be watching like a hawk. Showing weakness and subservience is no."

22. Verbatim text: "Birth certificate He is a Muslim No flags anywhere around him He says things he doesn't believe."

23. Verbatim text: "Dishonesty, negative history, unAmerican values, Islam values."

24. Verbatim text: "He has an unhealthy attitude toward Islam and it's relationship to our democratic society. He is a tax and spend liberal that continues to increase the debt of our nation. He is favorable toward disposing of human life through abortion. He is in favor of redefining morality in that he supports gay marriage. Etc. Etc."

25. Verbatim text: "he is not an american he is probably a muslim adn he does not have american values or christian values."

26. Verbatim text: "He's a Muslim radical set to destroy the country, replace the constitution with Shariha law, and become dictator. He is an illegal sitting as president and should be on trial for treason with the senile democratic leadership."

27. Verbatim text: "likes Muslims more than likes us, he's a dictator and a socialist// he's a liar//no."

28. Verbatim text: "pretends to be Protestant while having Muslim sympathies and Atheistic policies!"

29. Michael Tesler and David O. Sears, *Obama's Race: The 2008 Election and the Dream of a Post-Racial America* (Chicago: The University of Chicago Press, 2010), Chapter 7, "Method" section.

30. Tesler and Sears found an effect even among those who said that they knew he was not Muslim. *Obama's Race*, Chapter 7, "The Mistaken Identity Hypothesis" section.

31. Appendix, Table 6.1.

32. Appendix, Table 6.2.

33. A total of 48.6 percent of the ANES sample say that Mormons are not Christians.

34. Appendix, Table 6.2.

35. Appendix, Table 6.3.

36. Appendix, Table 6.4.

37. Appendix, Table 5.10.

38. Cindy D. Kam and Donald R. Kinder, "Ethnocentrism as a Short-Term Force in the 2008 American Presidential Election," *American Journal of Political Science*, 56, no. 2 (April 2012): 326–340.

39. Christopher S. Parker and Matt A. Barreto, *Change They Can't Believe In: The Tea Party and Reactionary Politics in America* (Princeton, NJ: Princeton University Press, 2013), Chapter 2, "Politics, Out-Group Hostility, or Fear of a Presidential 'Other'?" section.

Chapter 7

1. Erick Erickson quoted in Molly Ball, "Is the Most Powerful Conservative in America Losing His Edge?" *The Atlantic*, January/February 2015, 70.

2. In these analyses, individuals who "lean toward supporting" the Tea Party are considered Tea Party supporters. On a number of measures, these individuals are more similar to those who indicate that they have "strong support" or "not very strong support" for the Tea Party than to other individuals.

3. Author's estimates based on analyses of the 2012 American National Election Study and the voting-eligible population estimate from Michael McDonald's "2012 November General Election Turnout Rates," *United States Election Project* (http://www.electproject.org/2012g).

4. Theda Skocpol and Vanessa Williamson, *The Tea Party and the Remaking of Republican Conservatism* (New York: Oxford University Press, 2012), 77–82; Christopher S. Parker and Matt A. Barreto, *Change They Can't Believe In: The Tea Party and Reactionary Politics in America* (Princeton, NJ: Princeton University Press, 2013), Chapter 5.

5. Skocpol and Williamson, *The Tea Party*, 69, 70; Parker and Barreto, *Change They Can't Believe In*.

6. Will Bunch, *The Backlash: Right-Wing Radicals, Hi-Def Hucksters, and Paranoid Politics in the Age of Obama* (New York: Harper, 2010), 341.

7. See, for example, Bill Press, *The Obama Hate Machine: The Lies, Distortions, and Personal Attacks on the President—and Who Is behind Them* (New York: Thomas Dunne Books, 2012), 127, 196, 197; John Wright, *The Obama Haters: Behind the Right-Wing Campaign of Lies, Innuendo, and Racism* (Washington, DC: Potomac Books, 2011).

8. Skocpol and Williamson, *The Tea Party*, 68.

9. Ibid., 68–69.

10. Ibid., 70.

11. Parker and Barreto, *Change They Can't Believe In*, Chapter 3, "Mapping the Relationship between Freedom and Tea Party Support" section.

12. Skocpol and Williamson, *The Tea Party*, 54–68, 192.

13. Robert P. Jones et al., *What It Means to Be American: Attitudes in an Increasingly Diverse America Ten Years after 9/11* (Washington, DC: The Brookings Institution; Washington, DC: Public Religion Research Institute, 2011), 21.

14. Robert P. Jones et al., *What Americans Want from Immigration Reform in 2014: Findings from the PRRI/Brookings Religion, Values, and Immigration Reform Survey, Panel Call Back* (Washington, DC: Public Religion Research Institute; The Brookings Institution, 2014), 9.

15. Stanley B. Greenberg and James Carville, *Inside the GOP: Report on the Republican Party Project: National Research* (Washington, DC: Democracy Corps, 2014), 11.

16. Skocpol and Williamson, *The Tea Party*, 197–201.

17. Ibid., 70.

18. Jones et al., *What It Means to Be American*, 6, 11, 14.

19. While not all Tea Party supporters are conservative, more than three-quarters (77.1 percent) of them are. Thus, it makes sense to compare them with conservatives who are not supporters of the Tea Party.

20. Appendix, Table 7.10.

21. Ibid.

22. Appendix, Table 7.11.

23. Appendix, Table 7.17.

24. Appendix, Table 7.18.

25. Appendix, Table 7.19.

26. Appendix, Table 7.21.

27. Appendix, Table 7.22.

28. Appendix, Table 7.23.

29. Appendix, Table 7.10.

30. Appendix, Table 7.11.

31. Appendix, Table 7.13.

32. Appendix, Table 7.14.

33. These stereotype questions were limited to a subsample of the survey respondents.

34. Appendix, Tables 4.9 and 7.15.

Chapter 8

1. Appendix, Table 6.1.

2. For example, Philip Rucker reported, "At a recent town-hall meeting in suburban Simpsonville, a man stood up and told Rep. Robert Inglis (R-S.C.) to 'keep your government hands off my Medicare.'" "Sen. DeMint of S.C. Is Voice of Opposition to Health-Care Reform," *Washington Post*, July 28, 2009.

3. Appendix, Table 8.1.

4. However, these differences were not statistically significant in all cases. See Appendix, Table 8.1, for details.

5. Ibid.

6. Ezra Klein, "The Budget Myth That Just Won't Die: Americans Still Think 28 Percent of the Budget Goes to Foreign Aid," *Washington Post*, November 7, 2013.

7. Appendix, Table 8.1.

8. Appendix, Table 8.2.

9. Chye-Ching Huang and Chuck Marr, "Policy Basics: Where Do Our Federal Tax Dollars Go? [video]," https://www.youtube.com/watch?v=ZdHsA6hEP-U (Washington, DC: Center on Budget and Policy Priorities, October 25, 2012).

10. Appendix, Table 8.1.

11. Appendix, Table 5.3.

12. Appendix, Table 4.9.

13. Appendix, Table 8.3.

14. Appendix, Table 8.4.

15. Appendix, Table 8.5.

16. Appendix, Table 8.6.

17. Appendix, Table 8.7.

18. Appendix, Table 8.8.

19. Appendix, Table 8.9.

20. Appendix, Table 8.10.

21. Appendix, Table 8.11.

22. This analysis focuses on the ANES federal spending questions and one Comparative Study of Electoral Systems (CSES) federal expenditure question about defense spending. The other CSES questions were deemed redundant, unclear, or too associated with Obama's policy goals to be useful for the goals of this section.

23. Appendix, Table 8.12.

24. Martin Gilens, the author of *Why Americans Hate Welfare: Race, Media, and the Politics of Antipoverty Policy* (Chicago: The University of Chicago Press, 1999), points out that "welfare" is actually a fuzzy term. Although "welfare" is often debated, it is not clear what individuals may mean by it (Chapter 1, introductory section). Are the ANES respondents not aware that President Bill Clinton ended Aid to Families with Dependent Children? Do they wish to diminish similar programs like Temporary Assistance to Needy Families? Do individuals see things like low-income housing programs, the Supplement Nutrition Assistance Program, and Medicaid as policies for the poor or "welfare"? Robert Rector of the Heritage Foundation has defined "welfare" as any means-tested antipoverty program, including things like vocational training and medical assistance programs. He has identified 79 programs. For him, it appears that all aid for the poor is welfare. "Examining the Means-tested Welfare State: 79 Programs and $927 Billion in Annual Spending" (Washington, DC: Heritage Foundation, 2012).

25. Gilens, *Why Americans Hate Welfare.*

26. Appendix, Table 8.12.

27. Ibid.

28. Ibid.

29. Ibid.

Chapter 9

1. Ian Haney López discusses the rise of "color blindness" as a way to deny racial discrimination and to block efforts at integration in Chapter 4 of *Dog Whistle Politics: How Coded Racial Appeals Have Reinvented Racism and Wrecked the Middle*

Class (New York: Oxford University Press, 2014). López sees the social scientists Nathan Glazer and Daniel Patrick Moynihan as downplaying the significance of racial discrimination. Fred L. Pincus in *Reverse Discrimination: Dismantling the Myth* (Boulder, CO: Lynne Rienner, 2003, 52) finds that "[r]ather than seeing black inequality as caused by discrimination, [Glazer in a 1971 publication] argues that there is simply a lack of supply of educated, skilled black workers." Since the 1970s, Thomas Sowell has argued that cultural traits are the primary explanation of differences in the economic status of racial groups. See his *Race and Economics* (New York: D. McKay Co., 1975).

2. Xuan Thai and Ted Barrett, "Biden's Description of Obama Draws Scrutiny," *CNN.com*, February 9, 2007.

3. See the recent writings of Bill Cosby, Juan Williams, and Thomas Sowell, for example.

4. See Chapter 2 for examples.

5. Robert P. Jones et al., *Citizenship, Values, and Cultural Concerns: What Americans Want from Immigration Reform* (Washington, DC: Public Religion Research Institute, Inc.; Governance Studies at Brookings, 2013), 20.

6. Cindy Brooks Dollar, "Racial Threat Theory: Assessing the Evidence, Requesting Redesign," *Journal of Criminology*, vol. 2014, Article ID 983026 (2014): 7 pages; Chris Mooney, "The Troubling Reason Why Whites in Some States May Show More Hidden Racial Bias," *Washington Post*, December 19, 2014; Maureen A. Craig and Jennifer A. Richeson, "More Diverse Yet Less Tolerant? How the Increasingly Diverse Racial Landscape Affects White Americans' Racial Attitudes," *Personality and Social Psychology Bulletin*, 40, no. 6 (June 2014): 750–761.

7. Lawrence Mishel et al., *The State of Working America*, 12th ed. (Ithaca, NY: Cornell University Press, 2012).

8. This is the scapegoating theory of prejudice. Richard T. Schaefer, *Racial and Ethnic Groups*, 8th ed. (Upper Saddle River, NJ: Prentice Hall, 2000), 46–48. Joe R. Feagin and Clairece Booher Feagin, *Racial and Ethnic Relations*, 9th ed. (Boston: Prentice Hall, 2011), see this at work within the split-labor market theory. Michael Kimmel applies it to understand anger among white men toward people of color in *Angry White Men: American Masculinity at the End of an Era* (New York: Nation Books, 2013). Social psychologists have found some support for scapegoating in experimental research. Mara Cadinu and Cinzia Reggiori, "Discrimination of a Low-Status Outgroup: The Role of Ingroup Threat," *European Journal of Social Psychology*, 32, no. 4 (July/August 2002): 501–515.

9. Appendix, Table 9.1.

10. Appendix, Table 9.2.

11. Appendix, Tables 9.1 and 9.2.

12. Quoted in Mahzarin R. Banaji and Anthony G. Greenwald, *Blindspot: Hidden Biases of Good People* (New York: Delacorte Press, 2013), 57.

13. Ibid., 208.

14. Gary Orfield and Erica Frankenberg, with Jongyeon Ee and John Kuscera, *Brown at 60: Great Progress, a Long Retreat and an Uncertain Future* (Los Angeles, CA: Civil Rights Project/Proyecto Derechos Civiles, 2012), 10.

15. Gary Orfield, John Kucsera, and Genevieve Siegel-Hawley, *E Pluribus . . . Separation: Deepening Double Segregation for More Students* (Los Angeles, CA: Civil Rights Project/Proyecto Derechos Civiles, 2012), 19.

16. David T. Burkam, "Educational Inequality and Children: The Preschool and Early School Years," in *The Economics of Inequality, Poverty, and Discrimination in the 21st Century*, Robert S Rycroft, ed. (Santa Barbara, CA: Praeger, 2013), 385.

17. Orfield, Kucsera, and Siegel-Hawley, *E Pluribus . . . Separation*, 6.

18. Appendix, Table 9.3.

19. Walter Laqueur discusses the wide variety of stereotypes that have been applied to Jews, including ones that could be seen as positive but have been made negative when applied to Jews. Economic success, ambition, and competitiveness for non-Jews are usually seen as positive qualities, but the social and economic success of Jews led to fear and envy. Jews have been seen as "overly ambitious and competitive . . . always devious." *The Changing Face of Anti-Semitism: From Ancient Times to the Present Day* (Oxford: Oxford University Press, 2008), 158. For Asians, the danger of the "positive" stereotype of intelligence is clearly revealed in the character of Dr. Fu Manchu who "uses his Western intellect and Eastern cunning to try to destroy Western Civilization and beat it at its own game of world conquest." John Kuo Wei Tchen and Dylan Yeats, eds., *Yellow Peril!: An Archive of Anti-Asian Fear* (Brooklyn, NY: Verso, 2014), 5. Feagin and Feagin also point out that both Jews and Asians are seen as "devious." *Racial and Ethnic Relations*, 117, 287.

20. Appendix, Table 9.4.

21. Efrén O. Pérez, "Explicit Evidence on the Import of Implicit Attitudes: The IAT and Immigration Policy Judgments," *Political Behavior*, 32 (2010): 517–545; Irene V. Blair et al. "Assessment of Biases against Latinos and African Americans among Primary Care Providers and Community Members," *American Journal of Public Health*, 103, no. 1 (January 2013): 92–98.

22. Orfield, Kucsera, and Siegel-Hawley, *E Pluribus . . . Separation*, 19.

23. Orfield and Frankenberg, *Brown at 60*, 42.

24. Appendix, Table 9.5.

25. Appendix, Table 9.6.

26. Tesler and Sears, *Obama's Race*, Chapter 7, "Method" section.

27. Appendix, Table 9.7.

28. Quoted in Hughey, "Show Me Your Papers!" 172–173. Verbatim text: "His staff are doing a great job avoiding the real truth behind is illeged [sic] US Citizenship as well as other serious topics, bravo. Most of you want to play the race card for Mr. Obama in sympathy well that is a crock. Im [sic] a white male that was born and raised in this country ans [sic] my parents were and thier [sic] parents etc. and [sic] I cannot find a job I'm qualified for, nor can I get a free education because someone elses [sic] accent or skin tone needs to be addressed before mine and other whites like myself. And the funny part is is [sic] that I'm the minority now, not Mr. Obama and other non caucasian [sic] racial people of this country. [. . .] Caucasians have passed laws, and rules that try to be fair to every other race in the country which is more then ok with me, but we excluded ourselves, why is this? We will fail as a nation, regretibly [sic] because of soft sympathizers like you."

29. Quoted in Kimmel, *Angry White Men*, 45.

30. Appendix, Table 9.8.

31. Appendix, Table 9.9.

32. Pew Research Center, *A Year after Obama's Election: Blacks Upbeat about Black Progress, Prospects* (Washington, DC: Pew Research Center, 2010), 42.

33. Pew Research Center, *King's Dream Remains an Elusive Goal; Many Americans See Racial Disparities* (Washington, DC: Pew Research Center, 2013), 18.

34. **Hater Most Important Problem, Third Mention, 183.**

35. These figures are taken or calculated from Karen R. Humes, Nicholas A. Jones, and Roberto R. Ramirez, "Overview of Race and Hispanic Origin: 2010," *2010 Census Briefs* (Washington, DC: U.S. Department of Commerce, 2011), Tables 1 and 2.

36. *New York Times/CBS News, Complete Poll Results*, July 7–14, 2008, 27; http://graphics8.nytimes.com/packages/pdf/politics/20080716_POLL.pdf.

37. Feagin and Feagin, *Racial and Ethnic Relations*, 117–118. The Anti-Defamation League keeps track of anti-Jewish conspiracy theories claiming secret powers of Jews. "Anti-Semitic Conspiracy Theories," http://www.adl.org/anti-semitism/united-states/c/conspiracy-theories.html.

38. Carmen DeNavas-Walt, Bernadette D. Proctor, and Jessica C. Smith, *Income, Poverty, and Health Insurance Coverage in the United States: 2012* (Washington, DC: U.S. Census Bureau, 2013), Table 3.

39. While campaigning in 2007, then senator Barack Obama told a black audience: "Don't talk yourself out of [voting for me]. . . . If we said we can't do something, we'd still have segregated schools" (Katharine Q. Seelye, "Obama, Civil Rights and South Carolina," *The Caucus: The Politics and Government Blog of the Times, New York Times*, November 2, 2007).

40. These demands are derived from a flyer announcing the march from the national organizing office. See "March on Washington for Jobs and Freedom Announcement," The Martin Luther King, Jr., Research and Education Institute, http://mlk-kpp01.stanford.edu/index.php/encyclopedia/documentsentry/march_on_washington_for_jobs_and_freedom_announcement/. Other versions of the flyer and the organizing manual had similar but different demands. This flyer, one could argue, was the most specified and least redundant. This broader economic vision of the goals of the civil rights movement is shared by the civil rights historian Charles Payne. Payne argues "For local people, the movement was about freedom, not just [the legislative victories of] civil rights. At the very least, their conception of freedom would have included decent jobs, housing, and education" (*I've Got the Light of Freedom: The Organizing Tradition and the Mississippi Freedom Struggle* [Berkeley: University of California Press, 1995], 361).

41. See Title VII of the Civil Rights Act of 1964, http://www.eeoc.gov/laws/statutes/titlevii.cfm.

42. Voting rights have been under attack recently. While there is less racial discrimination in the labor market, it still exists. See the discussion of this issue in "Explaining Poor Employment Outcomes" in Janelle Jones and John Schmitt, "A College Degree is No Guarantee" (Washington, DC: Center for Economic and Policy Research, 2014), 13–14.

43. Algernon Austin, "The Unfinished March: An Overview" (Washington, DC: Economic Policy Institute, 2013).

44. Ibid.

45. Quoted in Mark P. Orbe, *Communication Realities in a "Post-Racial" Society: What the U.S. Public Really Thinks about Barack Obama* (Lanham, MD: Lexington Books, 2011), Chapter 8, "Negativity Based on Race" section.

46. Quoted in Shankar Vendantham, *The Hidden Brain: How Our Unconscious Minds Elect Presidents, Control Markets, Wage Wars, and Save Our Lives* (New York: Spiegel & Grau, 2010), 213.

47. Jennifer Steinhauer, "Volunteers for Obama Face a Complex Issue," *New York Times*, October 14, 2008.

48. U.S. representative Mo Brooks coined the phrase, but the sentiment underlies the white-victimhood mentality. As Jonathan Chait observes, "White racial victimization is a concept as old as racism itself. . . . The war on whites has raged continuously in the right-wing mind for more than two centuries." Jonathan Chait, "Republican Denounces 'War on Whites,'" *New York*, August 4, 2014.

49. Austin, "The Unfinished March," 2.

50. David Cooper and Doug Hall, "Raising the Federal Minimum Wage to $10.10 Would Give Working Families, and the Overall Economy, a Much-Needed Boost," *EPI Briefing Paper #357* (Washington, DC: Economic Policy Institute, 2013).

51. Economic Policy Institute, "Share of Workers Earning Poverty-Level Wages, by Race and Ethnicity, 1973–2013," *State of Working America* (online), Figure F4, http://www.stateofworkingamerica.org/chart/swa-wages-figure-4f-share-workers-earning/.

52. See Michelle Alexander, *The New Jim Crow: Mass Incarceration in the Age of Colorblindness* (New York: The New Press, 2012) for a discussion of this issue.

53. Robynn J.A. Cox, *Where Do We Go From Here? Mass Incarceration and the Struggle for Civil Rights* (Economic Policy Institute, 2015), Figure F.

54. Vivian Hunt, Dennis Layton, and Sara Prince, *Diversity Matters* (London: McKinsey & Company, 2014); see also the opening discussion and links in Algernon Austin, "Will the New Tech Economy Solve the Old Economy's Racial Problems?" (Washington, DC: Center for American Progress, 2015), https://www.americanprogress.org/issues/race/news/2015/01/14/104132/will-the-new-tech-economy-solve-the-old-economys-racial-problems/.

55. Heather Boushey and Adam S. Hersh, *The American Middle Class, Income Inequality, and the Strength of Our Economy: New Evidence in Economics* (Washington, DC: Center for American Progress, 2012), 8.

56. Robert Lynch and Patrick Oakford, *The Economic Benefits of Closing Educational Achievement Gaps: Promoting Growth and Strengthening the Nation by Improving the Educational Outcomes of Children of Color* (Washington, DC: Center for American Progress, 2014).

57. Stanley B. Greenberg and James Carville, *Inside the GOP: Report on the Republican Party Project: National Research* (Washington, DC: Democracy Corps, 2014), 11.

58. See Robert Costa, "House Conservatives: Border Bill Collapse One of Our Greatest Triumphs," *Washington Post*, August 1, 2014.

59. López, *Dog Whistle Politics*, 122.

60. Paul Krugman, "The Story of Our Time," *New York Times*, April 28, 2013.

61. The discussion here is a bit too-simple too. See Daniel Costa, David Cooper, and Heidi Shierholz, "Facts about Immigration and the U.S. Economy: Answers to Frequently Asked Questions" (Washington, DC: Economic Policy Institute, 2014), Questions 4, 7, and 11 for more details.

62. Editorial Board, "Immigrants and Small Business," *New York Times*, June 30, 2012.

63. Annette Bernhardt et al., *Broken Laws, Unprotected Workers: Violations of Employment and Labor Laws in America's Cities* (Chicago: Center for Urban Economic Development, 2009).

64. Council on American-Islamic Relations-California, *2014 Civil Rights Report: The Status of Muslim Civil Rights in California* (Los Angeles: Council on American-Islamic Relations-California, 2014), 1.

65. Arab American Institute, *American Attitudes toward Arabs and Muslims* (Washington, DC: Arab American Institute, 2014), 4.

66. Ibid., 5.

Afterword

1. Michael A. Memoli, "113th Congress Just Barely Avoids Being the Least Productive in History," *Los Angeles Times*, December 18, 2014.

2. Ed O'Keefe, "The House Has Voted 54 Times in Four Years on Obamacare. Here's the Full List," *Washington Post*, March 21, 2014.

3. Dhrumil Mehta, "Every President's Executive Orders in One Chart," *FiveThirtyEight.com*, November 20, 2014.

4. Zerlina Maxwell, "Obama Says He's Not 'President of Black America,'" *theGrio.com*, August 8, 2012; Jonathan Capehart, "Obama Can't Win with Some Black Critics," *Washington Post*, May 21, 2013.

5. The White House, *My Brother's Keeper*, http://www.whitehouse.gov/my-brothers-keeper.

6. The My Brother's Keeper Task Force reports state that the initiative was developed "to improve significantly the expected life outcomes for boys and young men of color (including Black Americans, Hispanic Americans, and Native Americans)" (12). In addition, it states, "The strategies and recommendations discussed in this report are designed in accordance with the fundamental principle that Federal and federally assisted programs and services may not discriminate on the basis of sex, race, color, or national origin" (11). At points, the report also highlights Asian Americans and Pacific Islanders. My Brother's Keeper Task Force, *My Brother's Keeper Task Force Report to the President* (Washington, DC: The White House, 2014). The one-year progress report mentions that 17 tribal nations are participating in the state and local component of the initiative. My Brother's Keeper Task Force, *One-Year Progress Report to the President* (Washington, DC: The White House, 2015).

7. See, for example, Kimberlé Williams Crenshaw, "The Girls Obama Forgot," *New York Times*, July 29, 2014; Room for Debate, "The Assumptions behind Obama's Initiative," *New York Times*, March 12, 2013.

8. My Brother's Keeper Task Force, *One-Year Progress Report to the President.*

9. Author's accounting from Office of the Press Secretary, "FACT SHEET: President Obama Applauds New Commitments in Support of the My Brother's Keeper Initiative" (Washington, DC: The White House, July 21, 2014). The *One-Year Progress Report to the President* states that the amount is "more than $300 million." My Brother's Keeper Task Force, *One-Year Progress Report to the President*, 3.

10. See Office of the Press Secretary, "FACT SHEET: President Obama Applauds New Commitments in Support of the My Brother's Keeper Initiative"; Office of the Press Secretary, "FACT SHEET: Opportunity for all: President Obama Launches My Brother's Keeper Initiative to Build Ladders of Opportunity For Boys and Young Men of Color" (Washington, DC: The White House, February 27, 2014).

11. Foundation Stats, "Aggregate Fiscal Data of Grants from FC 1000 Foundations, to U.S. Recipients, for Children & Youth, 2012" (New York: Foundation Center, 2015).

12. This calculation is based on the official poverty threshold, but the results are the same if one uses up to 150 percent of the poverty threshold.

13. Author's analysis of 2013 American Community Survey data from Steven Ruggles, J. Trent Alexander, Katie Genadek, Ronald Goeken, Matthew B. Schroeder, and Matthew Sobek. 2014. Integrated Public Use Microdata Series: Version 5.0 (Machine-Readable Database). Minneapolis: University of Minnesota.

14. Joe Romm, "World's Scientists Warn: We Have 'High Confidence' in the 'Irreversible Impacts' of Climate Inaction," *ClimateProgress*, November 2, 2014.

15. Coral Davenport, "Obama Builds Environmental Legacy with 1970 Law," *New York Times*, November 26, 2014.

16. U.S. Environmental Protection Agency, "EPA Proposes First Guidelines to Cut Carbon Pollution from Existing Power Plants" (Press Release), (Washington, DC: Environmental Protection Agency, 2014).

17. Bill McKibben, "How Green Is Barack Obama," *PoliticoMagazine.com*, December 10, 2014.

18. Ibid.

19. The White House, "Remarks by the President in Address to the Nation on Immigration" (Washington, DC: The White House, November 20, 2014).

20. American Immigration Council, "Executive Grants of Temporary Immigration Relief, 1956-Present" (Washington, DC: American Immigration Council, October 20, 2014).

21. The Pew Research Center estimates that it will provide temporary relief from deportation for 3.9 million out of 11.2 million unauthorized immigrants. Jens Manuel Krogstad and Jeffrey S. Passel, "Those from Mexico Will Benefit Most from Obama's Executive Action" (Washington, DC: Pew Research Center, 2014).

22. Public Religion Research Institute, "Roughly Three-Quarters of Americans Favor Goals of Obama's Immigration Action" (Washington, DC: Public Religion Research Institute, 2015).

23. U.S. Senator Marco Rubio, "The Border Security, Economic Opportunity & Immigration Modernization Act of 2013," http://www.rubio.senate.gov/public/index. cfm/immigration-reform?p=Get-The-Facts1.

24. Dara Lind, "The Campaign Promise That's Still Haunting Obama," *Vox.com*, June 9, 2014.

25. Reid J. Epstein, "National Council of La Raza Leader Calls Barack Obama 'Deporter-in-Chief,'" *Politico.com*, March 4, 2014.

26. For information on the record number of agents on the border, see U.S. Department of Homeland Security, "Border Security Results," November 1, 2013, http://www.dhs.gov/border-security-results; Louis Jacobson, "Barack Obama Touts Record High Border Agents, Lowest Immigration from Mexico in 40 Years," *Politifact. com*, October 17, 2012, http://www.politifact.com/truth-o-meter/statements/2012/ oct/17/barack-obama/barack-obama-touts-record-high-border-agents-lowes/.

27. Jonathan Capehart, "Boehner Refuses to Act on Immigration Reform," *Washington Post*, November 6, 2014.

28. Michael D. Shear, "For Obama, More Audacity and Fulfillment of Languishing Promises," *New York Times*, December 17, 2014.

29. Mark Landler and Michael R. Gordon, "Journey to Reconciliation Visited Worlds of Presidents, Popes and Spies," *New York Times*, December 17, 2014.

30. Barack Obama, "Transcript: Obama's Remarks on U.S.-Cuba Relations," *Washington Post*, December 17, 2014.

31. Marc A. Caputo, "Pro-Embargo, Cuba Hardline Is a Minority Stance in U.S., Polls Show," *NakedPolitics, Miami Herald* blog, December 23, 2014; Nicole Gaudiano, "Poll: Americans Favor Normal Relations with Cuba," *USA Today*, February 11, 2014; Gallup, "Cuba," http://www.gallup.com/poll/1630/cuba.aspx.

32. Harry Enten, "There Won't Be a Backlash to Ending the Cuba Embargo," *FiveThirtyEight.com*, December 17, 2014, http://fivethirtyeight.com/datalab/cuba-embargo-obama-backlash/; Caputo, "Pro-Embargo, Cuba Hardline Is a Minority Stance."

33. Nick Corasaniti, "Clinton Weighs in on Cuba: I Approve of Policy Change," *First Draft, New York Times*, December 17, 2014.

34. Mark Landler, "U.S. and China Reach Climate Accord after Months of Talks," *New York Times*, November 11, 2014.

35. Landler and Gordon, "Journey to Reconciliation."

36. Fredrick C. Harris, *The Price of the Ticket: Barack Obama and the Rise and Decline of Black Politics* (Oxford; New York: Oxford University Press, 2012), 140.

37. For example, Richard Kogan and Issac Shapiro note that Republicans show strong support for the "$1 trillion a year in tax expenditures (deductions, exclusions, credits, and other preferences), which disproportionately benefit high-income households and many of which essentially operate as entitlements provided through the tax code." "Congressional Budget Plans Get Two-Thirds of Cuts from Programs for People with Low or Moderate Incomes" (Washington, DC: Center on Budget and Policy Priorities, March 23, 2015).

Bibliography

Alexander, Michelle. *The New Jim Crow: Mass Incarceration in the Age of Colorblindness*, rev. ed. New York: The New Press, 2012.

Amato, John, and David Neiwert. *Over the Cliff: How Obama's Election Drove the American Right Insane.* Sausalito, CA: PoliPointPress, 2010.

Arab American Institute. "American Attitudes toward Arabs and Muslims." Washington, DC: 2014.

Aravosis, John. "Original 1989 Document Where Heritage Foundation Created Obamacare's Individual Mandate," *Americablog*, October 24, 2013, http://americablog.com/2013/10/original-1989-document-heritage-foundation-created-obamacares-individual-mandate.html.

Associated Press. "Palin: Obama Pals around with Terrorists," *USA Today*, October 4, 2008.

Austin, Algernon. "The Unfinished March: An Overview" (Washington, DC: Economic Policy Institute, 2013).

Austin, Algernon. "Will the New Tech Economy Solve the Old Economy's Racial Problems?" (Washington, DC: Center for American Progress, 2015), https://www.americanprogress.org/issues/race/news/2015/01/14/104132/will-the-new-tech-economy-solve-the-old-economys-racial-problems/.

Avlon, John. *Wingnuts: How the Lunatic Fringe Is Hijacking America.* New York: Beast Books, 2010.

Ball, Molly. "Is the Most Powerful Conservative in America Losing His Edge?" *The Atlantic*, January/February 2015.

Banaji, Mahzarin R., and Anthony G. Greenwald. *Blindspot: Hidden Biases of Good People.* New York: Delacorte Press, 2013.

Barras, Jonetta Rose. "He Leapt the Tallest Barrier. What Does It Mean for Black America?" *Washington Post*, November 9, 2008.

Barron, James. "9 Jewish Leaders Say E-mail Spread Lies about Obama," *New York Times*, January 16, 2008.

Bartlett, Bruce. "Barack Obama: The Democrats' Richard Nixon?" *The Fiscal Times*, July 22, 2011.

Berman, Mark. "Americans Increasingly Say Race Is the Country's Most Important Issue," *Washington Post*, December 19, 2014.

Bernhardt, Annette, Ruth Milkman, Nik Theodore, Douglas Heckathorn, Mirabai Auer, James DeFilippis, Ana Luz González, Victor Narro, Jason Perelshteyn, Diana Polson, and Michael Spiller. *Broken Laws, Unprotected Workers: Violations of Employment and Labor Laws in America's Cities.* Chicago: Center for Urban Economic Development, 2009.

Bertrand, Marianne, and Sendhil Mullainathan. "Are Emily and Greg More Employable Than Lakisha and Jamal: A Field Experiment on Labor Market Discrimination," *American Economic Review*, 94, no 4 (2004): 991–1013.

Bunch, Will. *The Backlash: Right-Wing Radicals, Hi-Def Hucksters, and Paranoid Politics in the Age of Obama.* New York: Harper, 2010.

Burkam, David T. "Educational Inequality and Children: The Preschool and Early School Years," in *The Economics of Inequality, Poverty, and Discrimination in the 21st Century*, Robert S. Rycroft, ed. Santa Barbara, CA: Praeger, 2013.

Bishop, Bill. *The Big Sort: Why the Clustering of Like-Minded America Is Tearing Us Apart.* New York: Houghton Mifflin Harcourt, 2008.

Bivens, Josh. "Abandoning What Works (and Most Other Things, Too): Expansionary Fiscal Policy Is Still the Best Tool for Boosting Jobs," *EPI Briefing Paper #304.* Economic Policy Institute, 2011.

Blinder, Alan S. "Keynesian Economics," in *The Concise Encyclopedia of Economics*, David R. Henderson, ed. (Library of Economics and Liberty [Online], Liberty Fund, Inc., 2008), http://www.econlib.org/library/Enc/KeynesianEconomics.html.

Blow, Charles M. "A Blacklash?" *New York Times*, May 3, 2008.

Boushey, Heather, and Adam S. Hersh. *The American Middle Class, Income Inequality, and the Strength of Our Economy: New Evidence in Economics.* Washington, DC: Center for American Progress, 2012.

Brodkin, Karen. *How Jews Became White Folks and What That Says about Race in America.* New Brunswick, NJ: Rutgers University Press, 1998.

Bump, Phillip. "The Chart Summarizing the 2014 Election That We Never Intended for You to See," *Washington Post*, December 8, 2014.

Burke, Megan, Maureen Cavanaugh, and Peter Schrag. "The Long View on American Attitudes toward Immigration," *KPBS.org*, May 10, 2011.

Caplan-Bricker, Nora. "Who's the Real Deporter-in-Chief: Bush or Obama?" *NewRepublic.com*, April 17, 2014.

Cashin, Sheryll. *Place, Not Race: A New Vision of Opportunity in America.* Boston: Beacon Press, 2014.

Cheng, Jennifer Y. "At Home and in School: Racial and Ethnic Gaps in Educational Preparedness," *California Counts: Population Trends and Profiles*, 3, no. 2 (2001) (San Francisco: Public Policy Institute of California).

CNN.com. "CNN Debunks False Report about Obama," January 23, 2007.

Cooper, David. "By the Numbers: Income and Poverty, 2013," *Working Economics* blog. Washington, DC: Economic Policy Institute, September 16, 2014.

Cooper, David, and Doug Hall. "Raising the Federal Minimum Wage to $10.10 Would Give Working Families, and the Overall Economy, a Much-Needed

Boost," *EPI Briefing Paper #357.* Washington, DC: Economic Policy Institute, 2013.

Cosby, Bill, and Alvin F. Poussaint, MD. *Come On, People: On the Path from Victims to Victors.* Nashville, TN: Thomas Nelson, 2007.

Costa, Daniel, David Cooper, and Heidi Shierholz. "Facts about Immigration and the U.S. Economy: Answers to Frequently Asked Questions." Washington, DC: Economic Policy Institute, 2014.

Costa, Robert. "House Conservatives: Border Bill Collapse One of Our Greatest Tri-. umphs," *Washington Post,* August 1, 2014.

Council on American-Islamic Relations—California. *Growing in Faith: California Muslim Youth Experiences with Bullying, Harassment, and Religious Accommodation in Schools.* Anaheim, CA: Council on American-Islamic Relations-California, 2014.

Council on American-Islamic Relations—California. *The Status of Muslim Civil Rights in California, 2014.* Anaheim, CA: Council on American-Islamic Relations-California, 2014.

Cox, Robynn J.A. *Where Do We Go from Here? Mass Incarceration and the Struggle for Civil Rights.* Washington, DC: Economic Policy Institute, 2015.

Craig, Maureen A., and Jennifer A. Richeson, "More Diverse Yet Less Tolerant? How the Increasingly Diverse Racial Landscape Affects White Americans' Racial Attitudes," *Personality and Social Psychology Bulletin,* 40, no. 6 (June 2014): 750–761.

Davis, F. James. *Who Is Black?: One Nation's Definition.* University Park, PA: Pennsylvania State University Press, 1991.

DeAngelis, Karen J., Bradford R. White, and Jennifer B. Presley. "The Changing Distribution of Teacher Qualifications across Schools: A Statewide Perspective Post-NCLB," *Education Policy Analysis Archives,* 18, no. 28 (November 2010).

DeNavas-Walt, Carmen, and Bernadette D. Proctor. "Table A-1. Households by Total Money Income, Race, and Hispanic Origin of Householder: 1967 to 2013," in *Income and Poverty in the United States: 2013,* U.S. Census Bureau, Current Population Reports, P60-249. Washington, DC: U.S. Government Printing Office, 2014.

Deslatte, Melinda. "Sen. Landrieu's Remarks on Race Anger Republicans," *Yahoo! News,* October 30, 2014.

Dobbs, Michael. "John McCain's Birthplace," *Washington Post,* May 20, 2008.

Dollar, Cindy Brooks. "Racial Threat Theory: Assessing the Evidence, Requesting Redesign," *Journal of Criminology,* 2014 (2014): 1–7.

The Ed Show. "Romney Tells Students to Borrow Money 'From Your Parents,'" *MSNBC.com,* April 27, 2012.

Edsall, Thomas. "The Anti-entitlement Strategy," *Campaign Stops* blog, *New York Times,* December 25, 2011.

Edwards, Ezekiel, Will Bunting, and Lynda Garcia. *The War on Marijuana in Black and White: Billions of Dollars Wasted in Racially-Biased Arrests.* New York: American Civil Liberties Union, 2013.

Epstein, Reid J. "National Council of La Raza Leader Calls Barack Obama 'Deporter-in-Chief,'" *Politico.com,* March 4, 2014.

Fabian, Jordan. "Obama: More Moderate Republican Than Socialist," *ABCNews.com*, December 14, 2012.

Fancher, Mike. "Times Won't Forget Readers' Reminder on Kwan Headline," *Seattle Times*, March 3, 2002.

Farley, Robert. "Fact Check: Obama on the 'Fiscal Cliff' Deal," *USA Today*, January 5, 2013.

Feder, Lester. "Dreams of My . . . Grandparents? Obama's Campaign Ad Omits All Mention of His Father," *Huffington Post*, June 28, 2008.

File, Tom. "The Diversifying Electorate—Voting Rates by Race and Hispanic Origin in 2012 (and Other Recent Elections)," *Population Characteristics: Current Population Survey*. Washington, DC: U.S. Census Bureau, 2013.

Finley, Laura L., and Luigi Esposito. "Conclusion: Obama and the Future of Progressivism in the United States," in *Grading the 44th President: A Report Card on Barack Obama's First Term as a Progressive Leader*, Luigi Esposito and Laura L. Finley, eds. Santa Barbara, CA: Praeger, 2012.

Galston, William A. "Why the 2005 Social Security Initiative Failed, and What It Means for the Future." Washington, DC: Brookings, September 21, 2007.

Gamboa, Suzanne. "How Many Latinos Are in the House of Representatives?" *Huffington Post*, February 5, 2013.

Gates, Jr., Henry Louis. "Introduction," in *Barack Obama: A Pocket Biography of Our 44th President*, Steven J. Niven, ed. New York: Oxford University Press, 2009.

Gentilviso, Chris. "Arnold Schwarzenegger 2016? Former Governor Mulls Rule Change Push to Run for President," *The Huffington Post*, October 19, 2013.

Gilens, Martin. *Why Americans Hate Welfare: Race, Media, and the Politics of Antipoverty Policy*. Chicago: The University of Chicago Press, 1999.

Giridharadas, Anand. "Immigrants, Nationhood and the U.S.," *New York Times*, May 26, 2014.

Glastris, Paul. "Introduction: Race, History, and Obama's Second Term," *Washington Monthly*, January/February 2013.

Goldsmith, Arthur H., Darrick Hamilton, and William Darity Jr. "From Dark to Light: Skin Color and Wages among African-Americans," *Journal of Human Resources*, XLII, no. 4 (2007): 701–738.

Goodstein, Laurie. "Without a Pastor of His Own, Obama Turns to Five," *New York Times*, March 14, 2009.

Gosztola, Kevin. "More Killing in Obama's 'War on Terror' Than Bush's 'War,'" *Firedoglake.com*, September 11, 2012.

Grant-Thomas, Andrew. "Does Barack Obama's Victory Herald a Post-Racial America?" *Colorlines.com*, December 5 2008.

Greenberg, Stanley B., and James Carville. *Inside the GOP: Report on the Republican Party Project: National Research*. Washington, DC: Democracy Corps, 2014.

Grunwald, Michael. *The New New Deal: The Hidden Story of Change in the Obama Era*. New York: Simon and Shuster, 2012.

Guess, J. Bennett. "Barack Obama, Candidate for President, Is 'UCC,'" *UCC.org*, February 8, 2007, http://www.ucc.org/barack-obama-candidate.

Healthcare—NOW! "What Is Single-Payer Healthcare?" (Philadelphia: Healthcare—NOW! n.d.), http://www.healthcare-now.org/whats-single-payer.

Henry J. Kaiser Family Foundation. "Massachusetts Health Care Reform: Six Years Later," *Focus on Health Reform*. Washington, DC: Henry J. Kaiser Family Foundation, May 2012.

Henry J. Kaiser Family Foundation. "Snapshots: Health Care Spending in the United States and Selected OECD Countries." Washington, DC: Henry J. Kaiser Family Foundation, April 12, 2011. http://www.health.ny.gov/regulations/hcra/univ_hlth_care.htm.

Herszenhorn, David M. "Congress Sends $801 Billion Tax Cut Bill to Obama," *New York Times*, December 16, 2010.

Hill, Mark E. "Color Differences in the Socioeconomic Status of African American Men: Results of a Longitudinal Study," *Social Forces* 78, no. 4 (2000): 1437–1460.

Hispanic Trends Project. "Table 1. Population, by Race and Ethnicity: 2000 and 2012" (Washington, DC: Pew Research Center), http://www.pewhispanic.org/2014/04/29/statistical-portrait-of-hispanics-in-the-united-states-2012/.

Horsley, Scott. "Obama Sticks with 'No Ransom' Strategy, Comes Out Ahead," *NPR*, October 17, 2013.

Hosenball, Mark. "Romney's Birth Certificate Evokes His Father's Controversy," *Reuters*, May 29, 2012.

Huang, Chye-Ching, and Chuck Marr. "Policy Basics: Where Do Our Federal Tax Dollars Go? [video]," https://www.youtube.com/watch?v=ZdHsA6hEP-U. Washington, DC: Center on Budget and Policy Priorities, October 25, 2012.

Hunt, Vivian, Dennis Layton, and Sara Prince. *Diversity Matters*. London: McKinsey & Company, 2014.

Hutchings, Vincent L. "Change or More of the Same? Evaluating Racial Attitudes in the Obama Era," *Public Opinion Quarterly*, 73, no. 5 (2009): 917–942.

Hutchings, Vincent, Gary Segura, Simon Jackman, and Ted Brader (principal investigators). *American National Election Study 2012* (electronic data file). Arbor, MI, and Palo Alto, CA: the University of Michigan and Stanford University, 2013.

Jacobson, Gary C. "Presidents, Partisans, and Polarized Politics" in *Can We Talk?: The Rise of Rude, Nasty, Stubborn Politics*, Daniel M. Shea and Morris P. Fiorina, eds. New York: Pearson, 2012.

Jacobson, Louis. "Barack Obama Touts Record High Border Agents, Lowest Immigration from Mexico in 40 Years," *Politifact.com*, October 17, 2012.

Jacobson, Matthew Frye. *Whiteness of a Different Color: European Immigrants and the Alchemy of Race*. Cambridge: Harvard University Press, 1998.

Jones, Robert P., Daniel Cox, Juhem Navarro-Rivera, E.J. Dionne, and William A. Galston. *Citizenship, Values, and Cultural Concerns: What Americans Want from Immigration Reform*. Washington, DC: Public Religion Research Institute, Inc.; Governance Studies at Brookings, 2013.

Jones, Robert P., Daniel Cox, Juhem Navarro-Rivera, E.J. Dionne Jr., and William A. Galston. *What Americans Want from Immigration Reform in 2014: Findings from the PRRI/Brookings Religion, Values, and Immigration Reform Survey, Panel Call Back*. Washington, DC: Public Religion Research Institute; The Brookings Institution, 2014.

Jordan, Winthrop D. *White over Black: American Attitudes toward the Negro, 1550–1812*. New York: Norton, 1977.

Journalism Project Staff. *The Media, Religion and the 2012 Campaign for President*. Washington, DC: Pew Research Center, 2012.

Kam, Cindy D., and Donald R. Kinder. "Ethnocentrism as a Short-Term Force in the 2008 American Presidential Election," *American Journal of Political Science*, 56, no. 2 (April 2012): 326–340.

Kantor, Jodi. "In Law School, Obama Found Political Voice," *New York Times*, January 28, 2007.

Keen, Lisa. "White House: New Federal Contractor EO Coming," *WindyCityMedia-Group.com*, June 18, 2014.

Keller, Larry. "Racist Backlash Greets New U.S. President," *Intelligence Report*, Spring 2009, Issue Number: 133.

Kim, Nadia Y. "Campaigning for Obama and the Politics of Race: The Case of California, Texas, and Beyond," *Research in Race and Ethnic Relations*, 16 (2010): 247–266.

Kimmel, Michael. *Angry White Men: American Masculinity at the End of an Era*. New York: Nation Books, 2013.

Klein, Ezra. "The Budget Myth That Just Won't Die: Americans Still Think 28 Percent of the Budget Goes to Foreign Aid," *Washington Post*, November 7, 2013.

Klein, Ezra. "Obama Revealed: A Moderate Republican," *Washington Post*, April 25, 2011.

Kochhar, Rakesh, and Richard Fry. "Wealth Inequality Has Widened along Racial, Ethnic Lines since End of Great Recession." Washington, DC: Pew Research Center, December 12, 2014, http://www.pewresearch.org/fact-tank/2014/12/12/racial-wealth-gaps-great-recession/.

Kravets, David. "Former CIA Chief: Obama's War on Terror Same as Bush's, but with More Killing," *Wired.com*, September 10, 2012.

Kristof, Nicholas. "How Romney Would Treat Women," *New York Times*, November 3, 2012.

Krugman, Paul. "The Boehnerization of Barack Obama," *New York Times*, October 16, 2010.

Krugman, Paul. "Conservative Origins of Obamacare," *The Conscience of a Liberal* blog, *New York Times*, July 27, 2011.

Krugman, Paul. "Orwell and Social Security," *Conscience of a Liberal* blog, *New York Times*, August 24, 2010.

Krugman, Paul. "The Story of Our Time," *New York Times*, April 28, 2013.

Lee, Valerie E., and David T. Burkam. *Inequality at the Starting Gate: Social Background Differences in Achievement as Children Begin School*. Washington, DC: Economic Policy Institute, 2002.

Linden, Michael, and Michael Ettlinger. "Obama vs. Bush: Who's the Bigger Tax Cutter? Different Cuts Reflect Different Philosophies." Washington, DC: Center for American Progress, September 13, 2011.

Lisheron, Mark. "Texas Stimulus Opponents Later Sought Stimulus Funds for Their Districts," *TexasWatchdog.org*, October 18, 2010.

Logan, Enid. "At This Defining Moment": Barack Obama's Presidential Candidacy and the New Politics of Race. New York: NYU Press, 2011.

López, Ian Haney. Dog Whistle Politics: How Coded Racial Appeals Have Reinvented Racism and Wrecked the Middle Class. New York: Oxford University Press, 2014.

Lynch, Robert, and Patrick Oakford. The Economic Benefits of Closing Educational Achievement Gaps: Promoting Growth and Strengthening the Nation by Improving the Educational Outcomes of Children of Color. Washington, DC: Center for American Progress, 2014.

Manning, Jennifer E. Membership of the 112th Congress: A Profile. Washington, DC: Congressional Research Service, 2012.

Marr, Chuck, and Nathaniel Frentz. "Federal Income Taxes on Middle-Income Families Remain Near Historic Lows." Washington, DC: Center on Budget and Policy Priorities, April 15, 2014.

Mauer, Marc. Race to Incarcerate. New York: The New Press, 2006.

Maxwell, Angie, Pearl Ford Dowe, and Todd Shields. "The Next Link in the Chain Reaction: Symbolic Racism and Obama's Religious Affiliation," Social Science Quarterly, 94, no. 2 (June 2012): 321–343.

Maxwell, Zerlina. "Obama Says He's Not 'President of Black America'—Turns Out He's Right," The Grio, August 8, 2012.

Mayorkas, Alejandro. "Deferred Action for Childhood Arrivals: Who Can Be Considered?" The White House blog, August 15, 2012.

McDonald, Michael. "2008 General Election Turnout Rates," United States Election Project, http://www.electproject.org/2008g.

Merida, Kevin. "Racist Incidents Give Some Obama Campaigners Pause," Washington Post, May 13, 2008.

Miller, Lisa. "Cover Story: Barack Obama's Christian Journey," Newsweek, July 11, 2008.

Mishel, Lawrence, Josh Bivens, Elise Gould, and Heidi Shierholz. The State of Working America, 12th ed. Ithaca, NY: Cornell University Press, 2012.

Mohamed, Rafik, and Erik D. Fritsvold. Dorm Room Dealers: Drugs and the Privileges of Race and Class. Boulder, CO: Lynne Rienner Publishers, 2011.

Mooney, Chris. "The Troubling Reason Why Whites in Some States May Show More Hidden Racial Bias," Washington Post, December 19, 2014.

Morgan, David, Roberta Rampton, and Susan Cornwell. "House Votes to Repeal and Eventually Replace Obamacare," Reuters, February 3, 2015.

Murphree, Adam, and Deirdre A. Royster. "Race Threads and Race Threats: How Obama/Race-Discourse among Conservatives Changed through the 2008 Presidential Campaign," Research in Race and Ethnic Relations, 16 (2010): 267–299.

Myrdal, Gunnar. An American Dilemma: The Negro Problem and Modern Democracy. New York: Harper & Brothers Publishers, 1944.

New York Times/CBS News, Complete Poll Results, July 7–14, 2008, 27; http://graphics8.nytimes.com/packages/pdf/politics/20080716_POLL.pdf.

Obama, Barack. The Audacity of Hope: Thoughts on Reclaiming the American Dream. New York: Three Rivers Press, 2006.

Obama, Barack. Remarks by the President at Morehouse College Commencement Ceremony. Washington, DC: The White House, Office of the Press Secretary, May 19, 2013, http://www.whitehouse.gov/the-press-office/2013/05/19/remarks-president-morehouse-college-commencement-ceremony.

O'Brien, Sharon. "Why Is Social Security Called the Third Rail of American Politics?" *SeniorLiving.About.com*, http://seniorliving.about.com/od/socialsecurity 101/a/socialsecurity.htm.

Ogletree, Charles. "Foreword," in *The Obamas and a (Post) Racial America?*, Gregory S. Parks and Matthew W. Hughey, eds. New York: Oxford University Press, 2011.

O'Keefe, Ed, and Robert Costa. "Jeb Bush, Scott Walker Emerging as Front-Runners for GOP Nod—and Rivals," *Washington Post*, March 10, 2015.

Orbe, Mark P. *Communication Realities in a "Post-Racial" Society: What the U.S. Public Really Thinks about Barack Obama*. Lanham, MD: Lexington Books, 2011.

Orfield, Gary, and Erica Frankenberg, with Jongyeon Ee and John Kuscera. *Brown at 60: Great Progress, a Long Retreat and an Uncertain Future*. Los Angeles: Civil Rights Project/Proyecto Derechos Civiles, 2012.

Orfield, Gary, John Kucsera, and Geneviève Siegel-Hawley. *E Pluribus . . . Separation: Deepening Double Segregation for More Students*. Los Angeles: Civil Rights Project/Proyecto Derechos Civiles, 2012.

Pager, Devah, Bruce Western, and Bart Bonikowski. "Discrimination in a Low-Wage Labor Market: A Field Experiment," *American Sociological Review*, 74 (October 2009): 777–799.

Parker, Christopher S., and Matt A. Barreto. *Change They Can't Believe In: The Tea Party and Reactionary Politics in America*. Princeton: Princeton University Press, 2013.

Parker, Suzi. "In Arkansas, Racism Cuts against Obama," *Washington Post*, May 25, 2012.

Parlett, Martin A. *Demonizing a President: The "Foreignization" of Barack Obama*. Santa Barbara, CA: Praeger 2014.

Passel, Jeffrey S., D'Vera Cohn, and Ana Gonzalez-Barrera. "Population Decline of Unauthorized Immigrants Stalls, May Have Reversed: New Estimate: 11.7 million in 2012." Washington, DC: Pew Hispanic Center, 2013.

Pew Research Center. *A Year after Obama's Election: Blacks Upbeat about Black Progress, Prospects*. Washington, DC: Pew Research Center, 2010.

Pew Research Center. *King's Dream Remains an Elusive Goal; Many Americans See Racial Disparities*. Washington, DC: Pew Research Center, 2013.

Pew Center for the People and the Press. "After Boston, Little Change in Views of Islam and Violence: 45% Say Muslim Americans Face 'A Lot' of Discrimination." Washington, DC: Pew Research Center, 2013.

Pew Social and Demographic Trends. *Blacks Upbeat about Black Progress, Prospects: A Year after Obama's Election*. Washington, DC: Pew Research Center, 2010.

Pincus, Fred L. *Reverse Discrimination: Dismantling the Myth*. Boulder, CO: Lynne Rienner, 2003.

Porter, Nicole D., and Valerie Wright. "Cracked Justice." Washington, DC: The Sentencing Project, 2011.

Powell, Michael. "Democrats in Steel Country See Color, and Beyond It," *New York Times*, October 26, 2008.

Press, Bill. *The Obama Hate Machine: The Lies, Distortions, and Personal Attacks on the President—and Who Is behind Them*. New York: St. Martin's Press, 2012.

Preston, Julia. "Report Finds Deportations Focus on Criminal Records," *New York Times*, April 29, 2014.

Public Religion Research Institute. "Roughly Three-Quarters of Americans Favor Goals of Obama's Immigration Action." Washington, DC: Public Religion Research Institute, 2015.

Raghavan, Gautam. "Obama Administration Statements on the Supreme Court's DOMA Ruling," *The White House* blog, June 27, 2013.

Recovery.gov. "Overview of the Funding," http://www.recovery.gov/arra/Trans parency/fundingoverview/Pages/fundingbreakdown.aspx.

Reed, Wornie L., and Bertin M. Louis Jr. "'No More Excuses': Problematic Responses to Barack Obama's Election," *Journal of African American Studies*, 13 (2009): 97–109.

Religion and Public Life Project. *Little Voter Discomfort with Romney's Mormon Religion*. Washington, DC: Pew Research Center, 2012.

Roberts, Sam, and Peter Baker. "Asked to Declare His Race, Obama Checks 'Black.'" *New York Times*, April 2, 2010.

Rockeymoore, Mary M., and Meizhu Lui. *Plan for a New Future: The Impact of Social Security Reform on People of Color*. Washington, DC: Commission to Modernize Social Security, 2011.

Rockquemore, Kerry Ann, and David L. Brunsma. *Beyond Black: Biracial Identity in America*. Thousand Oaks, CA: Sage Publications, Inc., 2002.

Romney, Mitt. "Why I'd Repeal Obamacare," *USA Today*, March 22, 2012.

Rubin, Richard. "Obama Delivers on Tax Cut Promises," *Bloomberg.com*, April 17, 2012.

Rutenberg, Jim, and Ashley Parker. "Romney Says Remarks on Voters Help Clarify Position," *New York Times*, September 18, 2012.

Sartor, Tricia, and Dana Page. "Obama Rumors Get More Press," Journalism Project. Washington, DC: Pew Research Center, July 17, 2008.

Schaefer, Richard T. *Racial and Ethnic Groups*, 8th ed. Upper Saddle River, NJ: Prentice Hall, 2000.

Schorr, Daniel. "A New, 'Post-Racial' Political Era in America," *All Things Considered, NPR*, January 28, 2008.

Schumacher-Matos, Edward. "NPR's Ombudsman on Diversity, Controversy and Leadership," *The Kojo Nnamdi Show*. Washington, DC: WAMU, June 4, 2014.

SDA: Survey Documentation and Analysis. Berkeley: University of California, Berkeley, 2014.

Seelye, Katharine Q. "Obama, Civil Rights and South Carolina." *The Caucus: The Politics and Government Blog of the Times, New York Times*, November 2, 2007.

Semm, P. Tom, and Christina Sanchez-Weston. "Waiting for Change: Obama and the LGBT Community," in *Grading the 44th President: A Report Card on Barack*

Obama's First Term as a Progressive Leader, Luigi Esposito and Laura L. Finley, eds. Santa Barbara, CA: Praeger, 2012.

Semple, Kirk. "A Killing in a Town Where Latinos Sense Hate," *New York Times*, November 13, 2008.

Sentencing Project. "Felony Disenfranchisement." Washington, DC: Sentencing Project, n.d., http://www.sentencingproject.org/template/page.cfm?id=133.

Shea, Daniel M., and Morris P. Fiorina. *Can We Talk?: The Rise of Rude, Nasty, Stubborn Politics*. New York: Pearson, 2012.

Shear, Michael D. "Obama Budget Is Dismissed by G.O.P. and Attacked by Left," *New York Times*, April 5, 2013.

Sinyangwe, Samuel. "The Significance of Mixed-Race: Public Perceptions of Barack Obama's Race and Its Effect on His Favorability," *Stanford Undergraduate Research Journal*, 11 (2012): 87–94.

Skocpol, Theda, and Vanessa Williamson. *The Tea Party and the Remaking of Republican Conservatism*. New York: Oxford University Press, 2012.

Smith, Ben. "Racists for Obama?" *Politico.com*, October 18, 2008.

Smooth, Jay. "TEDxHampshireCollege—How I Learned to Stop Worrying and Love Discussing Race [video]," November 15, 2011, https://www.youtube.com/watch?v=MbdxeFcQtaU.

Solomon, John, and Aaron Mehta. "Stimulating Hypocrisy: Scores of Recovery Act Opponents Sought Money out of Public View." Washington, DC: The Center for Public Integrity, October 19, 2010.

Sorensen, Eric. "Asian Groups Attack MSNBC Headline Referring to Kwan—News Web Site Apologizes for Controversial Wording," *Seattle Times*, March 3, 1998.

Steinhauer, Jennifer. "Volunteers for Obama Face a Complex Issue," *New York Times*, October 14, 2008.

Stimson, James A. *Tides of Consent: How Public Opinion Shapes American Politics*. New York: Cambridge University Press, 2004.

Sue, Derald, and Michel Martin. "Microaggressions: Be Careful What You Say," *Tell Me More*, NPR, April 3, 2014.

Swanenberg, August. *Macroeconomics Demystified*. New York: McGraw-Hill, 2005.

Tapper, Jake. "The Terrorist Notches on Obama's Belt," *ABCNews.com*, September 30, 2011.

Tesler, Michael, and David O. Sears. *Obama's Race: The 2008 Election and the Dream of a Post-Racial America*. Chicago: The University of Chicago Press, 2010.

Thai, Xuan, and Ted Barrett. "Biden's Description of Obama Draws Scrutiny," *CNN.com*, February 9, 2007.

This American Life. "Act Three: Union Halls," *Ground Game*, Episode 367 (radio broadcast) (Chicago: Chicago Public Radio, October 24, 2008).

U.S. Department of Homeland Security. "Border Security Results," November 1, 2013, http://www.dhs.gov/border-security-results.

Van de Water, Paul N. "Health Reform Essential for Reducing Deficit and Slowing Health Care Costs." Washington, DC: Center on Budget and Policy Priorities, 2010.

Vedantam, Shankar. "Does Your Subconscious Think Obama Is Foreign?" *Washington Post*, October 13, 2008.

Vendantham, Shankar. *The Hidden Brain: How Our Unconscious Minds Elect Presidents, Control Markets, Wage Wars, and Save Our Lives.* New York: Spiegel & Grau, 2010.

Waldman, Paul. "Republicans Are Beginning to Act as though Barack Obama Isn't Even the President," *The Plum Line* blog, *Washington Post*, March 9, 2015.

Wallsten, Peter. "Frank Talk of Obama and Race in Virginia," *Los Angeles Times*, October 8, 2008.

Wise, Tim. *Between Barack and a Hard Place: Racism and White Denial in the Age of Obama.* San Francisco: City Lights Books, 2009.

Wolfers, Justin. "What Debate? Economists Agree the Stimulus Lifted the Economy," *The New York Times*, July 29, 2014.

Wright, John. *The Obama Haters: Behind the Right-Wing Campaign of Lies, Innuendo, and Racism.* Washington, DC: Potomac Books, 2011.

Index

About the Author

ALGERNON AUSTIN consults on race, economics, and public opinion research and writing in Washington, D.C. He is the former director of the program on race, ethnicity, and the economy at the Economic Policy Institute.